AF361628

Ecological Moral Character
A CATHOLIC MODEL

Ecological Moral Character

A CATHOLIC MODEL

Nancy M. Rourke

Georgetown University Press / Washington, DC

The publisher is not responsible for third-party websites or their content. URL links were active at time of publication.

Library of Congress Cataloging-in-Publication Data

Names: Rourke, Nancy M., author.
Title: Ecological moral character : a Catholic model / Nancy M. Rourke.
Description: Washington, DC : Georgetown University Press, 2024. | Series: Moral traditions series | Includes bibliographical references and index.
Identifiers: LCCN 2023012601 (print) | LCCN 2023012602 (ebook) | ISBN 9781647124021 (hardcover) | ISBN 9781647124038 (paperback) | ISBN 9781647124045 (ebook)
Subjects: LCSH: Human ecology—Religious aspects—Catholic Church. | Ecology—Religious aspects—Catholic Church. | Environmental responsibility—Religious aspects—Catholic Church. | Environmental ethics—Religious aspects Catholic Church. | Virtue.
Classification: LCC BX1795.H82 R68 2024 (print) | LCC BX1795.H82 (ebook) | DDC 261.8/8—dc23/eng/20231108
LC record available at https://lccn.loc.gov/2023012601
LC ebook record available at https://lccn.loc.gov/2023012602

♾ This paper meets the requirements of ANSI/NISO Z39.48-1992 (Permanence of Paper).

25 24   9 8 7 6 5 4 3 2   First printing

Printed in the United States of America

Cover design by Nathan Putens
Interior design by BookComp, Inc.

Contents

Acknowledgments

I want to express my gratitude to my friends and colleagues at Canisius University. Thanks to the librarians who made the college feel like home, to the past and present members of my department, to the generous community of the sustainability initiative, and to Becky Krawiec and Sarah Woodside, my writing accountability partners.

This book results from many people's support. I thank the editors and blind reviewers at the presses of Georgetown University and the Catholic University of America and the scholars of the Catholic Theological Society of America, the College Theology Society, and the Society of Christian Ethics who considered my work and asked questions that helped me improve this book. I am grateful for your commitment to theology and ecological well-being.

I am grateful to the hardy, wise, and crafty American Catholics who persistently wheedle, organize, appeal, pray, whisper, and shout to move this Church away from fossil fuel use. I am grateful to the Catholic laypeople who fight for solar cells on church roofs and who gladly gather to read *Laudato si'* together. I thank my colleagues, including Erin Lothes Biviano, Charlie Curran, Dan DiLeo, Kathy Lilla Cox, Marcus Mescher, Daniel Scheid, Matt Shadle, and Tobias Winright. You give our world your skilled theological attention with care and hope, and for this we all owe you gratitude.

I thank my family, my parents and my sisters, Kate and Connie, and all the Rourkes, Bixbys, Greaneys, Giffords, and Chittys who have supported and encouraged me. I promise to keep listening for your guidance.

I am grateful for the places that have held and nurtured me. These are places that are embedded in current, ancestral, and stolen lands of the Kanienkehaka, Mohican, Haudenosaunee, Wampanoag, and Massachusett peoples. I have known these places as Bixby farm, Hudson Falls, Fort Edward, the

Adirondacks, Schenectady, Voronezh, Boston, Maynooth, Buffalo, and Swillburg. These places shaped me and helped me to learn about integrity. For them, I promise to keep learning to inhabit creation's places with attunement.

Finally, I am grateful for Lou "Butch" Chitty, my spouse and partner for twenty years. Butch, your openness, intelligence, strength, and love continue to inspire and embolden me. Thank you.

Preface

We humans are shaped by our planet, and we have shaped our worlds in it. Yet climate change will reshape us. Climate change is a significant moral challenge, and this book describes one aspect of a Christian response. The book covers both Catholic moral theology and ecological virtue ethics to expand our ecological and moral awareness in the hope that expanded awareness, as Pope Francis has said,[1] will help us face this challenge well. Because humans are participants in and constituents of environments, this virtue theory approach to ecological ethics offers a new vision of ourselves, specifically that aspect of ourselves that Roman Catholic virtue ethics calls moral character. We can work our way to considering moral character by thinking about our context.

The climate of our lives is changing. Our world's climate has warmed by about one degree Celsius since the Industrial Revolution.[2] One degree sounds harmless. However, as an average increase of averaged averages over intervals of years, a single degree moves only when a very large number of numbers have risen.[3] This warming results from human activity. Our energy source choices emit greenhouse gases into the atmosphere.[4] The resulting atmospheric makeup leads to higher average temperatures, more frequent extreme weather events, species extinctions, droughts, and changes in the oceans' acidity. The way we use and generate energy threatens life on the planet.

Earth's systems of life are resilient and adapt to change, given time. But the pace of our temperature increase is accelerating. The atmospheric warming trend is accelerating, with the increase in temperatures rising by about 0.2 degrees per decade.[5] In other words, each decade's temperature compared to the previous decade's increase is 0.2 degrees greater. Some efforts to slow this heating have begun, but we are running out of time to adopt better energy habits. We (inhabitants of Earth) will likely reach a warming of 1.5 degrees between 2030 and 2052 if humanity does not make sufficient changes.[6] An increase of 1.5 degrees is a warming above which we can expect disastrous consequences.[7]

We (humans) have caused this change through our interactions with the dynamics of the systems of our climate. When we increase pressure on these systems quickly, without counterbalancing against the effects, the systems can destabilize. If we change how we live, especially how we use energy and what sources of energy we employ, we can steer our trajectory away from self-annihilation.[8] The way we live is part of our planet's systems. Human choice, infrastructures, and systems shape our ecosystems' dynamics. The social and the ecological are not separate.[9] In other words, we and our environments constantly shape one another.

When I was a child, I used to imagine that the climate of a place deeply impacted the personality of societies that resided there. I believed that snowy mountainous places, such as my own places, led to tougher, colder folk. I thought perhaps that the Adirondacks, the topography of my youth, defined and shaped us in their own image. When I traveled the roads of New York state's Adirondack foothills, I often felt affection for the people I saw out and about in heavy coats and thick boots, trudging through icy sludge and driving with our rare skill through salt, ice, and powder. We pile on layers of gear and thrust ourselves out into hostile conditions in order to participate in the world as it is, with our eyes running, lungs stinging, and nose hairs freezing stiff. Some days I push through a wall of freezing wind with gritted teeth, and other days I whimper and shiver. We can choose how the wind and the cold shape us. We cannot choose whether it will shape us. When a person travels through freezing, wet wind, she will not likely arrive in a mood of serene, quiet optimism and calm. She will arrive damp, her heart pumping, her skin cold and prickly, her eyes tearing, and her glasses fogged. Her outlook will absorb something of her environments.

Later, encountering Catholic virtue theory (an idea developed over eight centuries of engagement with Thomas Aquinas), I recognized the human responsibility to be a good person. Of course, we are responsible for our actions and for the impacts of our acts. We also bear some responsibility for the kind of persons we turn out to be. At least some degree of personal development is up to us.

The lesson of virtue theory seemed to be that we can perfect a handful of virtues, adding them up to become good persons. We could accomplish this through our habits and by attending to God in our actions and decisions. But some factors lie beyond human moral agency: our environments, God's action, and even the internal dynamics, or all the motions within the moral character itself. Theological virtue theory works based on the conviction that we can steer our moral becoming, but it also offers language for those foggy regions where human agency meets its limits. Human self-development works in tandem with dynamics from the sacred and always takes place within (and is continually buffeted by) social and ecological contexts. In fact, human moral character is a kind of ecosystem, embedded within the ecosystems of the person. For this and other reasons, virtue ethics is a very useful approach to the moral problem of climate change.

ECOLOGICAL VIRTUE ETHICS

Ecological virtue ethics helps us think about morality in the face of ecological problems such as climate change. In secular ecological virtue theory, Philip Cafaro has described ecological virtues (such as patriotism, love of the land,[10] simplicity, and perceptivity[11]) that humans ought to cultivate. He has identified and described role models of ecological virtuosity. Cafaro's collaborations with Ronald Sandler led to compiled writings that jump-started ecological virtue ethics in English-speaking philosophical scholarship.

Ronald Sandler has defended ecological virtue ethics among (or against) other ecological moral theories.[12] His work demonstrates how ecological virtue thought can be used to think through pressing ecological moral questions (such as the legitimacy of genetically modified crops).[13]

Thomas Hill Jr. is best known for showcasing what virtue theory's view of morality recognizes (and what other approaches to ecological ethics miss). His story about a homeowner awoke many ethicists to virtue theory's efficacy. This homeowner, the story goes, paved over plants and grass for a blacktop surface that requires no effort or attention to maintain. Hill asks, "What is wrong with this?" Ultimately, an observer finds that the moral problem illustrated by such a homeowner is not one of rights to manage a home or land as one sees fit or of the benefits or harms of this choice. Rather, we best pinpoint the moral failure here when we think, "What sort of person would do a thing like that?"[14] Hill's work has demonstrated virtue theory's ability to name where the moral good is (and is not) in human actions and in attitudes toward our environments.[15]

Geoffrey Frasz has demonstrated the ecological virtues of benevolence,[16] of friendship (understood as a virtue) and of openness, which he argues (contra Hill) is a significant ecological virtue.

Louke van Wensveen's pioneering work in ecological virtue ethics avoided pitfalls into which other progenitors of ecological virtue ethics have fallen.

One such pitfall is a failure to look at ecological problems alongside and connected with problems not often interpreted as ecological. This error curtails ecological virtue theory's strength of helping us to see the interconnectedness of moral failures and successes across land use, social in/justices, human history, and psychology. The problem is most vividly evident in the later work of Cafaro, which argues against human population increase and against immigration into the United States.[17] Van Wensveen's 1991 "catalog" of "dirty virtues" demonstrated the progress made in ecological virtue ethics and recommended this approach to environmentalism with creativity and inspiration.[18]

Christian moral theology has also developed ecological virtue ethics, offering ways to help us think about ourselves and our place in this world. I will highlight two recent examples here.

Kathryn Blanchard and Kevin O'Brien's *An Introduction to Christian Environmentalism* offers a vision of ecological virtue ethics.[19] The book focuses on individual moral character, an important target for a project hoping to help all Christians and people of goodwill take charge of our own moral development in an ecologically attentive way. The book is packed with role models across the spectrum of political and theological angles, some well established in the canon of ecological models (John Muir, Bill McKibben, Wangari Maathai, and Naomi Klein) and others with interesting stories that deserve our attention (Brayton Shanley, Kent Busman, Sandra Steingraber, and Bjorn Lomborg). Blanchard and O'Brien take individualities seriously, demonstrating a way to sustain a productive dialogue that includes Christian subcultures that tend to face one another with hostility.[20]

More recently, Steven Bouma-Prediger's second volume of Christian ecological virtue ethics, *Earthkeeping and Character*,[21] offers a theologically grounded description of the virtues that balance together to shape an ecologically attuned moral character. Weaving biblical stories, shouts, and exhortations, Bouma-Prediger depicts virtues of wonder, humility, courage, compassion, fortitude, and hope. To sharpen our understanding, he also explains vices such as insensibility, austerity,[22] and ecological foolishness.[23]

Each of these ethicists has demonstrated that ecological virtue ethics is a particularly helpful way of thinking about moral issues. Let's consider three of the strengths of ecological virtue ethics. Ecologically attuned virtue ethics helps to link moral goodness and good living, presents morality in a way that encourages, and approaches moral goodness as a whole-body endeavor and experience.

First, ecological virtue ethics assumes that goodness and flourishing are related. This is a truth for Christianity, with our belief that God calls creation good. In addition, ecological virtue ethics carries a message that being good at being human is also an enjoyable experience. Flourishing feels good, and moral goodness and flourishing are intricately intertwined.[24] Moral effort and good feelings are linked. The motivating power of a moral theory is often overlooked but should not be. Virtue ethics values and mobilizes inspiration, feeding a resolution that can spread from person to person. Rather than a grim struggle to avoid dire evils, virtue theory's vision of doing good resembles a life of well-supported good.

Second, virtue ethics aims to make being good an easier, less effort-laden endeavor. The aim is to develop moral habits that sustain morally good actions and practices so that doing good and being our best is our default. Morality is not mostly about one-off, high-stakes choices between opposing forked paths. Virtue theory helps our view of morally good living sink into our first responses, shaping our prereflective thoughts, words, and deeds. Ease of moral goodness is another important and unfairly overlooked benefit of a good moral theory.

Finally, ecological virtue ethics works from a thicker embodied and embedded anthropology,[25] understanding morality as an aspect of thought but also of feeling, physicality, and layers of perception and interpretation lying below conscious or cognitive processes. Ecological virtue ethics integrates these aspects of human life. It is, as Louke van Wensveen said, an "integral discourse."[26] This is the most important benefit of ecological virtue thought. As van Wensveen put it, ecological virtue thought "fit[s] well with efforts to live out an ecological worldview."[27]

In fact, ecological virtue ethics offers the same vision that animates Pope Francis's 2015 encyclical *Laudato si'*. This encyclical describes a way for humans to live, through faith, in attunement with the interrelationalities of our world. The integral ecology is an ecological virtue theory aspiration.[28]

LAUDATO SI' AND ECOLOGICAL VIRTUE THEORY

Laudato si' begins with a call for greater ecological awareness. This call begins with a reminder that climate change demonstrates that we need a "profound internal conversion." Christians who ridicule ecological concern and Christians who ignore it both need this ecological conversion.[29] This conversion is a matter of living the Christian "vocation to be protectors of God's handiwork."[30] It is "essential to a life of virtue; it is not an optional or a secondary aspect of our Christian experience." As I demonstrate in chapter 7, the integral ecology, fundamental to Christian life, is a call for ecological virtuosity.

Though *Laudato si'* rarely refers to virtue, it frequently names specific virtues such as honesty, responsibility, sobriety, humility, innocence, self-control, willingness to learn, and gratitude. The encyclical often names good and bad "attitudes." It gives no technical definition of "attitude," but we can say that an attitude is a kind of inclination. Attitude is somewhat imperceptible because it is interior, influencing our way of interpreting our worlds, but it is also quite visible through the responses we tend to give to what we encounter. Attitude manifests in our gut reaction, our first assumptions. Even when not displayed, attitude is still present as a baseline. Attitude is habitual and is similar to a character trait. In many ways attitude is very much like a virtue.[31]

Pope Francis's call for an integral ecology is infused with comments about attitudes. His call sounds like a call for virtue, specifically for the virtue of ecological attunement. This integral ecology is a human habit of deliberately contextualizing ourselves and our interactions within our many environments: social, religious, ecological, political, liturgical, and economic environments, to name only a few.[32] This type of ecology is therefore a responsiveness to what we and other lives create and need. Integral ecology is both our awareness of interrelationality and our renewed and attentive self-integration within and among all our spheres of interrelationality. We are thus inspired to ask questions such as "What need does the earth have of us?"[33] This is not just an intellectual exercise. The radical connectedness required by an integral ecology "includes taking time to recover a serene harmony with creation, reflecting on our lifestyle and our ideals, and contemplating the creator who lives among us and surrounds us."[34] The integral ecology is both a participation in our global connections and the contemplation of these connections themselves. Chapter 7 therefore concludes this book by presenting the integral ecology as a demonstration of ecological virtue ethics.

Ecological Moral Character presents Catholic ecological virtue theory in order to help virtue theory think ecologically about moral character. The book develops ecological virtue ethics by offering a model of moral character that highlights its interactions with the world and its inner dynamics, or the interactions among its own constituent parts. We can improve our self-understanding as moral beings in a created world with an ecological model of human moral character. Here is the model: a moral character is like an ecosystem, and the virtues, vices, and other components of a moral character are like the inhabitants of or participants in an ecosystem. This model can help us recognize the contours of our lives as being embedded within our ecological and social contexts and thus see our moral selves as participants in these worlds.

A good model for thinking about moral character is important. A model can lionize select virtues at the expense of others. It can depict vices as rare and few or, on the other extreme, as inevitable and overwhelming. A model indicates the roles and significance of the intellect, the passions, and the will of a person. The stakes of the model we use are obvious when we look at an earlier conversation about the unity of the virtues within a moral character. Few moral theologians are still interested in the twentieth century's debates about the unity of the virtues. Of our many arguments about which version of Catholic moral theology is most faithfully Thomistic, this one is not the most interesting. However, I will risk reviving these discussions for the sake of this lesson: the way we imagine virtues' relationality matters.

THE DEBATES ABOUT THE "UNITY OF THE VIRTUES"

The debates about the unity of the virtues took the form of articles commenting on the virtues as collectives. Participants included Josef Pieper in the midcentury and John Langan and Gilbert Meilaender later on, and finally Jean Porter revisited the question.[35] The focus of these debates was to discern whether all the moral virtues are required in order for a moral agent to become virtuous or whether a person can have some but not all the required virtues and still be virtuous in character. In my view, much of this conversation involved misinterpretation of others' uses of terms such as "unity" and "interconnected." Straw man arguments proliferated. Mechanistic images of the moral virtues' unity led to the conclusion that having one virtue meant having all, which undermined any pathway that an imperfect moral agent might take toward moral improvement. Yet observation demonstrates that humans are able to improve our moral characters and our lives. Summaries of other ethicists' views about the virtues' unity insinuated that they drew human persons as either entirely perfect or thoroughly degraded. Often the debates seem to actually rehearse a hidden debate about when we can imagine a virtue model tightly and strictly, as with the gears of a clock, and when we must soften the model's application with observations that human morality is messier than clockwork. Yet that question was not central.

To be fair, the fuel for the unity of virtues debates was ignited by questions about Christology and the moral nature of the incarnate Jesus Christ.[36] I will not delve into that daunting question here. Instead, I want to show that these debates can teach us that the model through which we imagine moral character matters. Such a model is an important influence on our moral aspirations and is rarely examined directly.

Ethicists in the debates about the unity of the virtues all agreed that there is at least some cohesiveness among the virtues. They imagined the nature of that cohesion differently. Many defined the coherence through a central or prime virtue. For Langan, moral virtues are unified in charity. For Pieper (and Meilaender), they are unified in prudence. For Porter, the cohesion is in well-ordered links between higher and lower virtues, an arrangement that is managed by the virtue of prudence. A synthesis of these views is easy. A collaboration between prudence and charity stands in as the engineer of a moral character's structural coherence.

A foundational referent for these debates appeared in Augustine's correspondence with Jerome. Augustine, concerned about the Stoic error of finding all sins to be equal, noted that a single vice can make a moral agent non-virtuous.[37] The Cappadocians (Gregory of Nyssa in particular) continued this discussion. In a summary of this discourse, theologian Andrew Radde-Gallwitz offers a useful breakdown of positions that resemble the "unity thesis," noting that "unity debate" is often a misnomer.[38] Some ancients (the Stoics) held that all the virtues are the same, and Radde-Gallwitz calls this the "identity" thesis. But the unity thesis argued differently. It is a corollary of what Radde-Gallwitz calls the reciprocity thesis.[39] This was Gregory of Nyssa's position, defended as part of his idea that humans and God each have virtues. Gregory of Nyssa also identified multiple theses for how this could be. Radde-Gallwitz concludes that Gregory of Nyssa endorsed views that the virtues are reciprocal and inseparable.

Josef Pieper took up the question in the mid-twentieth century in order to address human morality only. The virtues of God were not his focus. For Pieper, the primacy of prudence was very important. He even argued that if prudence was not the first and foremost virtue of a person, then Christianity had not actually taken root in that person.[40] For him, a hierarchy of virtues held high stakes. A correct hierarchy of virtues would prioritize prudence, and there could be no valid view positing a mere "interdependence" of all the virtues. There must be a first among virtues, and prudence must occupy that place. We can see in Pieper's claim a preview of Alasdair MacIntyre's argument that the choice of which virtues to uphold is definitive of a society's morality.

Later, Gilbert Meilaender, working from Pieper, noted the importance of the debate about the unity of the virtues. It matters, Meilaender said, because the claim of unity springs from a confidence that creation itself has meaning.[41] For him, this was a necessary condition for proceeding with theological ethics of any sort. Meilaender thought that Pieper sometimes did seem to see among the virtues a unity and sometimes did not.[42] Either way, without an organized order of the virtues, there is no valid accounting for genuine moral disagreement and, more importantly, no foundation for a moral life. Meilaender echoed Pieper's view of the significance of prudence's centrality to the coherence of a virtuous moral character. Affirming that a unity of all the virtues does exist, as a result of this coherence, Meilaender nevertheless argued that this unity is not actually achievable because humans cannot attain perfect virtue in our lives. Meilaender's answer to the question of the virtues' unity is possible because he recalled the mortal and organic context of all moral virtues: living, growing, imperfect human beings.

John Langan engaged the debate in the 1970s, recalling Augustine's conversation with Jerome. Langan's reflection begins with a comment that all discussions of virtues employ a construct, a "theoretical entity" similar to a psychological state, through which we are able to talk about moral formation of humans.[43] Langan notes that mindfulness of the limitations of such analogies can restrain us from taking our discussions of these constructs' behaviors too far and too literally. To mind these limitations, Langan recommends distinguishing between two ways of talking about the virtues. We can refer to a virtue as an explanation for an act or as the entity that actually moves the action we are evaluating. When we speak of a virtue as an explanation of an act's moral quality, we have to think more carefully. Langan worries about the "interconnection" thesis, which says that virtues are not all "ontologically" the same but instead are interconnected. To Langan, this view makes moral formation appear too difficult.[44] This view can "totalize" our evaluations of a moral character, bringing us to conclusions about the whole moral character merely on the basis of an observation that one or two specific virtues exist.

While Langan creates a bit of a straw man argument here, taking the unity and the interconnectedness theses very literally, his resolution is creative and good for this reason: his test for a good view of the construct of virtues' interrelationality lies in what aides and what impedes moral growth.[45]

More recently, Jean Porter, drawing on Aquinas, noted that while moral perfection is not attainable, coherence of the moral character is important. For her, a good coherence lies in a proper relating of lower faculties to higher faculties. This order encompasses not only virtues but also the will and the passions. Because there is coherence, we can know that perfected virtues do not contradict one another.[46] Porter's thinking here is in continuity with the Scholastics' ways of addressing moral dilemmas in terms of sizing up the relative significance of the virtue upheld by an act against the virtue undermined by that act.[47] This is proportionate reasoning when it is being done in a virtue theory context (to evaluate action as reflective of a person's moral character).

The fault in some conclusions drawn in these unity debates is the assumption that any virtue in one moral character is the same thing that exists in another person. The question of whether a virtue in one person is the same when it exists in another person is not often acknowledged in these discussions, but it is important as a part of one's broader position on whether and in what ways a moral character has a structural coherence. The way we imagine the parts of moral character is a necessary piece of our discussions about the whole moral character itself. This book focuses on models through which moral character can be imagined and views virtues (and other participants of a moral character) in light of a moral character model.

MORAL CHARACTER MODELS

The debates about the unity of virtues remain significant in that their focus is the same question that centers this book: What is a good model through which to imagine a whole moral character? How do we picture the virtues, the will, the passions, and the diversity of moral characters that exist in the world? There are many models in the traditions of Catholic virtue theory. A moral character can be like a clock, a hill to climb with obstacles along the way to overcome, a pyramid of ruling and obedient components, or a pile of resources that can be of greater or lesser size and quality. It follows that we can choose among more or less helpful models. This is the metaethical question at hand. This book's model offers a new option: we can adopt a model of ecological integrity.

"Ecological integrity" is a familiar term. As chapter 7 notes, a concept of an "integral ecology" evolved before our eyes from Pope John Paul II through Pope Benedict XVI to Pope Francis and has found additional friendly habitats in the work of many theologians.[48] Chapter 7 traces that evolution. In this book, integral ecology is cultivated on a metaethical level. The book presents a model of moral character that encourages us to recognize ourselves as entirely embedded in our environments, from toes to scalp to conscience to culture. With this model, virtue theory can teach us about our own animality, our earthly citizenship, our Eden-descended createdness, our struggles, and our collaborations with God. This book describes an ecological model of moral character based on traditional Catholic virtue theory as it has been developed through centuries to today.

The language used to describe virtues involves dissection of a whole and a naming of constructed "pieces" that do not exist in any more real sense than the whole. I suggest that we not think of the pieces of a person's internal life as fitting together to create a character. Rather, the person is one. The person's internal world is some kind of a coherent whole. In virtue theory, we draw distinctions and divide a whole into parts. We visualize these parts as differentiable functions that together make a human person's moral character and move a person to act. This dissection is an epistemologically useful imaginary, as philosopher Jean Porter has noted. "Human perception is not to be understood in terms of distinct capacities which must somehow be brought together; rather, what is fundamental is the thinking and perceiving agent, whose unified act of perception can then be analyzed in terms of its distinct components."[49] What matters is the person, acting as a whole. A person's action can be analyzed for insight, but all fragmentation that we perform in order to be able to see this whole's parts is imposed by our observation. The unity deserves our focus. Next, we will consider how to imagine moral character well.

THE PROPERTIES OF A GOOD MODEL

Nicholas Kahm's meticulous discussion of the interactions between the passions and other aspects of a moral character exemplifies a careful navigation between the whole of a moral character and the motions of its internal "parts." For example, he correctly observes that Aquinas saw the various powers of the soul as parts of the soul's total power, not powers proceeding from a soul's parts.[50] A good model will help us to retain this view of the totality, the unfragmented moral character, while still allowing us to distinguish epistemologically between different motions, behaviors, and actions taking place within a moral character.

What are the characteristics of a good model for envisioning moral character? Ecological scientists discuss the traits of good models for use in describing and understanding ecological changes. In ecology, good models can move from one ecological subdiscipline to another; they fit the available data, help us to make inferences, and are not overly contrived.[51] This book also recommends a model for ethicists and moral theologians, but this recommendation is not meant to be taken as a final model sufficient for all times. New models will be needed as ages pass. They should be what is needed for the people of those ages. Our age requires a heightening of ecological awareness, and as we will see, an ecological model of a moral character is quite helpful for this and related needs. However, we can name the characteristics of a good model for moral character for any kind of age. We can describe what makes a good model.

First, a good model of moral character will help us to think about, hope for, and work toward continual moral growth. As we have seen, Langan followed this priority, choosing to evaluate visions of virtue unity on the basis of what helps a moral agent believe that moral development is possible. A good model will aid and inspire.

Second, a good model can encapsulate a whole and highlight dynamics between parts. A good model will reflect persons' totalities and offer ways to refer to a whole moral character's constituent participants.

Third, a good model of moral character will embrace and demonstrate complexity, reminding us that we are spirits as well as humans, animals, carbon dioxide generators, ecological consumers, and future decaying matter. We are not reducible to any one of these. We are ecological participants in creation.

Fourth, a good model works for general reflection and for scrupulous academic discourse. A good model will seem viable in terms of casual, commonsense observation, taking into account the unpredictability of moral growth and the possibility of good within imperfection. This ability in particular is weak in virtue theory today.[52] A good model will also resonate with the best of theological anthropology, psychology, and sociology and will be able to adapt as these disciplines continue to revise their descriptions of humanity.

Fifth, a good model of moral character will help us think about sinfulness. A good model also will not participate in unjust social systems, will flag authoritarianism for moral rejection, and will highlight cooperation between moral agents and across scales of human agency. Such a model will resist binaries and fragmentation, integrating moral, intellectual, and theological virtues as well as emotions and the will into a complex system. A good model of moral character will value a wide diversity of virtues as beneficial.

Sixth, a good model will help us grapple with scaled-up and scaled-down analysis of moral character without determinism and without atomistic anthropologies. A good model will help us to think about individuals and about societies.

Seventh, a good model will show how grace moves in a way that illuminates human collaboration with God. This means accounting for how the moral character is rooted in grace through the theological virtues. A good model of moral character will allow for ambiguity in the spaces where human and divine agency meet in the processes of moral growth.

This book argues that an ecological model fits these criteria and gives us a new imagination to help us bring integral ecology into metaethics. A description of the steps of the argument follows.

THE BOOK'S STRUCTURE

Chapter 1 explains what virtue theory means vis-à-vis a moral character, presents a few models used to describe moral character, and argues that a good moral character model improves virtue theory in two critical areas: it incorporates the unpredictability of moral growth and faces the difficulty of naming a clear telos or finality toward which we can aim in moral improvement. Chapter 2 introduces the concepts of ecology that we need for the book's proposed model: a moral character imagined as an ecosystem. Chapter 3 uses four traits of ecosystems that were defined in chapter 2 (weak and indirect causality, vague and porous borders, nestedness, and niches) to describe the structure of an ecologically modeled moral character. Chapter 4 describes the theological virtues in accordance with this model of moral character. Chapters 5 and 6 introduce the cardinal moral virtues, beginning with a discussion of cardinality and then defining prudence and justice (in chapter 5) and fortitude and temperance (in chapter 6). Chapter 7 adds specifics to the model, defining three subsidiary virtues (wonder, integrity, and solidarity). The chapter then presents ways in which *Laudato si'* demonstrates thinking similar to this book's approach to ecological virtue theory and concludes with some examples to demonstrate Catholic ecological virtue theory at work.

Focused scholarship in virtue theory usually relies predominantly or exclusively on one specific line of scholarship to extend one specific virtue theory tradition into the present, such as one scholar's reading of the virtues of Confucianism, Aristotelian thought, Augustine, or Aquinas's virtue system. Catholic moral theology draws on Aquinas's thought quite heavily, so I will pull from those traditions. But as a tradition, Catholic moral theology does not employ only one specific reading of Aquinas. No Thomistic traditions monopolize all of moral theology, despite efforts to claim an exclusive and correct trajectory of Aquinas's theological view. (Consider the many works on new natural law.) We (moral and other theologians) debate these traditions. There is no single scholarly tradition of Thomistic ethics that can be deemed synonymous with the Roman Catholic Church's entire moral theology. Therefore, in this book I will refer to "traditional virtue theories" to indicate the traditions that Aquinas inspired and informed as we, the communities of Roman Catholic moral scholars, have inherited and developed them over eight centuries. I draw on theological and philosophically interpreted strains of Thomistic virtue thought. While there are significant differences between these, this book's purpose is not to identify a correct or even more helpful interpretation of Aquinas. I have been particularly attentive to the works of James Keenan, Gilbert Meilaender, and Josef Pieper and have gained insights from Alasdair

MacIntyre and the works of Jean Porter for her care in distinguishing between some of the finer distinctions in Aquinas's thought.[53] I cite Thomas Aquinas's *Summa Theologica* as the most primary source of the "Catholic virtue tradition" to which I refer. This project ought to be applicable to several descendants of Aquinas's thinking about human moral character and virtue.

While this project's focus is moral development, I have not looked at the world of child psychology or development. Moral growth continues all through life's stages, and here I focus on adult humans. I hope to offer here openings through which virtue theory can continue to interact with moral psychology, particularly in the ways these two are already beginning to reach for one another. This is happening in the work of the University of Oklahoma's Institute for the Study of Human Flourishing under Dr. Nancy Snow's leadership and in the work of Dr. Jennifer Herdt.

We begin in chapter 1 with an overview of the idea of the moral character in Catholic virtue theory and some demonstrations of why a virtue theory model of moral character matters.

NOTES

1. Pope Francis, *Laudato si'*, para. 202 and 207.
2. More precisely, "Global surface temperature was 1.09 [degrees] higher in 2011–2020 than 1850–1900." IPCC, "Climate Change 2021," https://www.ipcc.ch/report/ar6/wg1/downloads/report/IPCC_AR6_WGI_SPM_final.pdf.

    Note that the first *Assessment Report* found an increase of about half that amount. See IPCC, "Climate Change: The IPCC 1990 and 1992 Assessments," https://www.ipcc.ch/report/climate-change-the-ipcc-1990-and-1992-assessments/.
3. A degree of global climate warming is a change in the temperatures averaged over a fifty-year period of averaged annual surface temperatures across all the globe's regions.
4. IPCC, "Synthesis Report of the IPCC Sixth Assessment Report (AR6)," IPCC, 2023. The gases most often specified are carbon dioxide (CO_2), methane (CH_4), and nitrous oxide (N_2O). CO_2 and N_2O are emitted when we burn fossil fuels (such as coal, natural gas, and oil) and wood. See also "Overview of Greenhouse Gases," Environmental Protection Agency, last updated April 13, 2023, https://www.epa.gov/ghgemissions/overview-greenhouse-gases. Methane is emitted as we produce and transport oil, natural gas, and coal and is also emitted from livestock. About 75 percent of greenhouse gases come from the energy sector. International Energy Agency, "Net Zero by 2050: A Roadmap for the Global Energy Sector," IEA, May 2021, https://iea.blob.core.windows.net/assets/deebef5d-0c34-4539-9d0c-10b13d840027/NetZeroby2050-ARoadmapfortheGlobalEnergySector_CORR.pdf.
5. IPCC, "Climate Change 2021," https://www.ipcc.ch/report/ar6/wg1/downloads/report/IPCC_AR6_WGI_SPM_final.pdf; and IPCC, "Global Warming of 1.5°C (SR15)," https://www.ipcc.ch/site/assets/uploads/sites/2/2022/06/SPM_version_report_LR.pdf.

6. IPCC, "Global Warming."

7. For example, at an increase of 1.5 degrees, the report projects species losses at 6 percent of insect species, 8 percent of plants, and 4 percent of vertebrate species (IPCC, "Global Warming.") Another example: the percentage of land area likely to become an entirely different ecosystem if our temperatures rose by only 1 degree is about 4 percent. With warming at 2 degrees, it will be 13 percent of Earth's land area (section B.3.2). For detailed descriptions of these consequences, see section B5 of the same source. IPCC, "Global Warming."

8. To slow, limit, or reverse the climate's warming, we must quickly lower our net annual greenhouse gas emissions. This means reducing the volume of greenhouse gas emissions we add to the atmosphere and increasing the volume reabsorbed from the atmosphere. This change is overdue but not too late to make a difference. On the other hand, if we only meet the goals we made in the Paris Agreement in 2015, our climate will exceed 1.5 degrees of warming. International Energy Agency, *Net Zero by 2050*, 13. The report notes that most of these Paris Agreement pledges have not been supported with necessary policy changes. This would be disastrous. More aggressive goals and changes are needed, and every delay makes it less likely that we will find a way to stay in range of safe climate temperatures. International Energy Agency, *Net Zero by 2050*, 3.

9. "Everything is connected." *Laudato si'*, para. 91, 117, 137.

10. Cafaro, "Patriotism as Environmental Virtue."

11. Cafaro, "Thoreau, Leopold, and Carson," 33–34.

12. Sandler, "The External Goods Approach to Environmental Virtue Ethics."

13. Sandler, "A Virtue Ethics Perspective on Genetically Modified Crops," 215–32.

14. Hill, "Ideals of Human Excellence," 47.

15. Hill, "Finding Value in Nature"; Hill, "Ideals of Human Excellence"; and Hill, "Comments on Frasz and Cafaro on Environmental Virtue Ethics."

16. Frasz, "Benevolence as an Environmental Virtue"; Frasz, "What Is Environmental Virtue Ethics That We Should Be Mindful of It?"; and Frasz, "Environmental Virtue Ethics."

17. See Cafaro's personal website, http://www.philipcafaro.com/ (accessed June 20, 2023).

18. Van Wensveen's work directly inspired this book's approach. See Van Wensveen, "Attunement"; Van Wensveen, "Cardinal Environmental Virtues"; Van Wensveen, "The Emergence of Ecological Virtue Language"; Van Wensveen, "Ecosystem Sustainability as a Criterion for Genuine Virtue"; and Van Wensveen, *Dirty Virtues*.

19. Blanchard and O'Brien, *An Introduction to Christian Environmentalism*.

20. This work exhibits a "both sides" -ism that may frustrate some. Blanchard and O'Brien accept conflicting ways to respond to ecological ethics because their aim is to help Christians collaborate across divisive disagreements. Productive compromise is prioritized over political or ideological slant.

21. Bouma-Prediger, *Earthkeeping and Character*.

22. Bouma-Prediger locates austerity where "desire per se becomes the target, not disordered desires." Bouma-Prediger, *Earthkeeping and Character*, 65–66.

23. Bouma-Prediger's descriptions of wonder and humility are particularly helpful. His definition of self-control is quite different from my own definition of temperance (covered in chapter 3), and his description of justice is less attentive to social structures than many that appear in Catholic moral theology, where Catholic social teaching has had a pervasive influence.

24. Rourke, "The Environment Within," 165–66.

25. Rourke, "The Environment Within," 178–79 and 82; and Rourke, "A Catholic Virtues Ecology."
26. Van Wensveen, *Dirty Virtues*, 9.
27. Van Wensveen, 8.
28. The following argument first appeared in Rourke, "Pope Francis' Encyclical and Catholic Magisterial Statements on Ecological Ethics." It will be developed further in this book's final chapter.
29. *Laudato si'*, para. 217.
30. *Laudato si'*, para. 117.
31. Thomas Hill has also implied this similarity when he refers to "attitudes." For an example, see Hill, "Ideals of Human Excellence," 51.
32. I am grateful to theologian Dr. Dan DiLeo, who in a private conversation helped me to think through this definition.
33. *Laudato si'*, para. 160.
34. *Laudato si'*, para. 225.
35. Pieper, *The Four Cardinal Virtues*; Pieper, *Fortitude, and Temperance*; Pieper, *Prudence*; Langan, "Augustine on the Unity"; Meilaender, "Josef Pieper"; Meilaender, *The Theory and Practice of Virtue*; and Porter, "The Unity of the Virtues and the Ambiguity of Goodness."
36. Radde-Gallwitz, "Gregory of Nyssa."
37. See Langan, "Augustine on the Unity," 84.
38. Radde-Gallwitz, "Gregory of Nyssa," 537–38.
39. Radde-Gallwitz, 537.
40. Pieper, *The Four Cardinal Virtues*.
41. In Meilaender's words, "An emphasis on the unity of the virtues comes naturally to those who believe that the moral life is harmonious, a seamless robe which must either be worn intact or not at all." Meilaender, "Josef Pieper," 117.
42. Meilaender, 118.
43. Langan, "Augustine on the Unity," 81.
44. Langan, 88.
45. Langan, 88. Ultimately, Langan resolves the problems with the reminder that no human can have perfect virtue.
46. Porter, "Unity of the Virtues," 155.
47. Kaczor, "Double-Effect Reasoning from Jean Pierre Gury to Peter Knauer"; and Kaczor, *Proportionalism and the Natural Law Tradition*.
48. See Deane-Drummond, "Living Narratives"; Miller, "Integral Ecology"; and Scheid, *The Cosmic Common Good*.
49. Porter, "Unity of the Virtues," 147.
50. Kahm, *Aquinas on Emotion's Participation in Reason*, 36–37.
51. For discussions of good ecological models, see McRae et al., "Using Circuit Theory to Model Connectivity in Ecology, Evolution, and Conservation"; Judson, "The Rise of the Individual-Based Model in Ecology"; Jessup et al., "Big Questions, Small Worlds"; and Johnson and Omland, "Model Selection in Ecology and Evolution."
52. Slingerland, "The Situationist Critique and Early Confucian Virtue Ethics."
53. Jean Porter approaches Aquinas as a philosopher, not a theologian, but I have used her work because of its careful attention to the interactions and relationships between the participants of a moral character.

1

The Shape of Moral Character

SHARPENING VIRTUE THEORY

This chapter describes virtue theory as an area of moral theology, with attention to some of the tools that virtue theory offers to help us think about morality with subtlety and inclusion of ambiguity. We will work our way toward virtue theory's tools by thinking first about goodness. The chapter first introduces virtue theory in general, focusing on the priorities (and dare I say hopes) of this approach to morality and describing its vision of the human person. Next, the chapter looks within the person at what virtue theory calls moral character and discusses models through which Roman Catholic moral theology often imagines and talks about moral character. This discussion highlights a commonality among these models: they often use spatial organization to analyze moral character. The chapter then demonstrates that the models we use to discuss moral character are powerful. Finally, the chapter notes two criticisms of virtue theory and argues that an ecological model of moral character offers unique assistance in addressing the more fundamental of these problems.

VIRTUE THEORY

Life is good. It is the fundamental gift, requisite for all experiences and understandings. Life is a good to receive, to give, and to be good at. We (human beings) are included in the scope of what God sees when God sees that it is "all good."[1]

Much of moral theology is about noticing different kinds of goodness well. Acknowledging goodness habitually and responding to it well is a good way to participate in life. We can participate in life's dynamics in ways that enhance it, and we can notice in our participation additional layers of good.

Goodness's fecundity can flourish in the environment of our lives. We can also live in ways that limit, diminish, impede, restrict, or deny the good. This ability to choose between these, to exercise moral agency, is another gift.

Because humans have moral agency, much of the goodness we bring carries a moral quality. Moral good is part of the "goodness" that exists in the life of creation among creatures who have moral agency. For such creatures, living well includes shaping a life that responds well to goodness. A good moral character is part of how a human person shapes a good life. Moral theology thinks about moral character using virtue theory.

Virtue theory links human action with human moral character.[2] In moral theology, we call a person a moral agent when highlighting that she or he *does* things. Because we are beings with temporal awareness, we discern histories, patterns, and accumulations of a moral agent's acts and act effects. In other words, because doing and being are connected, this "moral agent" identifier also highlights what people are like as individuals. It refers to their distinct traits and tendencies, or the patterns created around and within them by the way they choose to embed themselves into creation.

Virtue theory views the whole of these tendencies and patterns as a continuous, somewhat discrete and definable thing: the person's character. This character comprises a sentience, a subjectivity, and an individuality that grow and develop over a whole life, including the part of oneself that Aquinas called a soul.[3] Many of the dimensions of character are moral in nature, so virtue theory focuses on an aspect of a person called the "moral character." Like all aspects of a person, a person's moral character is continually in flux. Virtue theory claims the possibility of looking "within" a moral character, at the parts of which it, as a whole, consists. A moral character's internal dynamics constantly move: manifesting, shrinking back and developing, strengthening or weakening. The many "parts" of a moral character are continually growing new connections to their neighboring elements or hardening in isolation. In this way, virtue theory presents a moral character as always evolving, made of "parts" or, better, of participants who are always evolving. This vision supports our awareness that people change and offers us a way to look more closely at the dynamics that add up to different kinds of changes.

Virtue theory assumes that our moral character changes as a result of what we do. As we activate our better and worse traits, they gel to become something like tendencies or habits. "Habit" is a useful way to name a persistently and continuously existing phenomenon as a kind of characterizable entity. The sum or balance of all these habits is what we call a person's moral character. Therefore, we can deliberately shape our moral character by choosing which traits to exercise through our actions. The traits whose tendencies we exercise are strengthened. Our moral qualities emit outwardly through the acts we do, marking our worlds in different ways, and the moral quality of these actions also seep inwardly, becoming a part of what we are. In virtue theories, "moral character" is the name for that relatively stable moral totality that we shape through our actions and that also in turn guides the decisions we make. A virtue theory's image of a human person's moral character should help us to act well, inhabit the world's goodness well, and have goodness living well within us too. It should also resonate with our self-observations, with what we understand humans and morality to be.

Yet human experience teaches us that some qualities of a person seem to change beyond that person's own control (such as height and allergies). Other qualities seem remotely changeable, as if we could steer their development only with great difficulty and limited success (such as food, music preferences, interests, sexual attractions, and hair color). These qualities have a moral dynamic through their links to agency and personal history and social contexts. They are shaped by moral character and by many other factors, soft, visible, intractable, and deeply submerged into subconscious.

The effects of an individual's efforts to shape a good moral character do not simply and directly lead to a virtuous moral character. The efficacy of our efforts has limits. We can only steer sloppily. And as is typical in life, growth is not linear. If virtue theory is to help, it must use good images or models of moral character that reflect the complexity of this process.

Virtue theory claims that a character trait, such as a virtue or a vice, exists within a person only if it is manifested. As a tendency, a moral trait of a person can be said to exist only if the tendency actually ripples outwardly, outside the person, out in the world. On the other hand, we are always learning about ourselves, about what is within us, even to the point of reflecting on traits we lack or traits we have not exercised. We can reflect on what we do and what we do not do and, in that way, come to see what additional potential qualities and tendencies inhabit us. Consider a pair of examples.

One moral agent may have no particular awareness of her capacity for generosity, but in the right circumstances she may find herself giving of her time, money, energy, or attention for someone else's sake. Surprised at this or not, she could notice on reflection that she does in fact have the virtue of generosity. She acted from that inclination, and so that inclination must exist within her even if she had never known or named it. It has been recognized, given a name and a place. She now claims the virtue of generosity. With that recognition, the virtue gains potency.

Now, suppose that another moral agent genuinely lacks a good moral trait, such as patience. Virtue theory offers this moral agent a hope of acquiring it. Naming and giving space within oneself for a trait that does not yet exist has power.[4] A moral agent can cultivate the moral character she aspires to have by acting as if she already has a potential worthy trait such as patience, whether she feels that she has it or not. Naming something within herself as "patience," or a wish for patience, creates a space for patience to develop. A moral agent's awareness of a gap defined by this naming can carve out a space to be inhabited. Noticing an absence within our moral character, we are more likely to put to work what ought to be there. A virtue can begin to appear. Therefore, our attention to moral character has an effect on what the moral character does (or does not) include. Virtue theory assumes the efficacy of a bluff. Faking a trait we do not "feel" can make that trait begin to appear. A good virtue theory model of moral character should remind us of that possibility.

Virtue theory's interest extends beyond actions done and potential traits one could grow. What virtue theory calls a moral character also influences how a moral agent perceive situations, even before she sees a need for any sort of moral deliberation. Moral character and action mutually influence one another in a muddy kind of dialectic. Our attentiveness is shaped by our moral traits and the way we engage what surrounds us (what we have noticed and what we have not) in turn influences the shape of our moral character.

Further layers must be added to the virtue theory tool of moral character. First, social practices participate in moral agents' character development, but the way they do this is complex. Second, Christian virtue theories believe that God plays a role in character development.

Humans exist in contexts. We absorb traits from the societies in which we participate. Societies teach us, deliberately and accidentally, that certain virtues and vices matter and that as members of the societies we participate in practices through which we exercise traits that the society values. The specifics of this process are often debated.[5] Critical realism offers one promising way to bring virtue theory together with sociological theories that strive for precision and insight into human action and agency.[6] Individual moral agency and social structures meet in foggy and complex intersections. But at the very least we must agree that our moral formation is not entirely individually determined. Our character's shape is influenced before we have moral agency, and it continues through our lives on levels below our perception or understanding.

A practice is something we do but not every kind of thing we do. It means taking part in a social activity, such as playing chess, reading, voting, jogging, shopping, buying and using insurance, "liking" memes, cooking food, knitting, and marrying, activities that we know to do because it is done in our societies. Doing these things helps us achieve "the goals internal to" the practice (however "internal to a practice" is understood).[7] Practices propagate actions, goals, and a common valuation of these goals. So, practices help us grow in ways that our societies want. Good societies offer good practices. These influence the development of our own individual moral character.[8] We are subject to multiple feedback loops of excellence or corruption across the scales of our nested cultures and societies. A good model of moral character helps virtue theory to recognize the complexities of a person's social embeddedness.

We can also see that the development of qualities we already have is not easily steered. Development in one area of a moral character, such as a set of virtues pertaining to household management, can catalyze change in other areas. All the parts of a moral character are connected. For example, if we practice composting, we can get better at minimizing the amount of waste our household generates (with help from our intellect and the moral virtues). We might also get better at caring about the impact of the noncompostable waste we send into our environments. We may also develop a higher tolerance for engaging the "gross" materials (such as old peels and rotten vegetable cores) that are part of our survival. The nature of our repugnance responses might change. This change can play a role in other changes we experience, such as a shift in what we experience as ugly or beautiful. Our appreciation of what we call "clean" or "beautiful" can become more accurately attuned to what life itself needs.

For the final complicating layer, in Christian virtue theory, character traits are not simply exercised into existence. Seeds must be planted in order to be nurtured. Christian virtue theory says that God gives certain virtues, theological virtues, as gifts to persons. These virtues, often characterized as "infused," are steeped within each person because God has set them there. We can and do pray for stronger faith, for example, but the infusion of such a virtue's seeds must precede their growth. These virtues are gifted, then. Their appearance in a moral character is not a result of a person's exercise of moral agency.[9]

Moral virtues can also be strengthened through God's agency. Divine agency, primary causality itself, moves all moving.[10] Existence and life itself begin there. In that way, even the exercise of any moral trait involves both person and God. But God also moves with secondary agency, responding to creation and to life. Virtues' growth within a person does not result from that person's own efforts alone. God can take part in a moral agent's development. For example, a moral agent might pray for resilience while struggling through a lengthy healing process and find that resilience begins to take effect more prominently, as a gift from God, and that it is then strengthened as that gift is exercised.[11] Moral growth is always a collaboration, and exactly who is doing what is never precisely clear. We will work with this reality better when we use a moral character model that takes such collaboration and ambiguity into account.

These precepts of virtue theory demonstrate that the shaping influence we have over our moral development is not similar to choosing, measuring, and mixing ingredients together. We have limited and loose control over what we turn out to be like. Moral virtues need theological virtues to function, and these depend on God. For example, a moral agent can take a stand for radical justice if she has well-rooted, well-integrated, and well-aimed hope. The theological virtue hope marks a locus of collaborating between human and divine agency.

Understanding well how our morality evolves is important. It is part of our responsibility to live well. Taking responsibility for ourselves as morally well-cultivated beings requires awareness of the limits of that responsibility. We should notice the collaborations we inhabit with God and with our social and ecological contexts. Consider one detail we've already glimpsed: the shape of a moral character depends on the interactions of its constituent parts. With this observation, we are drawn to ask in what ways we imagine the interactions between the parts of a moral character. This is the aspect of virtue theory to which this book centrally attends. To delve into that task, we turn next to the models we use to imagine moral character.

MODELS FOR IMAGINING MORAL CHARACTER

Attention to the relationships between the moral virtues permits us to imagine where a virtue resides within a moral character. Imagining each virtue's collaboration with the other aspects of our moral character evokes debates about the unity of virtues. These were described in the preface. This book is not a call to settle these debates, but I will begin with a presumption that the virtues have some sort of unity. They are unified flexibly in a way not best viewed as a mechanical whole. The unity worth imagining is ecological in nature.

In early Western virtue traditions, the virtues were often spatially organized in a place, like a fenced-in pathway that goes up a hillside. This depicts moral character as a journey or a quest that one undergoes. The *Tale of Cebes'
Tablet* (from the first or second century CE) gives an example. In this tale, a sage's explanation of a painting of a hill describes the journey of moral growth. The hill is divided into levels and populated by people, paths, and obstacles.

The sage explains the paths that lead one through gates, past fortunes, up steep slopes, and near dangers and distractions. A traveler encounters vicious temptations, tricky and narrow gates, good and bad luck. Some persons eventually enter the higher and smaller areas of the hill. Very few are finally able to be with the virtues (depicted as women) in the upper gardens overseen by Wisdom herself.[12] Virtue-journey analogies such as this demonstrate models of virtues and moral character. They often parallel idyllic gardens and virtuous character, one way to imagine moral character environmentally.

In classic Thomistic virtue ethics, the moral virtues' arrangement implies a pyramid shape, which echoes the earlier tradition of a hill. Four cardinal virtues (at the top) oversee all the other virtues (along the pyramid's base). The cardinal virtues themselves are ranked hierarchically,[13] with prudence at the peak and justice, fortitude, and temperance arranged, in that order, below prudence. These cardinal virtues govern all the other moral virtues, which are therefore called subsidiary virtues.[14] Each cardinal virtue is in charge of its own subsidiary virtues. These virtues' positions in such models of moral character depict the subsidiary moral virtues in a subordinate role.[15]

Pyramid-shaped virtue structures helped nineteenth-century moral manualists to apply the principle of proportionate reason in evaluating a moral agent's acts. This principle compared the virtue upheld against the virtue violated by an act.[16] The relative authority of these virtues revealed the act's morality by naming what exactly is weighed against what when determining whether a proportionate reason justified an action.[17] We may write this off as a symptom of one theological era's love of hierarchies, but the idea that virtues are not all equally important pervades Catholic virtue theory. Virtues are often described in terms of hierarchical arrangements, such as height or altitude, their relative mass or area or size, or which virtues govern which. MacIntyre noted that virtues' relative significance demonstrates something definitive about different societies' morality.[18] Some virtues' content was deemed to carry less moral significance than others. The more highly ranked a virtue, the more important the values it upheld and vice versa.

These models of virtue arrangements all depict spatial relationships between the virtues. For example, generosity and temperance are both virtues, but temperance, as a cardinal virtue, is given more significance in moral theological literature. It is higher in a well-ordered moral character. Because it governs, includes, or oversees the formation of its subsidiary virtues, temperance encompasses more than do subsidiary virtues such as generosity. The relationship between virtues can be described in terms of their relative ranks, or which are within others or are managed by other virtues. In all cases, relative location demonstrates virtuousness.

My point here is not to call for a canonical hierarchy of the moral virtues. Neither will I propose that ecological virtues should be given greater prominence to improve our usual hierarchical virtues arrangements. My point is that the utility of a virtue theory lies not in its definitions of specific virtues but rather in its understanding of how they are arranged or, more to the point, how they interact. Virtue traditions imagine these interactions through different models of moral character. Therefore, the model through which we imagine moral character is powerful.

Yet the models we use are rarely scrutinized. The pyramid or hill hierarchies of virtues mirror the social and political structures of those societies that envisioned them. One can look at Cebes's tablet and hear its story and see the contours of its society's practices and assumptions about gender, social power, propriety, work and leisure, and the good life. The models we use to describe virtues' interrelationalities demonstrate our beliefs about what is and is not morally significant and therefore what is and is not morally good. Two contemporary examples can help us recognize this. Religion scholar Melanie Harris's womanist virtue theory describes interactions between virtues and values, with careful attention to a possible detrimental effect of binary thinking that may otherwise result. Environmental scholar Dale Jamieson's comments on causes of climate instability show us that the map of virtues' interactions carries more moral meaning than the list of which virtues are present in a moral character.

Melissa Harris's virtue theory offers a model of interacting pairs.[19] Drawing on Black women's literature, Harris outlines the priorities, emphases, and central virtues of a womanist virtue ethic. Her model is built in accordance with these explicit priorities. It aims to resist moral frameworks of a dominating society's racism and the wicked "morality" it perpetuates. Harris's model accounts for the moral development and well-being of both individuals and communities. It seeks these goals for the purpose of a clear overriding aim: survival. The model repeatedly emphasizes the link between the virtues (and vices) of a society and those of the individuals within that society. Given that one of the significant effects of racism is fragmentation across multiple scales and in many places, the wholeness that is reflected in the links between individual and society is important to Harris's argument.

This womanist virtue theory is necessary because in the United States, the dominant culture is thoroughly infected with the beliefs and practices of white supremacy. Virtues such as thrift, industry, and self-reliance are encouraged to further that system. Harris argues that these virtues only empower people with complete freedom. They do not make sense for Black women in the United States. Other virtues, such as generosity, compassion, justice, and spiritual wisdom, are required.[20] Harris also praises virtues of invisible dignity, quiet grace, and unshouted courage.

In order to resist prevailing white supremacist frameworks, this virtue theory also names several moral values that accompany the virtues. Wholeness is one of these values, meant for both the community and the individual. Virtues promoting "interdependence between the realms of spirit, history and nature" are needed.[21] Values of self-naming and of Earth justice are also identified.

In this virtue theory, the right values and virtues are woven together to form a "web-like interdependent structure" that creates a foundation for a womanist virtue ethic.[22] The virtues are those that tend to uphold and bolster these values, and the values in turn point to the right virtues.

The corrupted nature of the dominant society's understanding of good moral character burdens Black women with the additional task of rooting out where, how, and why their communities are threatened. Virtue ethics must therefore eliminate this moral discourse's damage to the development of Black people's health and character. Passing on the correct virtues and values is part and parcel of the responsibility to form one's own moral character.

Harris's focus is not on the structure of virtues' interactions. She attends to specific virtues and values with an eye to the resistance needed for survival. But the structure she describes is unique. Virtues and values inform one another, and her system's necessity of resisting a society requires her to attend to the social aspect of moral character with care and nuance. The structure of the model is one of resistance, pushing back, counteracting, and also secretly holding open a space within for subversive and joyful flourishing. Virtues and values cooperate to shape this. Harris recognizes the potential for a polarizing moral binary in this dynamic. Therefore, she also explicitly names values and virtues that are needed to avoid a polarized habitus such as the one that pervades a society of white supremacy. Harris names two binaries—heterosexist practices and assumptions of human supremacy on Earth—as two examples of moral failures that must end in order for a good moral community to flourish. Harris's vigilant attention to her moral character model's efficacy demonstrates her understanding of a model's power.

For the second example, we turn to environmental philosopher Dale Jamieson. Jamieson explains how we created our current ecological disaster. "Ignorance of science can give rise to excessive respect, which can quickly turn to disillusionment when science does not deliver the goods or when scientists turn out to be as petty and selfish as the rest of us."[23] Note the vices named here: ignorance, excessive respectfulness (a vice of excess), pettiness, and selfishness. The interactions of these virtues and vices is invoked to explain why we (humans of industrial societies) have continued to cause climate change even after we recognized the harm we are causing. An intellectual vice (ignorance, or insufficient knowledge) led to a moral vice (excessive respectfulness), and these two together nurtured disillusionment (another moral vice). Once disillusionment had taken root, we were ripe for manipulation in the hands of "those who make their living by manufacturing doubt and sewing [*sic*] discord." We became saturated with our "public apathy, dissatisfaction, and cynicism." Note that Jamieson implies that both moral virtues and vices brought us to this point of moral failure. The interaction between virtues and vices of different kinds shaped us badly. Note also that this evolution began with an intellectual vice, not a moral vice. Ignorance led to obsequiousness.[24]

Now, imagine a reverse progression. Imagine a society in which excessive respect for science led to scientific ignorance. This sort of society averted its eyes from reality out of obsequiousness. The society pictured in this scenario is quite different from the one Jamieson depicted (which began with an intellectual failure). The moral character of these two societies differ even though they share the same virtues and vices. It would follow that the best correction for each society's moral and intellectual failures would also differ. The model through which we visualize moral character and virtues matters.

ECOLOGICAL THOUGHT OFFERS BENEFITS TO VIRTUE THEORY

These two examples indicate the significance of the model we use to imagine moral character. A good model can help virtue theory to avoid some of its most notorious pitfalls. Next, we will consider three significant criticisms of virtue theory and find that a good model of moral character can help us grapple with the more significant of the three.

The first criticism is that virtue ethics does not supply moral norms to guide moral agents.[25] Steven Bouma-Prediger has argued, drawing on C. D. Meyers and Jason Kawall, that virtue theory does supply what we (moral agents) need for guidance in moral deliberation and reflection. A virtue theory view of morality avoids the Cartesian tendency to equate moral deliberation with intellectual work. This view relies on a richer anthropology,[26] recognizing the embodiment and the storytelling nature of humans for sources of moral insight.[27] Bouma-Prediger reminds us that character also shapes perception, which gives virtue theories an ability to address the moral dynamics in play before a moral agent is even aware of a need for conscious deliberation.[28] In his view, this criticism is simply not true and not cogent. He is not wrong. As I see it, a more fundamental problem with this criticism is that it holds other moral approaches as a standard that virtue theory ought to meet. This criterion faults virtue theory for lacking clear and absolute duties, or identifiable principles that can guide any moral agent in all similar situations. This critique judges virtue theory on the bases of other theories' priorities.

Were a virtue ethic to present concrete moral norms to guide action, it would contradict virtue theory's own main hope, which is moral agents' pursuit of moral growth by cultivating the virtues we need for a good moral character. Virtue theory encourages us (humans) to take seriously our responsibility to develop good moral character. We are to examine our own moral character, take stock, and carry out efforts to improve the balance of traits and abilities we see there. In such complaints, the criticism of virtue theory is that it is virtue theory and not deontology or principlism. Improving virtue theory will not answer critiques such as these.

But two other critiques do deserve our attention. Here is the first criticism of virtue theory that an ecological model of moral character can answer: virtue theory seems unable to describe clearly the flourishing or telos toward which a good moral character ought to orient itself. There is no sufficiently specific description of moral flourishing or well-being. The second criticism is that moral development seems quite nonlinear and erratic, and virtue theory does not account well for this unpredictability. Therefore, virtue theory does not offer specific and pragmatic guidance for us to improve our moral character even if the final end could be clearly visualized. Let's consider each of these challenges in turn.

Roman Catholic virtue theory has images of the telos, the ultimate and organizing end of human life. The ultimate end is the "beatific vision," or an encounter with God, the good itself.[29] This is not achievable in the context of a human life. It is eschatological or at the very least postmortem. Within the span of a human life, the telos offered by Catholic virtue theory is that one should aim to love: to love others because of the love for (and from) God.[30] But virtue theory does not suggest a turn-by-turn path to this. A life lived in the practice of love is referenced here, but exactly what that means for each individual is not specified. The telos on which morality depends is vague and broad. Let's consider this prospect in terms of ecological virtue ethics.

Ecological virtue philosopher Mike Hulme notes that virtue thought is not a "techno-fix," a "system for Earth governance," or an "exercise in social engineering."[31] It has a more biotic nature. Today's ecological crises (especially climate change) present the "challenge of embarking on a global project of climate management" even as "the very values required to design and deliver such a project are deeply contested."[32] But as Hulme argues, virtue theory brings a capability for such a situation. He points out that virtue ethics' particular aptitude for ecological ethics is that it "offers a more credible, situated and plural way—not necessarily an easier or a more universal way—of thinking about the intractable ethics of climate change."[33] In virtue theory, the specific telos to orient toward is locally defined. It is situated and therefore plural. Moral agents must recognize the versions of flourishing that are apt and discern the specific direction of moral growth that is needed for one in a given time and place to imagine, approach, and cultivate that telos.

It is possible to recognize more or less good things without a detailed description of our eschatological destiny. The fact that a universal human telos cannot be described in detail does not mean that it is not real or that it cannot guide us. Christian life in the "already/not yet" tension takes as a given that we are always hoping for and leaning toward a kind of life that we cannot clearly see. An overly specific telos for all should raise suspicion.

Because we are working our way toward an ecological model of moral character, it helps to notice that the disciplines of ecology share a similar problem: What is the meaning of "flourishing"? As it turns out, debates about the meaning of a healthy ecosystem proliferate. Some question whether it even makes sense to speak of a stable and perfected stage of any ecosystem's development.

Ecologist Edward Kormondy's comparison of two ecosystems demonstrates the difficulty involved in naming an ecosystem as healthy or less healthy. This basic comparison focuses on two ecosystems' systems of energy.[34] One is a bog, the other a clear-water river. The bog's autotrophic activity (that is, its processes of converting inorganic elements and energy into nutrients) is ten times more efficient than that of the river. That sounds like a hearty life cycle system. But the bog loses more than double the energy than the river loses. In the river, more unused elements are lost because they flow downstream. In the bog, more material is kept in the system than in the river, but the bog loses more of the energy it creates. So, which system is healthier? Even for such a narrow focus, attentive only to an ecosystem's energy conversions, the comparison does not help a reader to know which system is healthier. The energy conversion flow and use and the loss of energy is not enough information. When more energy is lost, compensation is needed somewhere or the system will not sustain. If it does not, this ecosystem will collapse.

But one ecosystem's collapse only means that different species will eventually appear and a new type of ecosystem will begin. So, in the end all one can conclude is that the bog is better at being a bog and that the river is better at being a river. This continues as long as each has a way of maintaining a stable cycle of energy. Neither bog nor river will be what they are forever. Their resilience will change, increasing or decreasing, as the species within succeed one another. Even when one can say that an ecosystem is at its most healthy by some defendable standard, that ecosystem is dynamic and in flux. The static perfection we might imagine of a "healthy" ecosystem never exists.[35] If it did exist, it would simply look as sterile as death or oblivion.

We can't easily say when an ecosystem is unhealthy and when it is in transition from one kind of ecosystem to another. Holmes Rolston III has noted that some "trajectory stability" might be the best we can hope for.[36] This is one obstacle to defining and recognizing flourishing in ecosystems. A brief discussion of additional obstacles to a simple and universal understanding of a healthy ecosystem follows.

In the ecological literature,[37] there has been an assumption that an ecosystem's health is signified by a balance of an ecosystem's complexity and its stability. Michael J. Auerbach identifies several flaws with this assumption.[38] One flaw is that these analyses have not predicted well. Healthiness exists when it persists. Sometimes an ecosystem considered healthy becomes demonstrably unhealthy. Auerbach notes inconsistencies in ecologist's ways of mapping the relationships between species (like chains of consumers or of those consumed) in order to construct a model that can demonstrate which ecosystems meet or fail the criteria of complexity and stability.

Daniel J. Rapport names problems with the goal of evaluating ecosystem health. As he asks, "Can part of nature be healthy yet contain unhealthy regions? Can a healthy ecosystem continue to remain so if it is surrounded by degraded systems?"[39] Rapport identifies three competing approaches to assess an ecosystem's health. Some look for specific critical characteristics that are shared by all ecosystems. Some aim to understand an ecosystem's ability to manage stressors (resilience). Some look for risk factors or the presence of dynamics or species that tend to threaten health. Rapport agrees that a few functions or structures can be considered necessary to any evaluation of ecosystem health. For example, one should consider the efficiency of an ecosystem's cycles of energy and nutrient transfer, as we saw in Kormondy's river/bog comparison above. The diversity of species is also important. However, not all kinds of species diversity is equally good, and diversity in ecosystems is not simply in direct proportion to that ecosystem's likelihood to survive. There are some traits that matter to all ecosystems, though mapping their quality is complicated.[40]

François Ramade argues that the motivation to categorize an ecosystem as healthy or not can itself be faulty.[41] Even stability, or a set of systems persisting over time, is problematic. Disruptions in stability are often good or necessary.[42] The first step in defining a healthy ecosystem is to decide about the time frame to be considered. Ultimately, he offers a list of maxims that could be part of an evaluation of an ecosystem's health.

To return to virtue theory, similarly, we cannot say with precision whether and when a person's moral character is developing, when it is evolving, when it is deteriorating, when it is static, or when its perfection is attained. But this is not a flaw with the claim that there are better and worse directions in which a moral character can evolve. Moral character is not fixed, and the peak of its perfection over a life span is knowable at best only when that life is over. For those of us who are alive, growth is the purpose, not finality.[43] Constant beatific union with God alone is perfection, and this condition does not exist for the living.

The kinds of ambiguity that prevent a clear, single, specific, and universal description of ecological flourishing reflects the ambiguity around human flourishing, including the flourishing of a moral character. Difficulties arising from this ambiguity can be ameliorated with a moral character model that can guide us in accordance with what is known and what can best be hoped for. This parallel of a moral character and an ecosystem is a good sign that an ecological model of moral character can help us navigate with a nonspecific, nonuniversal telos.

The second criticism we recognized above is that virtue theory does not successfully predict moral growth on any specific level. It fails to provide a manual with clear and unfailing instructions even to meet proximal goals in character formation. We cannot confidently recommend a specific practice or habit to a moral agent in order to help her to develop a single specific virtue. We cannot predict the shifts in virtues and vices that may arise with a society's evolving practices, or even whether a moral agent's newly adopted habit will affect her character. There is an element here of chaos, of wildness, that speaks of the power of apparently inconsequential consequences. Again, the same is true of ecosystems. The consequences of altering an ecosystem in some way are never completely predictable. Introducing or eliminating a species in an ecosystem begins changes that will compound the unpredictability the longer we watch. Too much randomness and complexity exist in ecosystems to account for what we observe with every change. We can make some good guesses but no promises. Again, the unpredictability of a moral character is similar to that of an ecosystem.

A moral character model needs to help the moral growth of the people in their contexts of time and space. In our age, growth in ecological awareness is needed. This is another benefit of an ecological model of moral character that enables a moral integration into our ecologies. The preface proposed several criteria for a good model of moral character, and the following chapters will describe an ecological model of moral character meeting these criteria. A moral character is analogous to an ecosystem. Chapter 2 lays out the ecological fundamentals we will need to imagine this model.

NOTES

1. Genesis 1:31.
2. This book draws on Catholic virtue theory traditions rooted primarily in Thomas Aquinas. The most significant sources along whose work I trace Catholicism's virtue theory traditions include the following: Meilaender, *The Theory and Practice of Virtue*; Meilaender, "Josef Pieper"; Pope, *The Ethics of Aquinas*; Porter, *Justice as a Virtue*; Porter, *Recovery of Virtue*; Porter, "The Unity of the Virtues and the Ambiguity of Goodness"; Pieper, *The Four Cardinal Virtues*; Keenan, *Virtues for Ordinary Christians*; Keenan, "Virtue Ethics and Sexual Ethics"; Keenan, "Virtue Ethics: Making a Case as It Comes of Age; Keenan, "Learning the Virtue of Justice"; and Keenan, "How Catholic Are the Virtues?"
3. For Aquinas, the "soul" of a person is that person's "animating principle." This book will focus on the moral character of persons, leaving aside consideration of Aquinas's definition and mechanics of the soul. Aquinas, *ST*, I, q. 75.
4. "Giving space" within oneself for a trait can mean giving energy or time to its exercise, giving the potential trait attention or intention, or siting a "place" among one's established traits where the new potential trait can be rooted.
5. See Narvaez, "The Co-Construction of Virtue," in Snow, *Cultivating Virtue*, and other essays in that volume. Theologian Lauren Winner demonstrates the dangers and the stakes of incomplete knowledge about the root of Christian practices as an important warning. See Winner, *The Dangers of Christian Practice*.
6. Daly, "Critical Realism, Virtue Ethics, and Moral Agency."
7. MacIntyre, *After Virtue*, 187.
8. Of course, we also shape our societies, a point developed further in chapter 3.
9. The theological virtues are causally more distant from action than moral virtues too, according to Thomistic virtue traditions. This contrasts with the discussions of faith, hope, and love in Blanchard and O'Brien's work, where actions are seen as proceeding directly from faith, hope, and love, described as virtues with a moral content. See Blanchard and O'Brien, *An Introduction to Christian Environmentalism*.
10. Aquinas, *ST*, I, q. 44 and q. 25.
11. Eric Cassell provides an insightful description of resilience not as a rubber "bouncing back" trait but instead as an ability to shift one's internal traits in a way that helps one to recover and persist after difficulty or tragedy. Cassel, "The Nature of Suffering and the Goals of Medicine."
12. I owe thanks to my colleague Dr. Thomas Banchich, professor emeritus of classics at Canisius University, for introducing me to this tradition. See Smyth, "The Tablet of the Theban Cebes"; Cebes, *Cebes' Tablet*; and Fitzgerald and White, *The Tabula of Cebes*.
13. Cessario, *The Moral Virtues and Theological Ethics*, 146.

14. For more on this virtues structure, see Rourke, "Prudence Gone Wild."

15. Keenan, "Virtue Ethics and Sexual Ethics."

16. See Kaczor, "Double-Effect Reasoning from Jean Pierre Gury to Peter Knauer"; and Kaczor, *Proportionalism and the Natural Law Tradition*. For more, see also Johnstone, "The Meaning of Proportionate Reason in Contemporary Moral Theology"; Hoose, *Proportionalism*; and Rourke, "Where Is the Wrong?"

17. No canonical ranking of all the virtues was ever definitively completed, which left proportionate reason no commonly held standard through which to work its magic. Arguably, this lacuna is part of the reason that Peter Knauer's mid-twentieth-century understanding of proportionate reason gained such traction. See Knauer, "The Hermeneutic Function of the Principle of Double Effect."

18. MacIntyre, *After Virtue*, 181ff.

19. Harris, *Gifts of Virtue*.

20. Harris, *Gifts of Virtue*, 55. Harris develops this into a more explicitly ecowomanist theory in *Ecowomanism, Religion and Ecology*.

21. Harris, *Gifts of Virtue*, 111.

22. Harris, 107.

23. Jamieson, *Reason in a Dark Time*, 4.

24. The point here is not whether Jamieson has accurately identified the causes of climate change. This account of our moral failures is only one of a few different explanations he presents. Jamieson elsewhere blames a mutual lack of respect between scientists and policymakers (*Reason in a Dark Time*, 62). However, he consistently identifies scientific ignorance as a root cause, and the progressions he describes are credible and specific. We can visualize the interactions between the virtues and vices he names to better understand where and how we became morally warped.

25. See, for example, Trimiew, "Presidential Address"; and Austin, "Normative Virtue Theory in Theological Ethics."

26. Bouma-Prediger, *Earthkeeping and Character*, 11.

27. Bouma-Prediger, 15–16.

28. Bouma-Prediger, 16.

29. Aquinas, *ST*, Supplement III, q. 92, and, III, q. 1, a. 2 (respondeo).

30. Aquinas, *ST*, II–II, q. 25.

31. Hulme, "Climate Change and Virtue," 303.

32. Willis Jenkins has made a similar point. See Jenkins, *The Future of Ethics*.

33. Hulme, "Climate Change and Virtue," 307.

34. Kormondy, *Concepts of Ecology*, 30–31 and 32–33.

35. Rapport, "What Constitutes Ecosystem Health?"

36. Rolston, *Environmental Ethics*, 166–76. See also Rapport, "What Constitutes Ecosystem Health?"

37. See Auerbach, "Stability, Probability, and the Topology of Food Webs"; Rapport, Gaudet, and Calow, *Evaluating and Monitoring the Health of Large-Scale Ecosystems*; Costanza and Mageau, "What Is a Healthy Ecosystem?"; and Ramade, "Qualitative and Quantitative Criteria Defining a 'Healthy' Ecosystem." We will consider a few of these shortly.

38. Auerbach, "Stability, Probability, and the Topology of Food Webs."

39. Rapport, "What Constitutes Ecosystem Health?," 128.

40. Rapport concludes that imagining an "ideal state" for an ecosystem is not helpful. In addition, assumptions about ecosystem health involve the human need for specific

ecosystem characteristics or species areas always involved in evaluations of ecosystem health. If we prioritize an ecosystem's sustainability, are we saying that human interventions in an ecosystem are antithetical to its health? If we disregard human interventions, are we forgetting that no ecosystem exists apart from the influence of human activity? Rapport concludes that there is no simple solution to this.

41. Ramade, "Qualitative and Quantitative Criteria Defining a 'Healthy' Ecosystem."

42. He notes that the definition of an ecosystem as a nonequilibrium system demonstrates that disruptions of ecosystems (such as fires and flooding) are necessary for the long-term life of some ecosystems.

43. The final good is that toward which growth (as opposed to deterioration) is oriented, but my point here is that moral life consists in moving toward what we can see down the road, not in cutting directly toward actual perfection.

2

Where Morality Takes Place

ECOLOGY AND ECOSYSTEMS

Chapter 1 argued for an ecological model of moral character. Next, we need some understanding of what ecosystems are and how they behave. This book relies on four particular characteristics of ecosystems, so this chapter introduces concepts used to understand ecosystems and then describes those four characteristics. In chapter 3, the book begins to imagine traditional Roman Catholic virtue theory's "moral character" idea into an ecological model.

Ecology is a category of scientific disciplines, including plant, animal, physiological, behavioral, molecular, population, and community ecologies.[1] Systems ecology, pioneered by Eugene Odum, appears today in fields of population ecology and community ecology (among others). Ecologists study places, but in order to look at places like they do, we need to shift our thinking to see systems instead of beings and things. We will begin with the difference between a bioregion and an ecosystem.

Any place can be called a bioregion. A bioregion can be anywhere and any size, so really the term "bioregion" refers to all places. Bioregions have living beings such as plants and animals (including us) and abiotic elements such as earth, rock and stone, water, sunlight, and air. These things are always located in bioregions, and by virtue of their proximity they interact with one another constantly. All these interactions, including those involving abiotic elements, make up what we could call a bioregion's life. Let's imagine one bioregion: a midsummer North American pond.

In this pond, a frog sits on a lily pad. The lily pad breathes in what the frog breathes out. Below them, fish nibble at the tiny creatures swarming around the stem of the lily pad. The fish and these tiny creatures watch for insects, but sometimes when one does arrive, the frog catches and eats it. When these tiny creatures die, they produce elements and materials that other lily pads and creatures will eventually use or consume. All these living beings exchange organic compounds and minerals and process within themselves everything they absorb from their coinhabitants. Everything they excrete and everything that the abiotic energy entities shed has an impact on the other beings and things around. All these interactions create complex webs of interrelationality. Webs of interrelationality are a bioregion's ecosystem. Everything in a bioregion participates in its ecosystem.

The terms "bioregion" and "ecosystem" refer to the same thing, viewed differently. "Bioregion" refers to what is present in a place: lakes, bears, rock, dung, grass, bees, worms, pools, and buildings. The term refers to all kinds of beings and things that are in proximity with each other. This is what most of us imagine when we think about places. The term "ecosystem" refers to what happens in this place. It means all the systems of interrelationality between, among, and within the lakes, bears, rock, dung, grass, bees, worms, pools, buildings, and so on. in a place. Schools of systems ecology observe behaviors, actions and dynamics, and the patterns these make over time. This ecological discipline examines ecosystems' characteristics as systems. The focus is events: motions, what happens, what causes something else to happen, and characteristics of these happenings such as speeds, frequencies, widths of influence of a happening, phases, numbers of pausing influences, and so on. The term "ecosystem" is a functionalist referent for a place, and in ecosystems there is always a lot happening everywhere.

In ecotheology, the standard is to use the term "ecological" over "environmental." "Ecological" reflects the processes and relationships of ecosystems rather than individual entities and better recognizes humanity's integration into creation, an important corrective for those of us who have learned to view humanity as separate from creation. Ecology looks at "relationships in the Earth environment," and that, not entities or beings, is our focus.[2]

ECOLOGY AND ECOSYSTEMS

The term "ecosystem" can refer to a place's systems as indistinguishable from the place itself. Therefore, every ecosystem is a set of many systems. Systems exchange energy between their participants and transform forms of energy into other forms of energy (such as solar, kinetic, and caloric). Ecosystems have nutrient cycles, cycles of succession among organisms, carbon cycles, and chemical cycles.[3] Ecological awareness entails noticing the loci and agents of many vectors of interactions.

Ecosystems are the webs of interrelationality, and ecology is a means of examining them. Because ecology is a category of disciplines that study ecosystems,[4] it is therefore a human activity. Ecology might mean carrying out an examination of an area's patterns of energy exchange or an analysis of all the cooperation involved in botanical reproduction in one field. Ecology could also refer to understanding the decomposers of a hillside or describing changes in a soil's acidity.[5] These patterns of life always take place among abiotic entities, such as inorganic elements and compounds, including water, oxygen, and phosphates, and the organic compounds that result from organisms' activities. Life's patterns also involve factors such as moisture, wind, currents, and solar radiation (light or heat). Some ecologists' focus is on systems that are barely affected by biotic systems at all, such as the hydrologic cycle.[6] For our purposes, population ecology and community ecology are the subdisciplines that are most helpful. Population ecology involves observation of a single species in an ecosystem. Population ecologists take interest in generations of a species, species-typical behaviors and reactions, and evolutionarily significant aspects of a species' individuals. Community ecologists study multiple species within an ecosystem. They notice interactions between individuals and cohorts of species, changes in the numbers or influences or behaviors of species, and how they affect or react to each other.[7]

The virtue model I describe in this book envisions moral characters as ecosystems, which means speaking of virtues as species and other participants in an ecosystem. The virtue theory version of a community ecologist would look at the interactions between virtues, vices, passions, and the will. A population ecologist would, in virtue theory, attend to something like the development or infusion of virtues, the diminishing or increase of a virtue's or a vice's strength, or the responses a virtue might give to presences or impulses or information received from other virtues, vices, or apprehensions, for example.

ECOSYSTEMS' BEHAVIORS

If an ecosystem can be any place regardless of location, size, or stability, what kinds of things could be said about them as generalizations? What kinds of things can be said about all ecosystems?

Ecosystems are complex and unruly. They are very difficult to describe in part and impossible to describe completely. They encompass everything and everywhere we think of as wild. It may seem that more distinguishes than unifies them. Holmes Rolston III has noted that ecology is not as "law" oriented as other natural sciences, like physics.[8] Laws such as that of gravity are exceptionless, but the wildness of life itself is less predictable. The few "grand theories" that ecologists use often "turn out to be … gross simplifi-cations," which are too abstract or riddled with exceptions to help ecologists deeply understand a specific bioregion. Ecology's necessarily interdisciplin-ary nature also inhibits ecologists from naming universal laws. "Chemical relations are studied according to different rules than are neurons; these rules differ from those needed to study organisms as wholes," and yet chem-ical reactions and neurons are both parts of ecosystems.[9] Environmental phi-losopher Bruce Morito tiredly concludes that "clarity of explanation cannot, therefore, be soon expected."

This does not mean that ecosystems are too chaotic to examine system-atically or to predict. Patterns appear and recur. For example, certain kinds of systems operate in all ecosystems. An ecosystem's energy requires producers. Producers are living beings that transform sunlight into carbohydrates that organisms (including themselves) can then consume and use as fuel for their own lives.[10] Producers can be plants or animals in aquatic or landlocked biore-gions. Their species vary with ecosystem, but their role is always essential. Consumers ingest producers, and the producers become consumers' energy. Grasses transform solar energy into carbohydrates, and geese eat them, trans-forming the energy of their own biological life systems. The nitrogen and phosphorus that producers absorb is also absorbed into a consumer that eats a producer individual.[11] Producers and consumers die, and then decomposers consume them after death, rereleasing these minerals into the environment. The flows of energy and of minerals complement each other in every ecosys-tem. These are the basic circles of life.

As ecologist Alain Pave has detailed, many systems ecologists examining these systems of exchange work with the precision of mathematical model-ing to describe and understand a place's behaviors.[12] For example, a study of a spring near Walden Pond observed that place's "energy income" (a unit of kcal per square meter of area per year). The study compared the energy income resulting from detritus with the energy income arriving in the form of solar radiation. A simple ratio can result from comparisons such as these, and modeling can tell the story of this ratio's history and future. A British ecologist in 1966 found that one gram of a particular mollusk contributes less than half the caloric energy produced by one gram of a particular micro-crustacean.[13] Slodobkin's concept of "gross ecological efficiency" boils down computations to a single percentage of energy transfers over trophic levels.[14]

While some ecologists distill observations into equations and charts, other ecologists work in a way that reflects a different sensibility, "deeply grounded in aesthetic intuition."[15] Both kinds of work happen in ecology. Ecosystems display both predictabilities and irregularities. Therefore, we can name a few gentle generalizations about ecosystems.[16] The complexity, diversity, and wildness of ecosystems do not prohibit methodical and quantitative descriptions of life in different places.

The "underdetermined" patterns present in different ecosystems can be tracked, compared, and generalized.[17] These patterns are the characteristics of ecosystems.[18] Some of these patterns or systems are cyclical, as with hydraulic, biogeochemical, and sedimentary cycles and the nitrogen and phosphorus cycles mentioned earlier. Patterns themselves can follow patterns too, because ecosystems have different degrees of entropy.[19] They can be more or less tightly organized. An ecosystem must be somewhat stable in light of its energy cycle. All ecosystems' energy cycles must be at least somewhat stable for life to persist, and all ecosystems have a way of using energy sources that come from beyond them: the sun or the heat from the earth. Although ecosystems differ, the patterns of life systems through which they evolve share common traits.

Christian ethicist Steven Bouma-Prediger and environmental philosophers Jason Kawall and Holmes Rolston III have compiled lists of ecosystems' traits.[20] Each of these lists is useful. To prepare a model for visualizing moral character, I offer here a distilled list of many ecosystem characteristics noted by ecologists. This list indicates ecosystems' varieties of interrelationality.

Interrelationalities, layered thickly to form the webs of life, make ecosystems. Some generalization about complex interrelationality is possible. For our aim of a model of moral character, we can begin with four specific characteristics of ecosystems' interrelationalities. First, in ecosystems, significant causalities are often complex, weak, diffuse, and reciprocal. Second, the boundaries between and within ecosystems are porous and imprecise. Third, all ecosystems are nested. And fourth, ecosystems self-organize through niches. The rest of this chapter will explain these four ecosystem traits.

When my students think about interrelationality, they tend to imagine such things as friends and members of families and organizations. Some also think of a person they see on their commute or their favorite barista or librarian. Many significant interrelationalities do not often occur to us. We easily forget that the air we breathe has already been breathed by others. Shared air is a form of relationship. We forget that what fuels us today was yesterday a leaf in the hands of a migrant worker or a grain packed in a truck a thousand miles away. Our experiences and the people involved in them continue to influence our decisions and habits even when we cannot remember the events. Race, religion, spirituality, gender, language, and caste all come through our interrelationalities. To think ecologically, we need to be more mindful of these forms of relationship. Consider Brian Swimme and Thomas Berry's image of a prenatal grizzly bear. "In the very shape of her claws is the musculature, anatomy and leap of the Chinook (salmon)."[21] Even before birth, this bear's relationship with salmon already develops. Interrelationality, fully understood, is the force behind evolution. As community members, we (living inhabitants of places) evolve through continual adaptation to the other beings and materials around us. Relationship is everything, and everything is relationship.

Causality

In ecosystems, causality is complex because significant causes can be weak, diffuse, and reciprocal.[22] This reality discomforts our usual ways of thinking about morality. We are accustomed to finding more moral (and legal) significance in strong and direct causality. We often rule out accidents and mildly impactful circumstances when we grapple with how and why things really happen. For example, many of our moral theories filter out complex causality involved in individual and corporate actions and behaviors. The principle of double effect, arguably the subtlest of our tools when it comes to discerning intention, names only two relevant intentions behind a moral agent's action. In many cases when this principle is applied, the directness of an agent's intention is even conflated with the mechanical immediacy of chain reactions. In metaethical debates about the moral relevance of consequences, we do not consistently or uniformly distinguish between the proximally and remotely caused consequences. We lack categories to examine gradients of intention for moral differences between harm we knew would follow an act and a harm that might follow. Morally significant consequences are immediate and perceptible, and we lack tools to incorporate more than two consequences of an act. Social ethics traditions offer language to consider the moral meaning of participation in corporate actions and systems, but the diffusion of responsibility convinces many to wave aside that meaning. What we've deemed too minor to be significant causes are still factors that live on, participating in the moral life of individuals and communities. We do not speak well about the cumulative effects of contributing to harms and benefits in ways that are slight, dilute, indirect, or reluctant, so these effects are often overlooked.[23] But these kinds of effects matter in ecosystems' causality. Consider an example.

Imagine that a horse was recently injected with a medication that tends to increase her anxiety. Right now she is napping in her fenced-in yard by the road. Suddenly a car on the road hits a couple of the fence poles, and the fence falls over. The startled horse wakes, immediately panicked, and runs out of the yard and into the forested hills beyond. She injures herself in her panic. Why did this happen?

Suppose we tried to answer this "why" question for legal purposes. As a social practice, the law's way of finding culpability demonstrates something of our society's view of causality. We would consider the property owner's culpability and discount it, because nothing wrong was done. The owner did choose the fence's location, shape, and construction. She also allowed the horse's medication and played a role in the conditions of the hillside behind the house. But none of these add up to legal culpability for the horse's flight. Ultimately we would conclude that the driver of the car is responsible for damaging the fence, which allowed the horse to escape, and therefore for the horse's injury. In a litigious society where recourse to financial compensation for harms incurred is carried out and encouraged, the driver would likely soon owe money to the property owner, and the amount of money owed might well reflect the driver's exclusive fault.

Many factors contributed to the horse's injury: the age of the fence, the side effects of the horse's medication, the condition of the road, the frequency of speed limit postings, the powerful scent of the sweet grass behind the house, and the horse's boredom during a long afternoon. These factors are only weakly or indirectly related to the event. We forget that they are in fact causally significant to the sequence of events leading to the horse's injury. We adopt tunnel vision and name the car's driver as responsible and even as exclusively responsible.

The legal realm performs social practices of blame that train us to think about causality. In automotive incidents and in environmental law, we seek to simplify our interpretations of events in order to find which single agent is responsible for harms incurred. We seek the same goal in Catholic traditions of action theory. This problem is impeding ecological justice.[24] My point here is that these practices cultivate within us a habituated blind spot. Our practiced resistance to complex causalities also impedes our ability to understand how and why things happen in the natural world. In ecosystems, weak, diffuse, reciprocal, and indirect causes are very important. As a result, we have extremely nuanced and sophisticated actuary tables to ground insurance policies and costs but a relatively basic common understanding of ecological patterns.[25] Addressing ecological effects of pesticides, Rachel Carson dryly described this problem decades ago: "While it is admittedly difficult, in dealing with human beings rather than laboratory animals, to 'prove' that cause A produces effect B, plain common sense suggests that the relation between a soaring rate of liver disease and the prevalence of liver poisons in the environment is no coincidence."[26] But courts rarely follow this sense. No direct vectors of causality link a specific volume of liver poisons with a specific individual's failing liver. Willis Jenkins calls this one of the "wicked problems" of environmental justice.[27]

So, what is wrong with valuing strong, direct, and exclusive forms of causality? Nothing. They are important. But when we take seriously only strong, direct, and exclusive causality, we are not be able to account for the ways of ecosystems. Most of what happens in this world can be understood only when indirect, weak, and diffuse causality is recognized and accounted for. Another example will help us to see the importance of causes such as these.

Imagine you are camping on the shore of Cranberry Lake in the Adirondack Park in upstate New York. You hope to hear a loon call while you are there. You know that loons live in the area, that they are seen around this lake every year, that they can be heard at this time of day, and that last year a loon couple had a nest somewhere in the corner of the shore where your tent is pitched. Yet so far the nights have been too quiet. What is the cause?

If one of the streams feeding the lake flooded last spring, the lake's water level might be too high for a loon couple to find the shore suitable for nesting this year. If the water level is too low, that can also deter them. The lake must also be large enough to supply loons with the quarter mile of "runway" of the water's surface in order to take off for flight.[28] The presence of too many competing predators, too many other loons, too little of the right sort of prey, or too much human activity too close to optimal nesting sites could all motivate loons to go elsewhere.

Cranberry Lake's water temperature and salinity this season might not be optimal for nesting. Even if it is optimal, it might not match the preference of the individual loons that are nearby. Studies have found that loons tend to choose nesting sites that are similar to their own first nests rather than only sites that are more likely to help them to produce healthy offspring.[29]

As for food supply, loons prefer to eat such fish as yellow perch and sunfish, including the pumpkinseed sunfish. These fish will be present if they have found good nesting places and if they find food supplies that suit them. Zooplankton species could be rich and numerous, with many individuals present. But if St. Lawrence County used road salt on Route 3 more heavily last winter, the species diversity among zooplankton could be lower this summer. Some species of zooplankton adapt very quickly to road salt in the water, but others do not.[30] The causal chains following road salt use create conditions that are more or less favorable to zooplankton and therefore to pumpkinseed sunfish and perch and thus to loons.

Perch and sunfish are eaten by other predators too. Larger fish (which loons might also eat) and other predatory birds, such as hawks, cormorants, and herons, also eat these fish. Some of these birds also prey on loons. So, the presence of these other bird species can influence the loon population in complex ways.

Perch are often brought to an area by human influence through such practices as boating and fishing with living fish as bait. So, humans fishing can increase the number of perch, which might attract more loons. On the other hand, humans who fish using sinker lures made of lead often leave the lures at the bottom of a lake, where the lead leeches into the water. Lead poisoning hurts loons. Therefore, human fishing can both enhance and detract from favorable conditions for loons.[31]

This brief list of weak, indirect, and uncertain causes reminds us that we would be wrong to assume that only direct or powerfully efficacious causes make a difference. Ecology teaches us that weak, diffuse, and indirect causality matters. Moral formation is at least as complex as loon life on Cranberry Lake. The mark of a social practice on moral agents differs from one individual to the next. Humans born and raised by the same parents often do not grow with identical or even similar moral characters. Moral lessons are not absorbed in the same way or with the same effect by all who encounter them. Moral formation is a complex dynamic interacting directly and indirectly with many other dynamics. Therefore, weak, diffuse, and reciprocal causality should be recognized and valued in an ecological model of moral character.

Borders and Boundaries

The second ecosystem characteristic is about borders and boundaries. In ecosystems, all boundaries are vague, porous, and permeable. This is true even to the point that identifying a stand-alone bioregion is not possible.

As we've seen, the concepts bioregion and ecosystem signify only constructed epistemological categories. The borders "defining" a place are not significant to that place itself. They matter only to those examining it. Ecosystems are spatially and temporally defined by an observer's driving questions. For example, consider ecologists who study cliffs. A cliff is a reasonable border between bioregions but it is also a bioregion in its own right. It has its own ecosystems.[32] So, for cliff ecologists, the places others see as boundary are an area of focus, and the boundaries around what matters are what other ecologists call bioregions. There is a flexibility to boundaries.

Even if we do for practical reasons imagine an ecosystem as a clearly defined ontological unit, the boundaries defining it remain porous. All ecosystems are open systems. Solar radiation originates outside of all our planet's ecosystems and plays essential roles.[33] Without the sun, producers make no calories, and nothing can eat. Furthermore, each ecosystem continually influences and is influenced by its neighboring ecosystems. We can more easily see why this is so when we are mindful of weak and diffuse causality. The interactions between ecosystems are significant, because ecosystems' participants and interactions flow across boundaries. Ecosystems "such as seas, cities and savannahs have structures and processes that blend into adjacent nature, often without discontinuities."[34]

Let's return to the hypothetical campsite by Cranberry Lake. An area of the shore around this lake can reasonably be called an ecosystem. In order to understand what is happening there, we need to know about every form of life inhabiting that area in the water, on the land, and in the air. We also need to understand the soils, air conditions, and the minerals that are present and how they interact. We need to know how the water's salinity, acidity, and temperature affect all these. Each of these details is defined by factors existing outside of the ecosystem.

Migrating birds nest in this area. Leaves fall from neighboring trees to provide decaying matter. New species arrive attached to the bottom of a boat or washed in with sewer water overflow. The air above and within brings influences from other places near and far. The rain includes particles from remote factories. In 1990 when the Clean Air Act began to limit the burning of coal in human communities, the water in this lake changed.[35] Methyl mercury levels of the water fluctuate with human industrial practices and with legislation.[36] Higher levels of mercury are absorbed by loons and other species, leading to death and lower reproductive rates. This changes the balance among all the species populating the area.[37]

In ecology, closed systems are not possible. All borders and boundaries are porous and permeable. Everything that happens on the shore of a pond can cause changes in the pond itself and far from the pond. Every boundary drawn to circumscribe an area for ecological study is continually trespassed by living entities, biological and botanic, and by chemicals, winds, energy exchange, and heat. Incorporating this characteristic into an ecological model of moral character helps us recognize the permeability of boundaries between and within a moral character. This gives us a model that reflects humans' interrelationality between individuals and across the scales of societies. It can also help us to think creatively about virtues and vices and about vague borders between collaborators within moral character, such as prudence and the intellect and faith and hope.

Nestedness

The third trait follows from the permeability of boundaries within and between ecosystems. All ecosystems are also subsystems of larger ecosystems. The difference between an ecosystem and a subsystem is one of perspective.[38] Like boundaries, this is a difference existing only in the observer's eye. The scale of an observer's focus defines an ecosystem.

Nestedness is an important category in ecological sciences because it pertains to species diversity.[39] In the mid-1990s, the significance of this trait became more widely understood.[40] Because diversity manifests on micro levels, awareness of nestedness helps ecologists recognize the "richness patterns" among species in an area.[41]

Naming an ecosystem requires choosing a scale of examination. At Cranberry Lake, we might want to look at an individual living thing (e.g., the tissues of the digestive system of a loon chick)[42] or a population (e.g., all the loons currently nesting at Cranberry Lake and around Silver Lake) or at one community within a bioregion (all the life in an area of six meters square adjacent to a loon couple's nest). Ecologists might examine the nitrogen cycle, a food chain, or the water temperature of the lake or its shores. Our interest fixes for us the size and scale of the region we will examine. In other words, we define each ecosystem by establishing the frame through which we observe.

Every observation of an ecosystem is also implicitly a study of that ecosystem's subsystems and its broader contexts. If we look at a loon chick's digestive system, we are also seeing the water he inhabits, the food he eats, the species that pursue him and pursued his ancestors, and the decomposers that will feed on his decaying body after he dies. All these things (foods, waters, species, family members) could be present in this lake's region or in a Yukon wildlife refuge or somewhere in between.

In choosing an ecosystem frame, we also determine which levels of the system we see most clearly and what we will view only partially or indirectly. Ecotheological ethicist Kevin O'Brien describes this as a trade-off between scale and resolution.[43] If we study the lake's food systems, we may easily see the effects of the water's acidity but might miss the impact of a visiting species' global migratory changes. If we examine the numbers of pumpkinseed sunfish over three years, we may note a change in the populations of its predators or prey, but we might not notice the disappearance of the ash trees in the Adirondack forest surrounding the lake. Naming an ecosystem means choosing what we will not see.

Yet an order resonates across the scales of ecosystems. Everything that happens on one scale will be reflected across all scales. What happens inside a bird's digestive system, in its predators' population density, in the average annual air temperature where the lake exists, and in the industrial regulations of states hundreds of miles away are all interrelated. This is why some describe ecosystems as superorganisms.[44] All ecosystems are subsystems of larger ecosystems. Nothing happens within only one scale of observation. Imagine that one zooplankton population of this lake disappeared. This is a change on a pretty small scale because these are tiny creatures, and there are many different such species. The effects of this disappearance would be evident on the scale of the whole area as this species' consumers adapt to this loss. We would see minuscule changes in the behavior, health, or unmet needs of each species in the area. Indirect consequences could appear in the reproductive systems of a plant that lives on the shore. Ripple effects may change the relationship between two normally cooperative bird species. Any one of these changes may be amplified in a feedback loop when it initiates a reciprocal causality process. This one species of zooplankton played many roles when it lived in this lake, and these roles participated in the lake's life on every level of scale. When it is gone, the billions of effects it created also disappear or transform, and other changes follow.

Bioaccumulation is another example. This is the phenomenon in which the concentration of a toxin (e.g., lead or mercury) increases across higher levels of a food chain. The smaller species absorb more minerals from lake water than the predator birds who live near the lake. Smaller fish eat these tiny life-forms, and larger fish eat those fish. Birds such as loons, hawks, and cormorants eat these fish, and larger birds eat smaller birds. Visualizing this, you can imagine the mineral and organic makeup of a tiny minnow that, once eaten by a larger fish, takes part in the life systems of that fish, which then will influence the makeup of the predator bird that eats him. At the same time, all these individuals are also directly ingesting the toxins in the environment. Each creature's organic and mineral makeup is taken in when eaten. Their bodies become nested within their higher-order predators. When we trace concentrations of toxins, we find that the concentration is higher in the larger creatures than it was in the smallest species' individuals. The bioaccumulation property of toxins in ecosystems is another example of how nestedness works in and among ecosystems.

Every ecosystem, from a single cubic meter at the lake's bottom to the acres encompassing the lake and its neighboring forests in Canada and New England, would respond to the loss of one tiny zooplankton species. This is a characteristic of ecosystems' nestedness.

Niches

Now that we've considered porous boundaries, loose causalities, and nestedness of ecosystems, we are ready to look at the fourth characteristic of ecosystems: niches. This term allows us to refer to a living creature in terms of its needs, behaviors, or functions.

For nonecologists, the term "niche" brings to mind a social space within which a person may uniquely and comfortably fit. A classroom can offer a familiar example. Imagine a small class into which a student has registered late. As this new student finds her place in a class, she learns which physical and social spaces fit her well while at the same time shaping these spaces to incorporate herself more comfortably. Physically, she arranges and shifts her desk and her chair's work space. Socially, she performs behaviors that seem good to her, informed by responses that her behaviors receive among classmates and the professor. As she "finds" her niche, the class's "personality" or dynamics also change in response. Other students may begin to fill new social roles or to behave somewhat differently. She might introduce a new levity or unique political views to discussions. Some students may become more competitive. A student who had been asking many clarifying questions during discussions might begin to speak less often. This dynamic, when observed over longer durations (generations instead of class periods), is similar to ecology's sense of the term "niche."

In ecosystems, a niche is also a kind of functionalist space. It is a role that a species might fill. As Eugene Odum explains, "The ecological niche . . . is the position or status of an organism within its community and ecosystem resulting from the organism's structural adaptations, physiological responses, and specific behavior. . . . The ecological niche of an organism depends not only on where it lives but also on what it does."[45] Niche flows from ecological interrelationality and is a way of naming a species' unique needs, contributions, and behaviors as functions that are carried out within a bioregion's systems. Species fill multiple niches because they are consumers, energy sources, and competitors (for example). Niches may be filled by multiple species too. Previously I noted that all ecosystems require producers (to transform sunlight into other forms of energy). The species filling the role of producer differ in grasslands and under pond water. Resilient ecosystems have larger numbers of species filling the role of producer. Therefore, a species may also occupy different niches in different places.

Consider Cranberry Lake again for a demonstration. The loons that nest on its shores likely eat fish such as perch and sunfish from the lake. They might also eat snails and insect larvae in the area. These loons are also potentially prey for other birds such as hawks and cormorants. They compete with other species for nesting places and food. Loons may cooperate with an aquatic plant by helping it to survive or procreate through their movements or through what they add into the water or on the land. Loons provide assistance to plant species whose seeds they distribute when they move or excrete them. In addition, loons feed decomposers after they die. When anything changes in any one of these relationships, all other relationships in which this bird population participates also change, even if only minutely, in response. If a migration pattern changes or if one year the loons arrive later, all the species with which loons interact will adjust with this change. Then, every species that has any sort of relationship with any of these species will also make adjustments. These changes ripple all throughout a bioregion on all scales, causing changes directly, indirectly, weakly, diffusely, and reciprocally, as we have seen.

Now, consider niches from the whole ecosystem's perspective. An ecosystem has needs that must be met in order for it to be a life system. These needs are processes that the ecosystem's participants both enact (by performing functions) and require (each for their own survival). Niches are steps of the process of life. When species' and systems' needs and roles meet, a niche is filled. When the niche is occupied, survival can continue.[46] Greater diversity (more species and functions and thus more niches) creates a more complex ecosystem, and that is a more resilient ecosystem.[47]

The needs of every species require that an ecosystem has a way for their bodies after death to be reincorporated into the ecosystem and a presence that resists their own population's growth. In order to endure over generations, species must encounter obstacles to individuals' continuing life. If no other factor of an ecosystem limits a species' reproduction and life span, that species will not survive. This is a law of ecological balance. When this balance fails, the whole ecosystem dies or evolves into a different ecosystem entirely.

What if there is a poor fit between the local population of a species and the ecosystem where it finds itself? This kind of failure can destroy that population or the whole ecosystem. For example, a new species may arrive in a bioregion where no appropriate niches for it exist. The roles it can supply are not helpful to existing systems, and the conditions it needs are not created by the place's species or abiotic elements. If the population of a species lacks some of what it needs to survive (such as food or adequate reproductive conditions), it will not last in that place. If the population's survival needs are met but no factors limit its reproduction or its individual's life spans increase, the ecosystem will be overwhelmed by this population. The ecosystem itself will be threatened and could die.[48] This is what happens with "invasive" species.

Invasive species are not particularly aggressive or invasive in character. They arrive in ecosystems (usually due to human action), and they threaten these ecosystems only because they do not fill and need the niches that are available or offered in the new places where they arrive.

If a species population adjusts over generations to the ecosystems in which it survives, it follows that the two different populations of the same species in two different places might become increasingly different from one another. This is called speciation. It is one of the ways a species can evolve divergently over generations to create different and more species. Niches change, ecosystems change, and species themselves change. "Each species alters its own environment and that of its associates . . . but in so doing, it provides a new set of conditions within the tolerance range of yet other species."[49] Evolution is always collaborative in this sense. Species become what they (we) are through coevolution.

As every species populations' individual members die, rot, feed, reproduce, cooperate, and compete in the places where they live and have lived,[50] an ecosystem and its participants evolve together. Niches shape species, and species shape niches; the whole ecosystem evolves as a community. In this way, ecosystems self-organize.[51] Therefore, understanding niches means thinking about the succession of species within ecosystems. A species can alter its habitat's conditions to the extent that the place becomes a poor fit for that same species.

The concept of niches helps us to think about a problem introduced in chapter 1. As we saw, an ecosystem's own telos is not easily definable. The definition of a "flourishing" ecosystem is debated, but some ecologists refer to a "climax community" to describe flourishing. A "climax community" is stable because the changes that are needed are taking place.[52] Such an ecosystem is not still or unchanging, having reached an ideal and now simply holding there. That is not how life behaves. Successions of generations and species occur, and the patterns of these successions can even be characterized. Ecosystems tend toward more diversity, more structural complexity, more organic matter, and more "metabolic stability." Life thrives in the kinds of stability that result from change, not from stillness or static conditions.

Of the four characteristics of ecosystems that will help us build a new model for moral character, the concept of niches is most valuable. Chapter 3 illustrates each of these four. Perhaps some parallels between ecosystems' traits and human morality are already apparent. At Cranberry Lake, we see a community of interacting species and abiotic participants, all living their lives and bumping into, using, and benefiting one another in all directions. This certainly sounds like our situation as humans navigating a complex world. Ecosystem dynamics call to mind many of the dilemmas that bring us to ponder morality in the first place. These similarities might be interesting, but they are not what we seek here. The bioregion is being held up not to mirror human communities but instead to model moral character. Our purpose is to imagine these species or niches as virtues or participants in a human person's moral character. Chapter 3 describes this model.

NOTES

1. The term "ecology" secondarily refers to the systems of life that these disciplines examine. Smith, *Ecology and Field Biology*; and Calow, *Blackwell's Concise Encyclopedia of Ecology*.

2. This definition is from Hart, *Sacramental Commons*, 214. For more definitions and understandings of ecology and for examples of ways it is approached in ecological sciences, see Schneberger, *The Black Crappie*; Krebs, *Why Ecology Matters*; Kormondy, *Concepts of Ecology*; McCann, *Food Webs*; Tribe, Eraut, and Snook, *Ecological Principles*; Spicer, *Biodiversity*; the classic text Odum, *Fundamentals of Ecology*; Cherrett and Bradshaw, *Ecological Concepts*; Worster, *Nature's Economy*; Odum, *Ecological and General Systems*; Slobodkin, *A Citizen's Guide to Ecology*; and Karban, *How to Do Ecology*.

3. Slobodkin, *A Citizen's Guide to Ecology*; Odum, *Environment, Power, and Society for the Twenty-First Century*; and Kormondy, *Concepts of* Ecology, 1–6. Drs. Slobodkin and Kormondy were professors of ecology.

4. Eugene Odum, sometimes called the "father of ecology," has called ecology "the study of organisms at home." Odum, *Fundamentals of Ecology*, 3.

5. Some who employ these terms outside of the ecological sciences differentiate between "ecology" and "ecosystem" less strictly. Ethicist J. Baird Callicott refers to the bioregion (or the ecosystem's component parts) as a "community ecology." Callicott, *Thinking like a Planet*, 42.

6. Kormondy, *Concepts of Ecology*, 36.

7. As a functionalist categorizer, community ecology and population ecology parallel sociology's theory critical realism. Both look at systems made up of interacting roles (or, ecologically speaking, niches). These roles are durably inhabited by individuals in sociology and by species in population ecology and community ecology.

8. Holmes, "Ecology," 299.

9. Morito, *Thinking Ecologically*, 77.

10. Kormondy, *Concepts of Ecology*, 2.

11. Kormondy, 3.

12. For an overview of the development of mathematical modeling in the ecological sciences, see Pavé, *Modeling of Living Systems*. Pavé discusses ecology's very gradual acceptance of this means of study and warns about some of the potential dangers of its use. "While modeling is not necessarily a form of theorization, the construction of a model may prove to be a determining element; however, we must remember that a formula or mathematical object must . . . be interpretable in biological or ecological terms" (2).

13. Kormondy, *Concepts of Ecology*, 33.

14. Trophic levels are like steps up and down a vertically imagined food chain. Kormondy, *Concepts of Ecology*, 31.

15. Morito, *Thinking Ecologically*, 71, quoting Theodore Roszak's *Where the Wasteland Ends: Politics and Transformation in Postindustrial Society* (1972).

16. For more on the problems of generalizations in ecology, see Cooper, "Generalizations in Ecology."

17. Kormondy, *Concepts of Ecology*, 2.

18. Morito, *Thinking Ecologically*, 177.

19. Kormondy, *Concepts of Ecology*, 33.

20. Bouma-Prediger, *For the Beauty of the Earth*, 18–21; Kawall, "Inner Diversity"; and Rolston, "Ecology," 295.

21. Johnson, *Ask the Beasts*, 119. She acknowledges here Swimme and Berry, *The Universe Story from the Primordial Flaring Forth to the Ecozoic Era*.

22. Weak causality is when a consequence is partly caused by an event. In diffuse causality, an event's consequences manifest as effects only after a delay, or indirectly. Reciprocal causality is a feedback loop, when an event's consequences cause the same event to recur.

23. We do practice consideration of differences between formal and material participation but only in instances of certain extreme moral violations. We do not expand our use of this distinction to consider moral participation in good acts or minor moral failures.

24. The journal *Biology and Philosophy* offered an excellent issue investigating areas of uncomfortable fit between biology (including ecology) and understandings of causality (particularly on the proximate and ultimate causes). See Dickins and Barton, "Reciprocal Causation and the Proximate-Ultimate Distinction"; and Laland et al., "More on How and Why."

25. Kormondy, *Concepts of Ecology*, 71.

26. Carson, *Silent Spring*, 192.

27. Jenkins, *The Future of Ethics*, 190.

28. Cornell Lab of Ornithology, "Common Loon Life History," All about Birds, accessed July 16, 2019, https://www.allaboutbirds.org/guide/Common_Loon/lifehistory.

29. Kuhn et al., "Modeling Habitat Associations for the Common Loon (Gavia Immer) at Multiple Scales in Northeastern North America," 4.

30. Coldsnow et al., "Rapid Evolution of Tolerance to Road Salt in Zooplankton." See also Stager, "Update on the Ecological Condition of Adirondack Lakes"; and Byrd, "Common Loon (Gavia Immer) Biogeography and Reproductive Success in an Era of Climate Change," 58–59.

31. Ecologists examine loons as an "indicator species" to help them see whether lead is present in high levels in a lake's water. See Kuhn et al., "Modeling Habitat Associations for the Common Loon (Gavia Immer) at Multiple Scales in Northeastern North America," 4; Schoch et al., "The Impact of Mercury Exposure on the Common Loon (Gavia Immer) Population in the Adirondack Park, New York, USA"; and Razavi et al., "Mercury Bioaccumulation in Stream Food Webs of the Finger Lakes in Central New York State, USA."

32. Larson, Matthes, and Kelly, *Cliff Ecology*, 1–15. Larson and others argue that the tendency to view cliffs as ecosystem borders means that we do not study cliffs themselves well enough.

33. Of course, the influence between sun and plant life is not mutual.

34. Odum, *Environment, Power, and Society for the Twenty-First Century*, 59.

35. Scrudato, Long, and Weinbloom, "Mercury Contribution to an Adirondack Lake."

36. United States Environmental Protection Agency and Office of Chemical Safety and Pollution Prevention, "Basic Information about Mercury," Overviews and Factsheets,

US EPA, August 20, 2015, https://www.epa.gov/mercury/basic-information-about
-mercury.

37. Karasov, "Digestive Physiology"; Schoch et al., "The Impact of Mercury Exposure on the
    Common Loon (Gavia Immer) Population in the Adirondack Park, New York, USA."

38. "What is a system, and what is a subsystem is an arbitrary characteristic of one's point of
    view. One person's system is another person's subsystem." Odum, *Systems Ecology*, 3.

39. Fontaine, "Abundant Equals Nested."

40. Worthen noted that nestedness, as a "composition pattern" rather than a number (such
    as abundance), was for a time overlooked. Worthen, "Community Composition and
    Nested-Subset Analyses."

41. Srinivasan, Tamma, and Ramakrishnan, "Past Climate and Species Ecology Drive Nested
    Species Richness Patterns along an East-West Axis in the Himalaya."

42. Karasov, "Digestive Physiology."

43. O'Brien, *An Ethics of Biodiversity*, 81–83.

44. Callicott, *Thinking like a Planet*, 41–44. In biological and ecological literature, see
    Powell, "How Ecology Shapes Caste Evolution"; Gardner and Grafen, "Capturing the
    Superorganism"; and especially Hölldobler and Wilson, *The Superorganism*.

45. Odum, *Fundamentals of Ecology*, 15. Kormondy defines a niche as a "unique multidimen-
    sional physical-chemical-biological formation." Kormondy, *Concepts of Ecology*, 159.

46. Callicott, *Thinking like a Planet*, 92.

47. Kormondy, *Concepts of Ecology*, 161, 163; and Rapport, "What Constitutes Ecosystem
    Health?," 129.

48. Ecologists debate whether this leads to a sick ecosystem, a dead ecosystem, or a different
    kind of ecosystem altogether. In any case, all agree that this is no longer a healthy ver-
    sion of the kind of ecosystem it was. Rapport, "Ecosystem Health," 5–31; and Rapport,
    "What Constitutes Ecosystem Health?"

49. Kormondy, *Concepts of Ecology*, 182.

50. Edwards, *How God Acts*, 24, 66, and 88.

51. "The ideas of natural selection and adaptation direct attention to the environmental
    context of species and their relationships with other species and with such physical and
    chemical aspects of the environment as temperature, moisture, salinity, acidity, and the
    like." Callicott, *Thinking like a Planet*, 54. "Context" here means niches. See also Morito,
    Thinking Ecologically, 70. In ecological literature, see Kutsch et al., "Environmental Indi-
    cation"; Roberts and Tregonning, "The Robustness of Natural Systems"; and Zhao et al.,
    "The Shaping Role of Self-Organization."

52. Kormondy, *Concepts of Ecology*, 158.

3

Earthly Moral Character
AN ECOLOGICAL VIRTUE MODEL

The ecosystem traits described in chapter 2 will help us structure a model of moral character as an ecosystem. This chapter describes this model's structure and dynamic. We will begin on the small scale of the virtues themselves. In an ecological model of moral character, virtues occupy and create niches. A virtue is more like a nexus than an entity.

An entity retains its traits (such as its shape or behaviors) more consistently in different contexts than a nexus. Entities have more autonomy from neighboring entities. But a systems focus helps us imagine virtues as dynamic nexuses. As a nexus, a virtue is a location where relationships meet and cross. Its behaviors result from the behaviors of neighboring points, the loci where the different relationships between others meet.

In fact, traditional Catholic virtue theories have often recognized that virtues are more a dynamic than a kind of entity.[1] We cannot directly name an essence of a moral virtue. A moral virtue is the right amount or the right strength of a certain trait balanced between its corresponding vices of excess and of deficiency.[2] So, for example, patience is "between" impatience and passivity. But what exactly is patience a good amount of? There is no term for that other than simply "patience," which does not answer the question. Let's take a closer look at traditional Catholic descriptions of a virtue.

HOW TO DESCRIBE A MORAL VIRTUE

Virtue theories use two methods to describe specific virtues. One method is to map out the interactions or relationships a virtue has with other participants of a moral character, such as the vices, the passions, and the will.[3] The second method is to refer to role models (real and imaginary) that demonstrate a virtue.[4] Sometimes this means naming moral exemplars such as saints or other role models, as demonstrated in work by Steven Bouma-Prediger, Kathryn Blanchard and Kevin O'Brien, and Bishop Robert Barron.[5] More often, we describe hypothetical moral agents doing things in order to show what a virtue is.[6] We use examples to illustrate what a virtue tends to motivate or enable. Every method of describing a virtue boils down to these two options, and both of these methods are necessary to convey what a specific virtue actually is. Let's consider why we need both methods to describe a virtue.

When we describe a moral agent in order to illustrate a specific virtue (using the second method just described), we can convey an image of that virtue's effect. Yet it is strange that this method works. Any act this hypothetical moral agent does could be enabled by more than one virtue. We might describe a person doing something dangerous in order to explain what courage is, but other quite different virtues (and vices) could come to mind from the example we describe. The moral agent we describe may seem to demonstrate determination, foolhardiness, obtuseness, or pride. So, a mere description of a person doing something brave will not successfully convey the content of the virtue we call "courage."

This is a good problem to have, because it reflects reality well. The problem arises from the complexity and ambiguity of a moral character's inner motions. No action uses only one virtue. Virtues are never actualized or exercised in isolation. (This is a very ecological trait.) Each act of courage may also require resolve, fortitude, or sensitivity or all these at once. Therefore, when we rely on hypothetical moral agents' actions to describe a virtue, our description remains ambiguous. This is why we also need the first method of describing a virtue.

When we use the first method, we explain a virtue's relationship to other aspects of a moral character, such as other virtues, vices, and passions. We might map out a few virtues' relative locations along a spectrum of intensity by saying, for example, that courage is between cowardice and brashness. Another step is to compare the virtue with others that are similar in some way. We might explain courage by saying it is similar to resolve. To be more specific, we describe a virtue's cooperations with additional virtues or with emotions or the passions. If we need to show how courage is not exactly the same as resolve, we can elaborate, adding that courage is like resolve but mixed with more fear. After these clarifications, the virtue's meaning is clearer.

The two methods—examples and relationships with other virtues—still do not let us name a specific virtue's content directly. When we refer to what it does or "where" it lives, we are showing how the virtue interacts or compares with its neighbors. If a virtue were an entity, we would be able to describe what it is made up of. We cannot. But we can say it does fit the properties of a nexus. A virtue is a behavioral location, such as a niche. More precisely, a behavioral locus, a virtue, is that which occupies a niche within a person's moral character. Therefore, in an ecological model of moral character, a moral virtue is like the local population of a species, or all the members of one species in an ecosystem. In other words, a virtue is that which contributes specific roles, such as behaviors, functions, and needs, to the dynamics of a moral character. With this understanding in place, we are ready to develop the moral character model further using the four traits of ecosystems that we examined in chapter 2: weak and diffuse causes are powerful, borders and boundaries are permeable and porous, nestedness characterizes ecosystems, and ecosystems self-organize through niches.

Causality in a Moral Character

Chapter 2 noted that in ecosystems, weak, diffuse, complex, and reciprocal forms of causality are significant.[7] In these systems, such causes have potency. This is also true of moral character. This is one reason that moral growth is not simple, straight, or predictable.

In the traditional explanations of virtue theory, we say that a person can acquire a moral virtue from practice.[8] For example, we can correct a corresponding vice of deficiency by exercising that particular trait so that it will strengthen. If I am impatient, I should practice waiting. Simple enough. But it does not seem possible to exercise only one single specific character trait. No action, much less practice, employs only one virtue. Our account of the development of virtues is thin here, as others have noted.[9] We are less able than we believe to name which virtues or vices are developed by which actions and practices.

One problem is that we cannot be certain about which virtues are exercised with an action or a practice. Moral agents can certainly be wrong about which moral traits they are actually exercising. Many who intend to practice compassion are actually patronizing or even enacting coercion. This happens for many different reasons, often linked to failures of other virtues, such as justice. Like species changing over generations through the processes of coevolution, moral virtues and vices are constantly shaping one another. No specific practice can be named as a reliable guide for any person's progress in growing a specific virtue.

Character formation steers wildly for yet another reason. Many virtues are impossible to exercise directly.[10] What does a person actually do when practicing a virtue such as gratitude? Ought a person say "thank you" more often until she feels genuinely (but not excessively) thankful? It seems at least as likely that practicing thanking more often would develop politeness, obedience, or discipline instead of gratitude. Perhaps a moral agent's outlook would remain only minimally grateful, but she would gain patience from taking time to thank people more often. Or perhaps she would become frustrated at her failure to feel more grateful because she thanks others out of duty. This could convince her that she actually has less reason to be grateful so that she grows in resentment instead.

A system in which weak, diffuse, and reciprocal causes have potency is complex. In such systems, growth does not occur as a linear process. Virtue theory has the capacity to work with this challenge. Religion scholar Edward Slingerland has noted that virtue theory's strength is its ability to account for an "aggregation effect."[11] This means that "a clear correlation between character traits and behavior may only begin to emerge over repeated observations over a long period of time." In other words, practices do not simply or directly cause virtues and vices to develop. An ecological model of moral character enhances virtue theory's ability to account for the complexities and wildness of growth itself because it acknowledges this cumulative effect as well as the ripples of nonlinear effects and complex responses within a person's changing character. Philosopher Daniel C. Russell likewise observes that "we should expect it [moral development] to be messy, piecemeal, varied, impure, culturally bounded, historically bounded, uneven, slow and difficult."[12] We can see an example of how virtue theory manages causality's complexity when we look at the interactions between the intellect and the will.

As a dynamic in a moral character, the will is among the participants of a moral agent's intellective power,[13] along with the intellect itself. The will's motions demonstrate weak, diffuse, or otherwise irregular causality.[14] Of course, a moral agent's participation in social practices can be quite deliberate. A moral agent might step forward and take part in a social practice that is new to her with the help of an emphatic exercise of will. However, more often, a moral agent will "fall in" to participate in social practices because they are known, familiar courses of action. She may be doing something intentionally, but her cooperation and participation in the social practice may not reflect her affirmation of the practice or its meanings. Even more often, a moral agent does things with no conscious deliberation as a matter of habit or routine. In all cases, the will is acting. Liturgies offer an example. Once a moral agent has chosen to attend a Mass, for example, her participation in each of that Mass's many practices often do not feel like distinct choices. Her presence is a kind of participation in each once she has arrived to participate in the whole sacramental performance. Here, the act of her will in arriving at the church building at 11:15 on a Sunday morning is the most recent cause of her participation, but it does not represent most of her will's motions toward participation in the Catholic sacrament of the Eucharist. Instead, her will's decision to become a Catholic, her reaffirmation of baptismal vows a month ago, and her pursuit of her desire to identify as a Catholic Christian each weakly contribute to the acts of will that led to her participation at any given Mass. Cumulative and indirect causes continue this participation.

The interaction between will and the intellect offers an example of reciprocal causality. The will and the intellect need each other to do everything that they do. The will represents a moral agent's ability to do actions deliberately. In order to initiate an external act, the will must be given a target first, a direction, from the intellect (with help from the senses). But the intellect needs the will to do anything because the will moves it.[15] Yet the intellect moves the will because the will is a kind of an appetite.[16] The collaboration of the intellect's participants is circular: a reciprocal causality matters here.

In ecosystems and in moral characters, the imperfect correlations of weak, diffuse, and reciprocal causality show us what Slingerland calls "the power and pragmatic usefulness of relatively small correlations."[17] Virtue cultivation is a wild enterprise, and we could account for it more usefully with an eye to the kind of causes that gradually shape forests, ocean floors, and grassy plains and carve continents.

Permeable Boundaries and a Moral Character

The second trait of ecosystems introduced in chapter 2 was about borders and boundaries. All boundaries in ecosystems are vague and porous. The place where one ecosystem ends and another begins is fluid. Boundaries within an ecosystem are just as unclear. The lines that differentiate habitats, distinguish between sources of energy, or demark species evaporate under scrutiny.

The boundaries of a moral character are likewise permeable. Lines defining the aspects of a moral character are not solid. This section will demonstrate this with a discussion of the passions. The boundaries between persons and between a person and God are also permeable. We will consider each of these kinds of boundaries after considering the passions.

Permeable Boundaries within a Moral Character

A moral character has virtues, the will, intellect, and passions. Because the passions are defined as the movements of the sense appetites, the concept of passions is already a functionalist term. The term "passion" indicates motion, not being. The passions are the moving that the sense appetites enact.[18] The passions represent Catholic virtue theory's effort to incorporate emotions, impulses, and other premoral reactions into a moral character. Their fundamental goodness is a bit unclear among different readers of Thomas Aquinas. Readers of Aquinas agree that the passions are good or bad depending on situations. They are good when they are obeying the reason and the will.[19] The question of their fundamental (unconditional) goodness inspires some disagreement. Jean Porter believes that Aquinas finds the passions to be not fundamentally good.[20] Servais Pinckaers says the passions are fundamentally good.[21] Nicholas Kahm equivocates but ultimately says they are good.[22] Kevin White describes Aquinas's comments on this in places where he addresses the passions as "perturbations" or areas of disorder within a person's moral character.[23] As a dynamic, the passions are categorized into four possible varieties of movement, either attraction or revulsion and either "concupiscent" or "irascible" in their formidability.[24]

How do the passions interact with other inhabitants of a moral character? Servais Pinckaers echoes the tradition's emphasis on the passions' integration with the reason and the will.[25] The passions can comply with reason, resist reason,[26] and preempt reason's input entirely,[27] as when a moral agent's body is able to influence the sense appetites powerfully and when the passions move to act or to experience or acquire something that reason has already previously vetoed. The passions do move when the will allows them to move, but at times it also seems that the passions have volition on their own. The passions can act as precognitive reflexes.

The tradition sometimes attributes virtue to the sense appetites themselves. Porter considers them "canny" in character.[28] Pinckaers says that there are virtues residing within some of the sense appetites. Temperance[29] and courage, for example, are within the concupiscent and the irascible passions.[30] Are they wholly encompassed by the passions, then? And if this is the case, ought we say that temperance and courage can likewise move without the will's propulsion? As a concept, the passions defy consistent characterization.

The passions belong both within and beyond moral evaluation. They both precede intellect and follow it. They work alongside the moral virtues, and they have moral virtues within them. The passions follow from what we see and know, but they also color what we see and know. Philosopher Steven Jensen insightfully notes that disagreements about the passions are always about what exactly is responding to what within the moral character.[31] As a kind of motion among motions, the passions are boundaryless and, for those of us seeking to define them, quite elusive. An ecological model of moral character, accepting the vagueness and permeability of all borders, can help us to think further about the roles of the passions and therefore about how to locate where within a moral character they are at work. As motions, they cannot be understood apart from their contexts' systems and conditions. We will consider the passions in more detail when chapter 4 discusses hope, chapter 5 discusses the cardinal virtues of caring and prudence, and chapter 6 discusses temperance and greed.

Permeability of Boundaries between People

Boundaries between moral characters, between persons, are also permeable. This is a significant aspect of virtue theories' understanding of moral character development. We will consider boundaries between individuals and groups in the next section, about nestedness. First, we will look at boundaries between individual moral agents.

Role models inform and inspire other moral agents. This kind of moral influence takes effect with and without a moral agent's cooperation and awareness. A neighbor who inspires us to grow can "rub off" on us when we emulate her strategically and also when we are not aware of being influenced by her moral character. Without even articulating the choice, we can decide to enhance or reject our own moral qualities upon observing them in action in another person's life. This is easier to observe among younger people whose moral character is changing rapidly, but it is also true of fully adult humans. As moral theologian Dana Dillon has noted, moral development never stops.[32]

Consider what happens when we are inspired by someone to become wiser, more creative, or more reliable or serene. This does not become for us a matter of copying what that person does or even of trying to respond as she might to our own situations. The process of actualizing the inspiration we experience is more like finding a way to fit within ourselves the excellences we see the other person display. In following this inspiration, we imagine how we could change the way our virtues or vices interact. For example, one moral agent might glimpse from watching a friend how her own passions (such as an aversion against appearing childish) could bolster her patience. Another might learn a way to mobilize her courage to aid her cultivation of serenity. We do not discard our moral character's components. We integrate the changes we desire, and everything within us shifts to adjust. This might be done through planning and care, but it might also happen without our full awareness. In other words, we absorb or reflect dynamics of other persons' moral character, both deliberately and subconsciously. Moral traits can in this way spread from person to person. We are able to do this toward our moral growth and also toward its detriment.

Permeability of Boundaries between People and God

A final aspect of boundaries' permeability lies in the boundaries between a person and God. Although virtue ethics, and therefore moral theology, is our first interest here, let's step back briefly to envision the wider context of a created being and God the Creator. When speaking of life and more so of existence itself, an ecological model of interactions does not sufficiently represent the situation. God introduces the possibility of a person's existence as well as the existence of everything needed to permit the person to be and to become alive. Theologies differ in emphasis, in starting points, and in their descriptions of the nature of God's agency as Creator. For Aquinas, the remoteness of God from creation is often emphasized. For Tillich, God's very "existence" is beyond existence, grounding it. But for ecotheologian Denis Edwards, God, particularly God's Spirit, continually sustains, in a sense doing and enacting our existing for us.[33] For all descriptions of God's creative agency, the person's utter reliance on God for existence does not translate fully into the ecological model of moral character, which is a matter of relationalities embedded within creation. At the same time, the systems of interactivity within a person reflect something of God, because Trinity-community also can be spoken of in ecological terms, as ecotheologians have demonstrated.[34]

Let's zoom back in to consider a more specific virtue theory focus: the relationalities between moral agent and God. Religious traditions pertaining to prayer speak of interactions between a person and God, an evolving relationship of giving, gratitude, truth, and forgiveness. Liturgically infused traditions such as Catholicism say that this boundary is crossed through participating in practices. The permeability of boundaries between God and person does not allow for mutual influence, because the human is not the divine. God is not shaped by humans to a similar degree or in similar ways that humans are affected by God. The source of life in Christian understanding does interact with creation, including with human moral character, but what passes through this porosity is not the same in both directions. As an analogy, consider the sun. As chapter 2 noted, solar radiation plays an irreplaceable role in creation, including the processes within creatures, but the life on our planet does not similarly impact the sun. The sun itself is not an ecosystem, nor is it fully contained within an ecosystem.

Human moral agency plays a role in our permeability by God. As the Body of Christ, the Church represents a millennia-old endeavor to mobilize our corporate identity and unity on the assumption that the practices we share (liturgical, evangelical, scriptural, sacramental, and otherwise) have a way of seeping into each of us. The actions we take in the form of participating in these will wildly, deeply, and unpredictably change us. This is due to the nature of participation itself and also to God's actions. God interacts with persons and, more to our current point, with each person's moral character. Our participation in religious traditions and practices further open our inner worlds to God's agency. This brings us to the theological virtues: faith, hope, and charity. The infused theological virtues are the most easily visible sign that a moral character, like an ecosystem, is an open system. Christian virtue theory recognizes these virtues as a fundamental way a moral agent's character is not self-contained but instead is fed by God's own participation in a person's internal worlds. Christian virtue theory cannot view a moral character as a unit sufficient to itself. A person's moral character is distinguishable from God's own being and actions, but the borders between them are porous. Chapter 4 discusses the traditional three theological virtues. The next section of this chapter identifies further implications of boundaries' permeability by looking across the scales of moral character.

Nestedness in a Moral Character

The permeability of ecosystems' boundaries appears not only between them but also within them. Ecosystems display nestedness. Therefore, in an ecological virtue theory model, that same permeability appears in the boundaries between individuals and societies. We'll consider the nestedness of individuals and societies first and then the nestedness of the cardinal virtues.[35]

Nestedness: Individuals within Societies

As Popes Francis and Benedict XVI noticed, "the external deserts in the world are growing because internal deserts have become so vast."[36] In other words, individuals' moral character is nested within ecosystems. What is happening within the smaller one is also happening within the larger context. A moral character is also nested within a person's societies. The boundaries differentiating individual moral character and the moral character of one's societies constantly allow seepage.

Think again about life in ecosystems. No organism is completely distinguishable from its environments. Our environment becomes our selves as we eat and breathe. Yesterday's groceries become tomorrow's fuel for today's aspirations of body, mind, and spirit. The nutrients and poisons located near us enter into us, inevitably. The COVID-19 pandemic and its predecessors have reminded us, even the most individualistic and isolationist among us, that what we have within spreads to enter into those close by as we sweat, breathe, sigh, and speak. Viruses even spread through our shared contact with abiotic elements of our environments, such as surfaces.[37]

The ecological model's greatest benefit to virtue theory is its ability to reorient our awareness of our virtues and vices (and passions, intellect, and will) as dynamics that function within ecological and social systems. An ecological analogy of moral character can account for a moral agent's absorption of societies' moral traits and for the influence of her own moral traits as they radiate outward. The ecological nestedness of moral character is one way that this model helps us imagine the reciprocal moral influences between individual and society.

A moral agent's moral character is nested within her societies. Therefore, her moral character soaks up the moral character of the societies she inhabits. She absorbs the virtues and vices of her societies. She does not absorb all of them and does not absorb only her own societies' traits, because the causality of this absorption is not certain or simple. Yet virtue theory does hold that social virtues and vices are absorbed by societies' participants through our practices and participation.

Societies' moral character seeps into individual moral agents' moral characters. This happens in multiple ways. A moral agent internalizes the views, attitudes, beliefs, and prioritizations implicit in her surrounding social structures, reactualizing them within in many ways.

Teachings do this, as when a social norm is explicitly described. We do this through signage, stories, memes, product advertisements, lessons for children, and overt command statements. "Remember to share!" tells a person that the current context is one in which sharing is expected. Social reinforcement in the form of major and subtle rewards and punishments also passes socially held moral and semimoral ideals from society into individuals' characters. Body language, verbal and nonverbal cues, and even forms of eye contact send messages continually, forming a complex environment with layers of acceptance, approval, discomfort, or rejection through which every person navigates all through her life. These inscribe the range of acceptable ways that we wait in line or how, where, when, and why we travel and all manner of our self-representations in public spaces (to name only a few examples).

In virtue theory, practices are a widely acknowledged means through which commonly held expectations, including moral expectations, are absorbed by individuals. Explicitly communicated teachings are communicated intentionally. Body language and indirect or minor verbal cues could be leveraged intentionally or involuntarily as a society's participants bolster conformity to the sets of standards they prefer. The mechanics of religious practices such as rituals follow threads of intentionality and unintentional participation to create a complex interplay between ritual and doctrine on social and individual scales.[38]

Are individuals' moral character deliberately shaped by societies? Yes and no. Specific virtues, those held by a democratic society, for example, are enacted and carried out through such practices as representation, voting, maintaining and meeting transparent governance standards, and creating and respecting a freedom of information process. These practices encourage attention to political news, education of communities, and organizing to inform and advocate in response to changing conditions. Virtues such as attentiveness, thoughtfulness, care for the common good, and a sense of ownership of places, structures, and symbols result. Other moral traits also result: regional pride, ambition (if a moral agent senses an opportunity in the structures of political representation), and apathy (if a moral agent senses that the number of voters or structure of representation regions makes her own ballot irrelevant). The messaging employed to maintain and encourage the practices of a democracy can also serve to heighten xenophobia, hyperindividualism, or moral relativism (as each individual's vote or view carries as much weight as any other's). An entrenched two-party system can draw individuals toward polarized views, reliance on definitions by negation, and a less imaginative and binary frame for experiences.

The explicit and deliberate nature of some of our ways of infusing society's moral traits into individuals makes them easy to identify. Commuters recognize and affirm that the seats on a bus are a common good, and the practice of standing in line to board buses instills and reinforces that recognition. The subtler means, particularly the practices, by nature of their invisibility are rarely interpreted as matters of choice. They are read by participants in society as neutral or normal and therefore as beyond acceptance or rejection. These means are quite powerful. We reenact the values buried in such practices through the movements of our bodies and affirm them without recognizing that we are doing so.

This interrelating can be quite physical too. For example, a society's practice of adding fluoride to the public supply of water helps a moral agent's teeth last longer. Taxpayers, voters, public works employees, and water users participate in this practice. This practice also shapes a moral agent's cognitive view of the proper functions of local government, and becoming accustomed to this practice, invisible though it is, shapes her sense of what counts as normal and safe water.

Practices give rise to other practices. A social practice of using chemicals that erode the atmosphere's ozone layer can cause a moral agent's skin to become cancerous, lead to an additional practice of using sunscreen vigilantly, and cultivate in her a (reasonable) fear of sunshine. The practice of a Sikh gurdwara's community gathering to pray and to feed all who have come, believers and nonbelievers alike, shapes one's awareness of how to serve and eat with others in sacred spaces, with good, filling, vegetarian food, eaten together, while seated on the floor.[39] This practice (called langar) led to gurdwaras cooking and serving food on large scales during the pandemic and in the service of Black Lives Matter protests.[40] The moral (and physical, linguistic, etc.) traits of a society seep into its people. A moral agent's participation in social structures changes that person. Across all the scales and dimensions of her existence, she constantly absorbs and integrates into herself what is in the atmosphere, morally speaking. These effects are not always what the practices' participants aim to cultivate, but they are powerful.[41]

The nestedness of moral character means that this influence is reciprocal across scale. The participants of an ecosystem alter their habitats and therefore also their ecosystems' surrounding supersystems. The moral virtues within a moral agent are thereby also functioning within that moral agent's societies and ecosystems. The effects of her presence and actions are unpredictable and minute, but they are real. Of all the challenges facing an ecological virtue theory's model of moral character, the most difficult might be to account for the relationships between individuals and societies.

Problems for Virtue Theory's View of Individuals in Societies

No model is perfect, and certain aspects of ecosystems do not translate well into a model of a moral character. An ecological model of moral character does not resolve the tension we encounter between the need to account for individual moral agents and the societies that they create and by which they are shaped. This is not grounds to reject an ecological model, because our traditional virtue theory models have not managed this tension well either. Moral theories, including virtue theory, struggle to explain the relationships between an individual's moral character and structures of sin,[42] or society's moral failings, the processes through which we reject and deny the good. Theologian Theodora Hawksley efficiently summarizes the problem: "The more social the concept [of sin] becomes—taking account of the automatic and unconscious ways in which systemic evil acts on moral agents—the less the activity of those moral agents appears as sin, traditionally understood. The more like sin it becomes—involving individually identifiable acts committed in freedom and knowledge—the less clearly its social and systemic dimensions appear." The result is this: "'Social' and 'sin' appear to be two notions heading in opposite directions."[43] Individuals' moral character or moral development processes cannot be simply scaled up.[44] What makes this so difficult? I can see three reasons.

One reason is intention and agency. Virtue theory efforts to engage social scales of morality might imply or attribute an intention to a society's practices, but there is no clear accounting for whether or how this can be. Is there a corporate will, after all? I argue that we can only say that there is in a very limited and qualified sense. This is an area in which virtue theory needs guidance from other disciplines such as psychology and sociology, for it does seem after all that societies demonstrate virtues (e.g., creativity) and vices (e.g., short-sightedness). We will return to this shortly.

A second reason that moral character cannot be simply scaled up to model societies' moral character is that participation in a society's practices is not a simple matter of intention and corresponding outcomes for societies (or even for individual persons). We might say that participation in the Eucharist brings a person awareness of the Church community, but it is demonstrably true that this awareness does not always result. Some humans are capable of demonstrating disregard for the Church and for humanity despite a lifetime of habitual participation in the sacraments. Sports practices purport to shape communities' healthy competition and excellence, but none of these result inevitably from participation.[45] Practices shape character unpredictably. The unpredictability of individuals' efforts to shape society is also clear.

Finally, the third reason is that society and individual moral character are each distinct potential targets of virtue theory analysis. The reasons we focus on an individual moral agent differ from our reasons for attending to societies' moral characters. At times, the moral character of a society can be virtue theory's ultimate aim. In such cases the problem of the will remains, as noted above. But when the individual person is the focus, should virtue theory attend to an individual's moral character and evaluate it in terms of the person's societies' values or not? If so, how? If not, why not?

To address the third problem, I argue that virtue theory should be able to analyze and evaluate moral character as a system to be recognized in its contexts, within specific societies or cultures. Virtue theory should also be able to analyze and evaluate moral character on its own, as something influenced by many factors including its societies' particularities, but which calls for evaluation in accordance with goods that may not be recognized in that person's societies.

Consider a wealthy and generous parish that is often able to muster significant support for community members facing cancer crises. This is certainly virtuous, and the effects of this society's generosity will probably appear among many of the parish's individual members. Suppose there is a group of friends in the parish who want instead to address the reasons for high rates of cancer in a neighborhood. Their focus may seem to others to compete with or even undermine the church's readiness to respond to individuals undergoing cancer treatment. Virtue theory should be able to analyze each level of this complex dynamic: the parish, the whole town, and the environmentally minded and vocal minority cohort of parishioners.

For an academic example, in grading student work, we might evaluate a paper on a curve or without any attention to the work of students' peers. Both constitute grading, and both can help students to learn and improve. Both methods can be good, and our way of grading ought to be able to manage either as circumstances and goals require. A student's work can be good on its own, and it can be good in relation to peers' papers. It can be both, and it can be one or the other.

Virtue theory can find help in modeling the relationship between individuals' and societies' moral characters from sociological tools. The concept of moral luck is one way to conceptualize the relationship between an individual's moral character and her society's moral traits.[46] This concept is used to imagine how an oppressive society might affect an individual's moral development. Feminist ethicist Lisa Tessman has used this idea from philosopher Claudia Card to support one way of imagining how unjust social structures might affect a person's moral character development.[47] Moral theologian Kate Ward has further developed the tool,[48] summarizing a few versions of this method and showing how their emphases and intended audiences influence their view of moral luck. Ward concludes that for Christians, consideration of grace's role in moral luck is essential. Incorporating some awareness of the dynamics of moral luck will help us to think more fluidly about the interplay of grace on the levels of both individual and society.

This is an important corrective and one that can work well with the loose forms of causality that are necessary in an ecological model of moral character. Consider an example. Ecologically speaking, one could compare the biodiversity of two plots of land in front of two different houses in adjacent neighborhoods in a city. One plot exists in a block that has been traditionally privileged economically and socially and in the allocation of the city's resources, and the other's block has been traditionally underresourced and exploited. Social norms for residents of the first house establish conditions leading to a high likelihood that the front lawn will be heavily treated with chemicals and highly controlled in favor of botanical homogeneity. This lawn impedes biological diversity. It will more likely be a toxic presence, and it also meets prevailing aesthetic ideals: thick and uniformly cut green grass and frequently treated shrubs, meticulously shaped. The second house's front lawn is influenced by different social conditions in which the same degree of control and chemical intervention is neither highly valued nor socially enforced. Due to this and other social conditions, this second plot of land is more likely to host a more diverse array of species. It is less likely to be a toxic presence and also less likely to be "read" by passing citizens as representative of aesthetic ideals of a "nice home." These trends may or may not be evidenced in each house's neighboring lawns. The social conditions do not lead inevitably to these results. But they do make these results more likely. These differences would also be reflected in the attitudes held by residents of each of these streets and even in the moral evaluation they might have about what makes for a good front lawn or a nice home. We know that marks of the society's moral outlook inscribe onto a person as that person learns and adopts practices that define and hold societies together. Some marks result from social practices that dehumanize targeted persons and social groups.[49] These are moral wounds, harming every member of a society shaped by such practices. In a dualistically arranged oppression, the moral wounds that are borne differ between members of oppressed groups and members of oppressive groups. These differences should be part of our own views of how societies' and individuals' moral characters are related. The moral luck concept has the potential to work with individuals' nestedness within societies to examine the ways moral development proceeds.

Sociology's critical realism is another analysis tool that can help an ecologically informed virtue theory think about individual-social nestedness. Critical realism offers several concepts that could prevent the wrong conclusions of simple determinism (the view that context simply shapes individual's moral character, like a printing press marking paper) as well as any flat assertions that a person's moral qualities are mostly independent of her societies' practices. Critical realism's way of defining society, culture, structures, and social positions demonstrates good potential to work with the ecosystem virtue model.

Theologian Dan Daly notes that critical realism, developed from the work of philosopher Roy Bhaskar,[50] holds three beliefs to which virtue theory also adheres. First, both critical realism and virtue theory hold that actions shape context (such as social structures and cultures). Second, both hold that structures affect the agency of individuals. And third, both hold that culture affects both structures and individuals. With these points of agreement, a solid partnership between these analytic tools is possible.[51]

In critical realism theory, the term "culture" refers to "ideas, objects," and knowledge.[52] These are the social elements through which persons are able to carry meaning.[53] The term "social structures" refers to the relationships between social positions. Critical realism theory is a tool for examining not individuals or even people but rather social structures' mechanisms, so the concept of social positions is particularly important. Social positions are roles that could be occupied by specific individual persons. Positions are like slots (or niches) that are inhabited by persons.[54] The theory eliminates any view that individual persons create positions. Daly highlights the help these concepts can offer virtue theory: keeping the moral agent and the social position conceptually separate allows us to see clearly how person and position might interact.[55] Persons participate in structures by means of their different ways of inhabiting these social positions. Daly suggests that we think about "position-practices" to see how and where individual moral agency does and does not manifest in societies.

According to theologian Daniel Finn, this theory has not settled a position on corporate moral agency. That is, there is no consensus on whether a group of persons such as a society has agency (and if so where that might reside). But individuals are moral agents. Therefore, critical realism's assistance to virtue theory can be in highlighting "how our daily *choices* . . . are . . . shaped . . . by the social structures within which we live."[56] Structures offer to individuals or inflict on them "restrictions, opportunities, and incentives." Social structures' positions do not themselves have moral agency.[57] A person experiences social structures in accordance with which positions she inhabits. Culture is an important piece of this dynamic, accounting for some of the ways a moral agent experiences and acts within these contexts of positions and structures. Sociocultural interaction is critical realism's way of imagining people's engagement of moral agency. Cultural systems and their elements are tools through which people act meaningfully.[58]

With critical realism's help, we can see, for example, that an individual moral agent's ability to engage her cultural system is enhanced or worsened by her society's structures. Daly describes how this "position-practice" system lens can help virtue theory.[59] Among other benefits, this concept lets us see that a moral agent's position both restricts the person (because the person must occupy this position in order to occupy it) and opens up possibilities for a person (because a position offers its occupant forms of power and opportunities). Daly also notes that critical realism will help us see virtues as emerging, not simply an "aggregation of a person's actions."[60]

"Moral luck" and critical realism are two lenses that can help ecological virtue theory to describe the nestedness of a moral character within cultures and within societies. Though I can offer no definitive description of the ways moral character's nestedness behaves, these approaches work well together to aid analysis while also upholding the indeterminacy of how a society's moral traits affect each moral agent who participates in it or encounters it and, potentially, vice versa.

Nestedness: Virtues in Moral Agents

Nestedness also characterizes the dynamics within a moral agent. Within a moral character, any boundaries between moral virtues are permeable. As nexuses, virtues are essentially interreliant. Again, an ecological model of moral character imagines virtues as nexuses of a web. Individual virtues are identifiable only through their relationships with other virtues. One virtue's changes always changes other virtues, directly and indirectly. In fact, nestedness characterizes the relationships between some moral virtues. Following an insight from ecological virtue ethicists Louke van Wensveen and Ronald Sandler, the ecological virtues model imagines cardinal virtues as "areas" within which "subsidiary" virtues participate.[61] In other words, in an ecological model of moral character, cardinal virtues are communities of virtues.[62]

Cardinal virtues "order" the virtues by establishing a mean of the virtues that comprise them.[63] They are not more important or more authoritative than other moral virtues,[64] despite our tradition's tendency to describe them as commanding or directing the subsidiary virtues. Understanding cardinal virtues as sets of virtues helps us to think more creatively about the kinds of virtues we do and do not value.

To visualize cardinal virtues as sets, think of a cardinal virtue as a circle laid out on the ground using a rope. Each area is a set of all it contains. In one place the described area is cold, buried under snow, with a single daffodil. In another place the rope circles hot, dry sand with a crab scuttling through. Another circled area has ants, mud, water, and a dead beetle. The area's location where we laid the rope establishes what the circle will contain. The encompassed participants, with all their interactions, establish the circled area's character.

To think ecologically, we must focus on functions, and descriptions of what is happening are also predicated by the circle. In one rope circle ants carry off the beetle carcass. Elsewhere a crab leaves organic bits on some grains of sand. The first circle's daffodil has formed a dimple in the snow. The relationalities enclosed by each circle form its mean, in the sense of an average character of the described place. Despite a daffodil, the first circle is a cold and wintery area. A crab's presence impacts the beach area's character, but it is still basically sand, saltiness, and warmth. These are the general characteristics of the area, but some specifics stand out as unusual, or contrary to the mean. The presence of the daffodil raises a question about the snow. Is this place really just a frozen, dead-of-winter setting, or is it about to change? Organic bits in a crab's trail evidence where the crab was before crossing this area. The bits he brought are now participants within this area, but they also link the area to something of what lives outside the circle. A powerful exception or aberration reveals something of the area's broader context or of its past. In that these outliers have an effect on the area, they also speak to and can even (weakly) influence the area's future.

The general character of each circle is a continually shifting compromise between parts and whole. At the heart of this analogy, we must also remember that we chose where to lay the rope in our naming of the traditional cardinal virtues. In a virtues ecology, cardinal virtues are areas within which virtues and vices form a set of participating traits. They are a community. The mean of these aggregated traits is normativized by the whole, or the cardinal virtue that contains the virtues community. The power of this normativization rests on our naming of cardinal virtues. This decision deserves further attention, for we must notice which kinds of moral traits we have overlooked by our naming of the cardinal sets. Where might our attentions have created empty niches in our vision of a good moral character?

Traditional descriptions of moral virtues do not often argue that the member virtues of one cardinal set interact only or even most often with one another. But the relationships that the communities of these particular virtues have with the passions differentiates them from one another. At the same time these four cardinal virtues give not only good moral tendencies for the moral character that has them but play a role in the process of moral formation itself. Prudence is an obvious example, with its skill of balancing the virtues of the moral agent, but the other traditional three also are needed for the moral agent to grow in new ways. They help with that struggle of moral development. Yet our construction of an ecological model of moral character should keep in mind this question: What more could we learn about moral character if we attended to the relationships between the "subsidiary" virtues residing in different cardinal sets?

Niches of a Moral Character

In an ecological virtue theory's model of moral character, the niche is a help-ful concept for imagining how the participants of a moral character mutually shape one another. Chapter 2 noted that in ecology, a niche is a behavioral location, or a role that a species might occupy in an ecosystem or require of an ecosystem. In ecosystems, a species' population can occupy several different niches. The same is true with moral virtues: they are not the same in each moral agent who has them. The interactions and relationships between moral virtues and vices differ within each moral agent. For one person, courage might be closely paired with loyalty, because in her the two tend to inspire or activate each other. For someone else, courage may sprout from an extraordinary capacity for patience, because she often mobilized patience to encourage other virtues to grow.[65] Consider the virtues of thrift and fortitude as examples.

A well-formed virtue of thrift may be bolstered in one person by a well-attuned sensitivity to the life conditions of people who live in poverty. For another person, thrift may arise from a restlessness that causes her to enjoy repairing and repurposing existing possessions. For a third person, thrift could flourish because of a well-rooted (but recently moderated) habit of hoarding resources out of anxiety over her family's wealth. In the case of the third person, practices that had served to feed a vice actually enabled her to form a related virtue as she learned to change her responses to this anxiety. The roles a virtue plays in one person's life can look quite different from that same virtue's behavior in another person's moral character.

The niche concept can work with our awareness of nestedness to help us to think about a cardinal virtue. For example, within fortitude there exist niches for subsidiary virtues. Fortitude names a realm of a moral character, functionally speaking. The niches within that area must be filled in order for that realm to operate as a coherent cardinal virtue. These niches should be occupied by moral virtues for fortitude to behave like a moral virtue.[66] A fulfilled virtue of fortitude requires its niches be filled with the necessary virtues, but exactly which virtues are needed varies with each person. In a persistent moral agent there is less need for endurance, so a weaker endur-ance suffices to allow for a healthy virtue of fortitude. In another moral agent persistence and endurance may be anemic, so courage could fill an empty niche by performing more roles than courage performs within the first moral agent. This means that persistence, endurance, and courage themselves each look very different from moral agent to moral agent. Virtues, like participants in ecosystems, are therefore universally individuated. Philosopher Sandrine

Berges's summary of Heloise's virtue thinking observed this phenomenon: "The mean has to be found for each individual according to the instincts she has to moderate."[67]

Because we name virtues in accordance with their functions within the moral character, some virtues signify something that is needed by all persons, because some functions seem indispensable. The subcommunities we name as cardinal virtues answer this need because they have roles related to organizing and balancing all the moral virtues. They are not the same thing in each person, but there must be commonality between them if we are to recognize them as the different versions of the same thing. The niche idea helps us see virtues as role fulfillers and role creators rather than independent entities, shows us that every change within a moral character leads to cascading further changes, and hints that the mean that makes a trait a virtue (not a vice) is a shifting "amount," linked always to its neighboring traits.

Because moral character is embedded in societies, the niches of virtues are too. Psychologist Darcia Narvaez notes that "virtue is co-constructed by those around" us.[68] This coconstruction takes place through social reinforcement, involving all the social, physical, spiritual, and other conditions into which we are born and through which we move. Epigenetics describes one example of how coconstruction takes place.[69] Our virtues and vices settle and resettle together within our character in response to our external ecological and social environments as they also develop. Virtues and vices self-organize through niches: they create and occupy niches for each other within a moral character. This is a virtues ecology's way of describing the interactive and dynamic balance of virtues.

The more niches are occupied, the more resilient the moral character will be. Good moral character is not like a checklist of a finite number of virtues. Redundancy is beneficial. Growth is about cultivating as many as we can, in a good variety, and to see that they thickly interact. Well-integrated virtues are healthy and active participants in a moral character, and the diversity of virtues is key to a moral character with resilience.

We (moral agents) fill and create niches in our ecological and social contexts through the shifting dynamics within our character. Our virtues and vices adjust to our contexts. The niches that are occupied by the virtues and vices of our moral character likewise respond to our contexts. They also motivate and inspire us to fill certain exterior niches offered by these contexts, in other words, to occupy the roles that we notice in our societies and ecosystems. The niches offered by our contexts motivate our moral, intellectual, and theological development. This motivation is only that, a motivator, not an inevitability—and we exercise moral agency in this process. As we become more aware that our way of filling spaces within our worlds changes who we are,[70] we can learn to identify social and ecological niches with an eye to our moral growth.

Meilaender's way of linking moral development with vision is helpful here. He observes that virtues do not only influence how we behave in situations. They are not only about our reactions. They also shape the kinds of situations we are likely to encounter, because our virtues (and vices) influence how we interpret our contexts.[71] Niches self-organize, and virtues have the power to shape character and the world around us through our interpretation.

We can to some extent creatively prioritize the ecological niches we fill. Understanding ourselves as niche occupants or niche satisfiers also helps us to practice a kind of solidarity with nonhuman animals. We often approach emerging situations while seeing ourselves primarily as a human person or as a specific kind of human person (such as a mother, a pastor, a resident, or an educated citizen). But we can also see ourselves primarily as oxygen breathers, as participants in the nitrogen cycle, as mammals, bipeds, water drinkers, or carbon producers. After all, these are also ecological niches we occupy.

This kind of choice can improve our theological anthropology. As Narvaez notes, "Our heritage of human virtue will be incomplete" if we do not extend it "to the natural world—to all entities."[72] She calls us to "a sense of partnership" as mammals within our "evolved developmental niche."[73] Taking ourselves as mammals among other mammals, for example, helps us to remember many overlooked aspects of what we are and do as neighbors and coevolvers in ecological communities. When we aspire to shape moral character in ways that are needed by our communities, part of the shape we must strive to fit is that of mammal participant within the ecosystems of our lives. A virtues ecology reminds us that we, moral characters and all, are participants in creation's ecosystems. We are participants in life itself.

THE UNIVERSAL DIFFERENTIATION
OF A GOOD MORAL CHARACTER

Like the systems of a bioregion, a moral character is populated by many participants, all living in dynamic balance with one another. The parameters of a good balance for each participant of a moral character depend on its context. A virtue's context includes the moral character within which it participates and that moral character's broader context, meaning the ecosystems and societies the moral agent inhabits and the history or trajectory of the moral agent's moral development.

As chapter 2 explained, the meaning of "flourishing" differs widely in ecology. In one densely populated bioregion, many species of plants and animals may live noisily in a dynamic balance. Sometimes a good moral character is aggressively expressive. In another bioregion fewer species or individuals exist, and all seems quiet and still. Similarly, a good moral character in other contexts is less expressive and more passive. For all bioregions, a variety of residents is essential. Life requires differentnesses.

Like individuals, bioregions differ. A temperate deciduous forest has a large number of species and well-developed soil,[74] but a tundra has fewer species, and over the course of a year the population density of these species will vary a great deal.[75] But no one ecosystem has all species, and there is no correct amount of species or individuals for all contexts. Analogously, there is no ideal strength or degree of prominence of any one moral virtue, such as perseverance or thrift, that is good for all moral characters. The key to an ecological virtue ethics is not to identify and develop the virtues that seem most pertinent to our climate crisis. The key is the interactions between a moral character's participants: we want more collaborations for diverse, thick arrays of virtues.

In Christian virtue theory, the good toward which a flourishing moral agent grows is God. Virtues need roots. This brings us to the theological virtues, the topic of chapter 4.

NOTES

1. Aquinas, *ST*, I–II, q. 55, a. 4.
2. Aquinas, *ST*, I–II, q. 64.
3. See, for example, Aquinas's descriptions of moral virtues, which are sometimes parts or potential parts of other virtues, commanding or commanded by others or (for vices) as opposites of one another, or sharing an aim with one another while differing in the ways they support that aim. Aquinas, *ST*, II–II, q. 48, q. 80, q. 128, and I–II, q. 60.
4. An example is in Aquinas's response to the first objection in *ST*, I–II, q. 55, a. 2, as he refers to a hypothetical agent.
5. See Barron, *The Priority of Christ*, chs. 17–20; Blanchard and O'Brien, *An Introduction to Christian Environmentalism*, in which each chapter offers examples across the political spectrum; and the introduction to each chapter in Bouma-Prediger, *Earthkeeping and Character*.
6. Aquinas, *ST*, I–II, q. 55, a. 1, links virtues with acts and habits with the assertion that the quality of a virtue can be known through the acts it motivates.
7. Note that the realms of causality discussed in this section pertain to human action and moral development. The primary causality of God's agency is taken as a given here.
8. Aquinas, *ST*, I–II, q. 51, a 2.
9. Daly, "Critical Realism, Virtue Ethics, and Moral Agency."

10. The discussion in chapter 5 on wonder, integrity, and solidarity engages this issue in more detail.
11. Slingerland, "The Situationist Critique and Early Confucian Virtue Ethics," 138.
12. Russell, "Aristotle on Cultivating Virtue," 41.
13. Aquinas, *ST*, I–II, q. 10, a. 2.
14. Aquinas, *ST*, I–II, q. 10, a. 4, describes an example in its consideration of divine agency's influence on a moral agent's will.
15. Catholic virtue theorists disagree about this, but Nicholas Kahm notes that Aquinas himself did not see this relationship consistently all through his life. Kahm identifies development in Aquinas's thought about the relationship between the will and the reason. In earlier writings, Aquinas envisioned the will as obeying reason (carrying out what reason commands). In later work, though, he thought that the will itself exercised some agency in its collaborations with reason. Kahm, *Aquinas on Emotion's Participation in Reason*, 11–12 and 228.
16. Gallagher, "The Will and Its Acts (Ia IIae, qq. 6-17)"; and Aquinas, *ST*, I–II, q. 9, a. 3.
17. Slingerland, "The Situationist Critique and Early Confucian Virtue Ethics," 139.
18. Aquinas, *ST*, I–II, q. 23, a. 4, and *ST*, I–II, q. 37, a. 2.
19. Aquinas, *ST*, I–II, q. 26, a.1.
20. Porter, *Justice as a Virtue*.
21. Pinckaers, *The Pinckaers Reader*, 274–79 and 287.
22. Kahm, *Aquinas on Emotion's Participation in Reason*, 9, 76, 175, and 282.
23. White, "The Passions of the Soul," 104.
24. Aquinas, *ST*, I–II, q. 23, 25.
25. Pinckaers, *The Pinckaers Reader*, 276.
26. Aquinas, *ST*, I, q. 81, a. 3, particularly objection 2.
27. Aquinas, *ST*, I, q. 81, a. 3, re. 3.
28. Porter, *Justice as a Virtue*, 109.
29. Aquinas, *ST*, I–II, q. 61, a. 4, and *ST*, II–II, q. 141, a. 3.
30. Pinckaers, *The Pinckaers Reader*, 314.
31. Jensen, "Virtuous Deliberation and the Passions."
32. Dillon, "The Vital Cell: Subsidiarity and a Family-Centered Approach to Accompanying Persons with Mental Illness."
33. Edwards, *Ecology at the Heart of Faith*, 30–31; and Edwards, *How God Acts*, 24–25 (on Jesus Christ) and 39–43 (on God as Creator).
34. Edwards, *Ecology at the Heart of Faith*, 75–76.
35. Nestedness also can help virtue theory to integrate with participatory theology for an account of human agency. Two potential loci of integration between these are the following: First, participatory theology offers a view of creaturely life in the context of being as participation in God. Certainly the nestedness of a moral agent in creation resonates with this lens. Nestedness can work with a participatory theological anthropology by giving a view of human personhood and morality that sees us within being, as a form of our participation in God, by virtue of our existence. Second, nestedness offers to participatory theology a way to think further about moral choices as a human exercise of the will best imagined as a form of collaboration in divine agency itself. See Davison, *Participation in God*.
36. Pope Francis, *Laudato si'*, para. 217, quoting Pope Benedict XVI, "Homily for the Solemn Inauguration of the Petrine Ministry" (April 24, 2005).

37. Centers for Disease Control and Prevention, "SARS-CoV-2 and Surface (Fomite) Transmission for Indoor Community Environments," April 5, 2021, https://www.cdc.gov/coronavirus/2019-ncov/more/science-and-research/surface-transmission.html.

38. See Bell, *Ritual Theory, Ritual Practice*, chap. 5.

39. Stephen, *Religion Matters*, 132–36.

40. Priya Krishna, "How to Feed Crowds in a Protest or Pandemic? The Sikhs Know," *New York Times*, June 8, 2020.

41. Theologian Lauren Winner has described significant US Christian examples of how central Christian practices can incorporate and perpetuate moral failures. See Winner, *The Dangers of Christian Practice*.

42. Pope John Paul II, "Sollicitudo Rei Socialis," para. 36.

43. Hawksley, "How Critical Realism Can Help Catholic Social Teaching," 13.

44. See Wimberley for an example of a psychologically grounded attempt to advise individual persons' moral formation, based on Callicott, with an eye to social and ecological flourishing. Wimberley's account offers interesting specific questions or concerns to incorporate into guiding another person's moral formation, but it does not include a thick description of the mutual interaction between person and society and ecosystem. Wimberley, *Nested Ecology*.

45. Laura Winner offers an insightful discussion of Christian practices with attention to the factors that can make Christian practices (e.g., the Eucharist, prayer, and baptism) damaging. Her argument focuses on how these Christian practices damage in ways that are characteristic of the practices themselves. Practices, embedded in history, carry within themselves human sinfulness. Her argument is important. My point here is that we cannot draw a straight line between a practice's stated purpose and its effects on each practitioner. See Winner, *The Dangers of Christian Practice*.

46. Claudia Card's "moral luck" and Lisa Tessman's modified "constitutive moral luck" are concepts used to integrate social and individual layers. The indeterminacy of social practices' moral impact is incorporated through the "luck" idea (individuals of social privilege and socially marginalized and oppressed individuals have different odds for encountering helpful and harmful structures and experiences), but the reciprocity of nestedness is not incorporated well. See Card, *Virtues and Moral Luck*; Tessman, "Critical Virtue Ethics"; and Tessman, *Burdened Virtues*.

47. Tessman, *Burdened Virtues*, 24.

48. Ward, "Toward a Christian Virtue Account of Moral Luck."

49. Tessman, *Burdened Virtues*.

50. Finn, *Moral Agency*, vii–xiii and 16.

51. Dan Daly's chapter in Finn demonstrates the potential that critical realism offers to virtue theory. See his "call to papers" to begin this effort at the conclusion of his chapter. Daly, "Critical Realism, Virtue Ethics, and Moral Agency."

52. Finn, *Moral Agency*, 48.

53. Finn, 30.

54. Daly, "Critical Realism, Virtue Ethics, and Moral Agency," 92.

55. Daly, 94.

56. Finn, *Moral Agency*, 39 (emphasis added).

57. Finn, 40.

58. Shadle, "Culture."

59. Daly, "Critical Realism, Virtue Ethics, and Moral Agency," 92.

60. Finn, *Moral Agency*, 97. The emerging dynamic of virtues noted here is a significant point for further development, particularly as a connecting point to the broader world of ecotheology.

61. Van Wensveen, *Dirty Virtues*, 13–14; and Van Wensveen, "Cardinal Environmental Virtues."

62. Chapters 5 and 6 on the cardinal virtues will develop this further.

63. Aquinas, *ST*, I–II, q. 61, a. 2, and the response in a. 3.

64. Keenan and Fullam's pleas for attention to subsidiary virtues demonstrate that the tradition has considered the cardinal virtues more attention worthy. See Fullam, "Sex in 3-D"; and Keenan, "Virtue Ethics and Sexual Ethics."

65. Perhaps the interactions and relationships between a moral agent's virtues reflect the specific progression of her own history of moral development.

66. Fortitude is defined in more detail in chapter 6. I suggest that fortitude comprises strength, endurance, perseverance, and patience and draws deeply on hope, bolstered by imagination.

67. Berges, *A Feminist Perspective on Virtue Ethics*, 51.

68. Narvaez, "The Co-Construction of Virtue," 211.

69. Narvaez, 253.

70. *Laudato si'*, para. 85, 116, and 226, describe examples of how we might do this.

71. Meilaender, *The Theory and Practice of Virtue*, 11.

72. Narvaez, "The Co-Construction of Virtue," 267.

73. Narvaez, 254.

74. Odum, *Fundamentals of Ecology*, 300.

75. Odum, 299.

4

Where Roots Meet Source

THE THEOLOGICAL VIRTUES

Chapter 3 began to illustrate a moral agent's moral character using the ecological model of moral character in broad strokes. This chapter describes the theological virtues in accordance with this model. We will begin by considering these virtues (faith, hope, and love) as a whole without differentiating carefully between them. Next we will note how the theological virtues are unique among virtues, and then the chapter will describe each in turn in a way that resonates with an ecological model of moral character.

In an ecological model of moral character, the theological virtues offer a view of the dynamics of human-divine collaborative participation in a person's moral growth. In theological and philosophical ecological virtue theories, the moral virtues are the elements of a moral character that guide action, but how they guide and to what ends depends on what they take as good. In Catholic virtue theory, the theological virtues link a moral agent to the good. They receive and share.

Moral character, like an ecosystem, develops by means of a collaboration between multiple agencies. Catholic theology locates God's role in character formation by referring to the theological virtues. These are the virtues through which a person believes in God, centers herself in God, and notices and accepts direction from God. Through the theological virtues, a person receives what God gives. In addition, these virtues are themselves a gift from God infused into a moral agent. If the theological virtues are integrated into the whole moral character, functioning responsively with neighboring participants of the moral agent's character, then the moral agent participates well in God's continuing creation of the moral agent and of her world. The theological virtues' integration into a moral character opens a kind of conduit, a channel through which the moral agent draws on the dynamics of God's love. Active, integral, and living theological virtues feed the moral virtues and root the moral agent in the good itself. Through the theological virtues, God's cooperation in the evolution of that person's moral character is accepted as the moral agent is attuned to the good.

This chapter presents the three theological virtues as participants in the moral character of a believing moral agent. Because we are building an ecological model of moral character, this presentation will emphasize first how these virtues function as a community in mutual cooperation with one another. Later the chapter will describe each one in more detail. The theological virtues are open to God. This virtues community is a locus where human agency and divine agency combine. They represent the flow of two agencies—divine and human—to create a dynamic of their own. Like the moral virtues, the theological virtues are characteristics of a human moral agent, but the way they function, when they are open to God, is as a dynamic. It is a flowing that is made possible by God, then assented to by the human person, and thereafter shaped by the relationship between person and God, including the person's responses to that relationship.

Traditional Catholic virtue theory says that faith connects one to God; hope draws on faith,[1] bringing its connectedness forward to charity;[2] and charity offers what faith has taken to inform prudence and the moral virtues.[3] An ecological model of moral character can describe the theological virtues similarly. A moral character, like an ecosystem, is an open system. Its dynamics are not completely self-contained. Theological virtues represent the active opening through which God's divine agency seeps into a person. The ecological moral character model can imagine that opening and seeping as proceeding "through" each of the three in a sequence similar to that of traditional Catholic virtue theory: faith holds open a person's receiving of God's grace, and hope draws on what faith brings and pulls it into more specificity, conveying what was received onward to the virtue of charity. Charity accepts and carries what faith received toward the moral virtues so that it will serve as fuel and flavor for the moral agent to accept and pass along. Like a conduit, this flow channel is alive and moving when open to God and to the person's moral character. When fully open, a person accepts God's presence and gifts and actualizes them and their effects into creation through her own doing and being.

Most of this book's description of a moral character focuses on the moral virtues. That effort continues in chapter 5. This chapter describes the theological virtues. The theological virtues, as a set, differ from the moral virtues in significant respects, so we will take stock of those differences before looking at each of the theological virtues individually. Unlike the moral virtues, the theological virtues are infused into the moral agent as gifts from God.

Their excellence is not best imagined as a balance between extremes, and their "actions" are always internal to the moral agent (that is, the theological virtues are less immediately linked to a person's external action).

DIFFERENCES BETWEEN THEOLOGICAL AND MORAL VIRTUES

As infused virtues, the theological virtues are gifts, given to a person. Moral virtues result from a moral agent's efforts to practice being virtuous, but the theological virtues' appearance in a moral agent do not result from the person's own efforts. If theological virtues are a receiving openness, it is not the moral agent herself who first opens the passage. That is God's work.

A person has this openness definitively as part of what she is: a created human being, loved by God. If this weren't the case, no person could look to God, because no person would know in which direction to look or even how to recognize God wherever God shows up. The theological virtues can be developed or improved through a person's own efforts, but it is God who begins this possibility. When a moral agent draws on God's gifts and presence through the theological virtues, these virtues evolve to better conduct what God offers into the person with more openness or with a stronger flow. The theological virtues can grow so that a moral agent lives in greater participation in and with God, to live more responsively to God's reaching for the person, but the openness through which a person experiences God's giving is itself a gift.

Moral virtues and theological virtues are each imagined in different terms. Each moral virtue is defined as a "mean" or balance between opposing extremes.[4] A moral virtue, such as honesty, is a balanced trait whose imbalances would be vices (the vice of deceit is a corresponding vice of deficiency, and tactlessness is a corresponding vice of excess), but theological virtues are not. This is the second difference between moral virtues and theological virtues. Faith, for example, is not a balance between disbelief and excessive belief. Christianity does not warn against excessive reliance on God. The improvement of the theological virtues is not a matter of balancing their strengths against other things. Instead, the growth of the theological virtues is a matter of improving accuracy and increasing participation in the flow of grace that comes from God. For the theological virtues, improvement is about how well these virtues aim at their source and object (God) and how well they take in and integrate what God offers. A healthy faith is one that orients its person well to God. Orientation and thickness are the excellences that matter here. The theological virtues, rooted well in a connection to God, hold open and widen the flow of God's grace into and through the person. The theological virtues also participate in the flow itself, integrating it into the person with the moral virtues. Theological virtues are shaped by a moral agent's relationship with God, and their integration of God's love into the person can change the dynamics of the moral character. (This is described in chapter 5's discussion of prudence.)

The third difference between the moral and theological virtues is that while the moral virtues' behaviors have a close causal link to external human actions, the theological virtues' actions are always internal to the person, strictly speaking. When the theological virtues act, we do not say that the person "does" something. The theological virtues do influence the moral agent's external actions through their interaction with prudence and the other moral virtues, but their niche in the moral character is to channel what God offers to the moral character, or to integrate divine and human agency. Therefore, while external actions can illustrate what a moral virtue is, the theological virtues can be said to perform only internal actions. They inhabit relationships with the other participants of the moral character, and their behaviors are events to be imagined in terms of those relationships.

With these traits in mind, we need a reminder of the limits of our ability to describe virtues, including the theological virtues. As we saw in chapter 3, the virtues are universally individuated.[5] They are different within each moral agent. All virtues in an ecological moral character model are responsive intersections. They move as they do in relationship with the other participants of a person's moral character. The virtues of each moral agent's communities are different, and so the theological virtues of each person are also unique. For example, the process of faith's development differs with each moral agent in whom faith lives because it is aided by the other virtues.[6] For another example, humility may help one person to accept what the theological virtues offer her, but in another person the growth of the theological virtues might arise from a reckoning with one's own dependence on her neighbors in creation. So, we cannot say that humility only arises from faith or that it only fosters faith. Theological virtues can tend to pull one person toward calm and stillness but in another person may function to excite or animate.

To put this in the terms we set in chapter 3, the theological virtues occupy many different niches in moral agents. But we can to a limited extent describe the role each theological virtue plays in a moral agent, beginning with faith.

FAITH

Before describing faith as a theological virtue, we will first consider what, ecologically speaking, is at stake in this concept. Faith, as a broadly defined character trait, is highly valued in ecological ethical writings within and outside of religious discourse.

Within theology, many note causal links between ecological failures and lack of faith or misdirected faith. As Elizabeth Groppe observes, even before magisterial calls for "ecological conversion,"[7] as appeared in *Laudato si'* and Pope John Paul II's 2001 general audience,[8] Christian biblical texts have linked agrarian cultivation with virtue cultivation. Groppe adds that our liturgical life suffers when we allow ourselves to be severed or split from agrarianism, or as farmer-philosopher Fred Kirschenmann put it, when we are "divorced from the soil."[9]

Theologians such as Groppe and Norman Wirzba have highlighted many connections between faith and the human practices of eating.[10] Outside of overtly theological contexts, Wendell Berry has demonstrated complex connections between faith and farming.[11] Eating is a human practice, and it is also a creaturely necessity that intimately links all species, including humans, and ecosystems. For humans, it is therefore also a locus of important engagement with faith. Pope Francis's ecological encyclical, *Laudato si'*, comments that this was also true of Jesus of Nazareth.[12]

Faith has ecological significance beyond theology too. Even Carl Sagan urged people of faith to engage their faith for the good of Earth in his urgent "appeal to the world religious community."[13] His appeal was made precisely because of the "religious dimension" of ecological problems. If our eating and farming practices exhibit causal links to faith, then we can conclude that humans' faith affects ecosystems and that ecosystems, in turn, affect faith.

Thomas Berry's legacy and the Journey of the Universe project,[14] which compellingly continues his work, demonstrate that the stories we tell about creation (and about ourselves) must, for the sake of our future, incorporate both scientific and religious forms of knowledge.[15] A description of life with no spiritual component will surely evolve into extinction. Ecological survival is made possible by belief. As ecotheologian Denis Edwards has noticed, "Any contemporary theology of the human . . . will need to situate the human within the community of life."[16] The ecological conversion for which he and Pope Francis plead integrates humanity, faith, and all creation together.

These are the stakes. Faith requires ecological health, and planetary ecological health requires creaturely faith. Next, let's look at faith specifically as a theological virtue that participates in an ecologically imagined moral character. Faith's relationship to God is definitive of what faith is. We have seen already that the theological virtues together connect a person to God. Faith refers to that interaction from the human side of the encounter. Faith fills a moral character's need for something that perceives and receives God and is the means through which one affirmatively orients toward God. Faith is a kind of knowing, and as such it inhabits the intellect in traditional Catholic virtue theory.[17]

Faith's openness, first instilled by what God gives, is distinguishable from what it receives. Through faith's openness, a moral character receives, or assents to accept, what God gives. The Holy Spirit offers grace, and faith assents to receive it.[18] God's agency is what makes faith important. Yet traditional Catholic virtue theory's explanations of faith emphasize human agency. Faith needs us to "nourish" and "reinforce" it,[19] which implies that we can also not nourish faith and that it can become anemic. Faith, once given, is said to "remain . . . in one who has not sinned against it."[20] We can indirectly improve or degrade this locus of openness through our actions and practices. God and human must both act in order for a person to have faith. This makes human faith a result of divine-human collaboration. Faith is given by God, and it must be habitually drawn on by the person. The motion of God's love widens the porosity of the boundary through which God's love seeps. The person's drawing on what is given has that same effect. God is the target and the source of this orientation. A person can resist it, draw on it, or increase its capacity, performing response actions with different degrees of assent to take in what faith receives. In other words, she can widen or narrow the openness through which God's Spirit reaches to participate in her internal worlds. Faith is the name for that openness, and it works only when both God and human tend to it. But more help than this is also needed.

Faith's development involves other moral agents. This includes persons who witness to God's creative, redemptive, and sustaining activities. For Christians in our era, a few millennia's worth of these participants are required. Additional sets of moral agents might also be needed to persuade the person to draw on what faith is supplying.[21]

I argue that even vices can be a part of a moral agent's means toward developing faith. Consider a moral agent whose impatience has caused for her many experiences of undesirable consequences. She may find in the reservoir of faith a way to balance her impatient tendencies against something with a depth sufficient to hold them in check. Faith is often drawn on when we are scrambling or flailing about, morally speaking. Making use of what faith offers widens its capacity, acclimating a person's moral character to that which belief helps her to know.

As a moral agent's openness to drawing on God's love, faith is the most deeply rooted of the theological virtues. It is also the theological virtue that is most remote from the activities carried out by the moral virtues. Faith interacts with hope and with charity by carrying what it receives to them, and with them through them.

An ecological model of moral character demonstrates a wide range of relationships among a moral character's inhabitants. For example, let's look more closely at the interactions between faith, the intellect, and the will. In traditional Catholic virtue theory, faith resides within the speculative intellect. As an aspect of the intellect, faith enacts the intellect's assent to God.[22] In that way, faith, as a participant of a person's intellect, acts to perfect or fulfill the efficacy of a person's intellectual capabilities.

Faith is never a lonely actor. The ecological model can help us see faith's functions and effects as results of cooperation between human and God. At times, though, we (wrongly) seem to value faith as a powerful and independent force, as if it is stronger when it is acting on its own, unbolstered by other participants of a moral character. Our discourse sometimes valorizes faith as acting without or even against reason. This error is preventable with an ecologically understood moral character. Faith is not independent in any way. It is all about connectedness, dependence, a drinking up of what is good. Faith allows what it encounters to change the person. That connection is what keeps the flow of life moving. At the same time, faith cocreates a locus of porosity through which God's dream for the world becomes that much clearer. The human theological virtue of faith is the raw convergence between God's offer of love and the human response.

HOPE

Like faith, hope is highly valued by ecologically attuned moral theorists, whether they understand it as a theological virtue, a moral virtue, or something else. Louke van Wensveen found hope to be among the most frequently mentioned virtues in ecological virtue ethics.[23] Hope is essential to all forms of justice work and for survival itself.

Our climate's trajectory does not favor our (humanity's) survival.[24] Because the most powerfully impactful societies have been unwilling to change our food, energy, and transportation infrastructures as quickly or dramatically as necessary, the composition of our planet's atmosphere will not change in time to prevent climate instability. It has already begun. In my own nation, a well-funded campaign of doubt and misinformation successfully impeded the public's understanding of how our practices affect our atmosphere, disincentivizing the necessary changes in policy, lifestyle, and infrastructure. Individuals who do want to make the necessary changes often find them prohibitively difficult, and the minor changes that smaller communities can implement do not seem to add up to enough to prevent the coming disaster. The lifestyle and practices of North Americans have created social, economic, and ecological conditions from which refugees are now fleeing. New disease vectors, crop failures, species extinctions, and superstorms already threaten the lives of people whose economic positions give them no safe way to escape.[25] Globally many have died, and many more will. Our current trajectory is self-extinction, beginning with those our religion teaches us to love most.

Hope is ecologically necessary. Philosopher Jonathan Lear illustrates the kind of hope we need now with a description of the role model of Chief Plenty Coups.[26] This Crow chief is held up as a leader who, facing imminent cultural annihilation, was able to reinterpret his society's moral resources to enable his people's survival. Lear describes his work of swiftly refitting his people's virtue heritage for the telos required to survive genocide.[27] Lear argues that Chief Plenty Coups was able to do this because he believed that there was helpful work he could both identify and actually carry out. This audacious presumption, facing the reality of powerful elite people's attempts to culturally exterminate his communities while also rejecting the inevitability of cultural death, has exemplified for some ecological ethicists the radical hope we need. Hope is necessary because our task now is to seed change with no certainty that change will sprout.

Theologian Steven Bouma-Prediger names Jane Goodall as a model of hope.[28] He notes the opposition to her research's findings, her ability to disregard her colleagues' methods of devaluing the primates that were her research subjects and companions, and the many factors that could have led her to despair over the survival of endangered species.[29] Yet she persisted. Bouma-Prediger describes Goodall as resolute, inspiring, and determined. When asked about her source of hope, Goodall gave four reasons: first, the marvels of our human brains; second, nature's resilience; third, the energy and commitment of younger humans; and finally, the human spirit's determination, demonstrated by individuals with courage, persistence, compassion, and love.[30] This description of hope reveals what we would expect to see in an ecologically attuned understanding of hope. It is fed by the activity of other virtues, by knowledge about the natural world, and by the presence of others who are acting from their own hope.

As a theological virtue, hope is what faith becomes for mortal beings, including humans, who are embedded in time. Our nature of being bounded in time's motion makes hope both possible and necessary. As a theological virtue, hope draws on what faith receives, engaging what it finds within a person. No person can hear the good of promises without hope. As Pope Benedict XVI noted, "Faith is Hope."[31] Hope is what faith senses forward in time.

In this book, hope is a virtue that deserves particular attention, because moral growth is our main interest. Imperfection and flaws are definitive for postlapsarian human nature. We cannot even love perfectly. Our moral improvement cannot be certain. We can aim our moral growth with a hope that we will develop in the ways that are good and necessary when they are needed, but we can do this only on the basis of a knowledge that reason alone cannot provide.

Hope is an orientation toward that which faith brings into the person. In other words, hope attends to faith's discovery, hearing it and passing it along toward action and vision. As a virtue, hope persists over time, fueled by faith in even the most dire and threatening situations. Hope attunes the person to take as direction not only the intellect's and the passions' understandings of the moment but also that which faith specifically presents about a moment's larger meaning.

One might feel as though hope ignores reality. Ecological philosopher Allen Thompson voices this view, saying that hope, properly formed, works against an accurate description of reality. He argues that radical hope is "a form of commitment against what may be justifiable despair."[32] For him, radical hope works against reason to help us build a future using apparently unlikely or impossible expectations. In a certain mood, even St. Paul seems to agree.[33]

But Christian ecological virtue ethicist Steven Bouma-Prediger has argued that hope is entirely realistic because it assumes a real truth: that God is at the center of everything.[34] All of creation can run in the wrong direction, poisoned, heartless, and lost, but being realistic means remembering that God remains God: center, ground, beginning, and, in some way, end.[35] In the face of extinctions, hope is critically important. Hope is what helps us to situate ourselves within creation in such a way that the future, the as yet unseen opening of God's intention for creation, changes the present. Given the power of this virtue, its orientation toward faith is extremely important.

Identifying hope is not always easy. Counterfeits and semblances of hope proliferate, so we need to look deliberately at what hope is not in order to prepare ourselves for the search for hope. Erroneous versions of hope fuel injustice and weaken faith's integration of God's gifts into a person. An

Afro-pessimist theological view offers irreplaceable expertise in humanity when it comes to hope.

In the United States, an open and legal practice of chattel slavery of Black humans evolved into housing and imprisonment practices to cultivate wealth disparities and a malicious belief system that still deeply inform how and where we live today. These attitudes and beliefs propagated further economic, political, ecological, religious, geographical, theological, and medical reinforcements of racism and a broad white supremacist ethos.[36] In such a context, hope must direct action and must be understood well. The Church's official responses have been inadequate,[37] but Black scholars' work can help the Church take a theological turn toward sanity. Therefore, our next step is to consider theologian Vincent Lloyd's work on hope. Lloyd identifies errors that conflate hope with desire, affect, and rhetoric.

When hope is equated with desire, it becomes a matter of individual preference and pins itself to a desired good's likelihood instead of to a true good itself. This cannot be sustained over time and cannot be a habit and is very far from the theological virtue of hope.[38]

Affect misinterpreted as hope makes hope into a "personality type" or a mood;[39] it is a feeling. This particular hope counterfeit does bring benefits. It can be infectious and could evolve to become belief. But its link to action quickly erodes. Social and cultural contexts can (and do) replace its object with something other than truth. Affect is not a virtue.

Rhetoric as hope is the most common misunderstanding of hope in the United States, argues Lloyd. This hope counterfeit combines affect with reasoning. Rhetoric masquerading as hope offers a desirable future as an inevitability, undermining our necessary work for justice. This hope counterfeit closely resembles the theological virtue of hope. Because its object is some sort of apparently radical transformation, it even conveys the appearance of an eschatological aspiration. But its function is to support feelings of optimism, not action. True hope's effects lead to a moral character's external acts.[40]

With these cautions in place, we can begin a good description of hope as it would appear in an ecological model of moral character. As before, we begin with hope's interactions with the other participants in a moral character. In traditional Catholic virtue theory, hope resides within the will. Hope's source is not the things we understand only through our intellect. Rather, hope moves from the connection with God that faith offers. As such, hope is a kind of orientation or vector. Because hope is the way that faith's discovery translates into a person's life, it is essentially a willingness, an openness to what faith brings to it and a motion to further pass that along into the moral agent's character. Hope lets us cling to the incomprehensible goodness that faith allows in and, because goodness is both dynamic and fuel, hope is also strengthened by what it receives and passes along.

Hope's participation in a person's moral character flows from God's offerings,[41] but hope does seem to have a dash more of human agency than faith does. Through hope, we draw on what faith holds, and the way we draw on it steers hope's development. Hope's work engages our imagination (another ecologically significant virtue),[42] passions, and perceptions of what, how, and where we are.[43] Lloyd notes that when faith is open and hope is mixing with grace, our practices and, importantly, our aesthetics will evolve.[44] As a result, in a world of white supremacy and ecological degradation, the affective experience of drawing on hope will not feel like optimism. This is an important consequence to name correctly and an important reason to understand correctly what hope is. This is Lloyd's insight: we must learn to accept despair.[45]

Lloyd argues that despair "offers training in hope."[46] This despair must be authentic. It is an honest recognition that the true good, even after a moral agent has learned to hope for it accurately and well, cannot actually be attained through one's own efforts. Despair is therefore an important symptom of the theological virtue of hope for Lloyd. When we are in despair with no affective experience of hope, the theological virtue of hope is all that remains.

Another example to illustrate Lloyd's point is a moral agent with depression. For persons in depression, there is only the theological virtue of hope. No emotional support or motivation for hope can gain a foothold when the mind is unable to feel joy, content, or assurance.[47] The decision to remain alive, to persist in living, is made over and over again and often with great difficulty. This kind of persistence is a powerful demonstration of raw hope and therefore of faith. Medical treatments and therapies exist to help people with depression to find their (our) way to a life with optimism and enjoyment. This is good and right, because depression is an illness. Depression impedes flourishing. But the experience of depression's despair does demonstrate that the lack of an affective experience of positivity simply does not correlate with loss of the theological virtue of hope, much less with a weaker faith.[48] On the contrary, persistence in living with depression is a sign of powerful hope.

Some may recall that the Catholic catechism states that despair is a sin against hope.[49] This passage's use of "hope" assumes and reinforces a mutual contradiction between hope and despair. But I argue that if a person in despair continues to seek health and to remain alive, then faith is still at work, and therefore hope is too. The human experience of persisting even when one feels despair raises a question about this binary. If hope integrates and conveys what faith has received, its consequences will be perceptible but might not manifest in emotions or mood. The virtue of hope certainly interacts with passions and emotions, but it must not be defined contingently on affect.

An ecological model of moral character would not identify a single moral vice as utterly antithetical to a theological virtue. The relationalities between virtues and vices are too complex to allow for a universal mutually oppositional relationship between a theological virtue and any moral vice. An ecological model of moral character also critically examines any Christian traditions that overemphasize hopeful feelings or optimistic outlook as a sign of theological virtuosity or superior faith. Hope interacts with passions and emotions but is not the same as them. As an "inhabitant" of the will, hope has a willingness to it, and hope's willingness is directed not toward optimism but instead toward faith. Hopefulness is a desirable and enjoyable emotional state, but it is not the same thing as the theological virtue of hope.

CHARITY

The third traditional theological virtue in Catholic virtue ethics is charity. As we have seen with the other theological virtues, charity is also often praised in ecological ethics.[50] Van Wensveen listed charity or love first among the virtues found in her catalog of the "dirty virtues" that were unearthed by ecological virtue ethics.[51] Ecotheologian Sean McDonagh and Wendell Berry both emphasize love.[52] This is a virtue whose ecological significance is recognized beyond moral theology.

As a theological virtue, charity fulfills the moral agent's openness to God. Charity draws on what faith receives and conveys that grace to the moral virtues. Using a more mechanical metaphor, we could say that charity completes the circuit between faith and action, allowing the mix of grace and human acceptance to encounter one's moral virtues. Charity is that through which we are able to love and propels the flow of God's reaching for us so that love passes through us to touch creation beyond ourselves. God's gifts flow with faith and hope into and through a moral agent. When charity is open to what it senses from hope, it draws that onward. Charity does not merely move God's love along dispassionately. Charity is also changed by what it encounters from God. The goodness that charity encounters and passes along to the moral virtues fuels and reshapes charity itself.

Because we are created beings, charity is synonymous in us with love. As a theological virtue, love is not an affect or mood. Charity has a vector quality, with God as its first source and its content, and creation as its recipient. Charity is a directing of love outward, toward others in creation (at least as well as a human person is able to do this). As moral theologian James Keenan puts it, charity's "focus is extroverted."[53] The target of this virtue is easy to guess: other people; vulnerable forms of life; communities that we know, including bioregions; and all the participants in creation's systems of life. Whatever God loves, charity helps us also to love.

Creation is quite lovable, and each moral agent's loving is unique even though the source for all is the same.[54] Charity takes up what faith absorbs and what hope conveys, brings it into specific embodiment as it changes the moral agent, and moves God's love outward, to others, through that moral agent's action.[55] As a theological virtue, charity is infused into persons and is meant to be nurtured by what we do in response to this encounter.[56] As we saw in defining faith, divine and human activity meet and collaborate in the virtue of charity. Charity also mixes with and propels the received good onward to the moral virtues through prudence. Charity, fueled by grace, motivates and shapes prudence. In charity, something of God is received, integrated, and sent onward toward embodiment in action. Charity cooperates with prudence and with a person's exercise of moral agency.

Charity meets prudence to bridge the theological virtues with the moral virtues. In traditional Catholic virtue theory, charity brings to prudence what hope has sent to it, and inspired by charity, prudence shapes action. A moral agent's action response to God begins in prudence. So, in a theological model of moral character, the theological virtue of charity is a locus of complex collaboration involving the person's agency in more ways than do hope and faith. Two related questions arise at this point. These questions deserve attention, although this book does not seek to give them definitive answers: How and where does the will interact with the theological virtues? Is the collaboration between prudence and charity the only place where a moral agent's internal world of moral virtues interacts with the theological virtues?

For the first question, we should note that Christian theologies cover a multitude of ideas about how (and whether) grace and the will interact. For the purposes of ecumenical dialogue, this proposal of an ecological model of moral character allows some ambiguity on this question. It seems reasonable to dialogue about moral character across disagreements about exactly where and in what ways the will and charity interact.

Yet one wonders whether, in an ecological model of virtue theory, the will cooperates with the theological virtues only through charity's connection to prudence. Might the will not also reach farther upstream, or farther in, to interact even with hope and faith? Some form of agency is at work in the behaviors of these virtues. We speak of hope and faith as at least indirectly responsive to a moral agent's choices. At times, virtue theory's descriptions of these virtues' behaviors even imply that the virtues themselves have volition. Theological virtues are said to connect, link, listen, and assent to God, and it seems that a moral agent can also not do these things. Do theological virtues then contain their own particular will?

At stake here is a moral character model's aptitude to help the theology it serves. This question is about how humans participate in the life of God and creation. A good model will value the collaboration between God and human. In my view, a good model will also recognize the impossibility of discerning completely between these collaborating agencies, at least on the level of responsiveness. Chapter 3 recommended participatory theology as a useful collaborator for this moral character model. A vision of human agency as a form of participation in divine agency offers a way to describe where and how the will functions among and between the theological virtues.[57] The priority ought to be in finding the description that seems accurate and that encourages and inspires moral growth. The insufficiency of human agency to manifest in action or consequences can be at times forgotten in moral theology because of its emphasis on responsibility and exercise of the will. Work in participatory theology can collaborate with this proposed model of moral character to help us think about how divine and human agencies interact. Ecotheology's attunement to the agency of life's systems, even when it is a secondary agency, offers a different view that might also lead to insight about how and where the will interacts with divine agency, with creation, and with the theological virtues of a moral agent.[58]

The second question asks whether prudence and charity's link is the only locus of cooperation between theological and moral virtues. An essential function in a bioregion is usually enacted in more than one way. Indirect cooperations and collaborations are powerful, and redundancies proliferate. The life systems of an ecosystem are not animated through mutually exclusive relationalities. An image of only one link between the theological virtues and the moral virtues, however thick that link, does not reflect the complexity and webs of ecological systems.

An image of attunement as a trait that proliferates all through a moral character can help us to envision a diversity of fine relationships between the theological virtues and many moral virtues at many different points in a moral character. Chapter 5's description of prudence in an ecological moral character model will address this connectivity.

Divine and human agency are mingled in the virtue we call charity. The experience of expressing love for creation, for this world and this universe, is an amplification of God's love into creation. The acts that cultivate this way of being also impede our ability to poison, neglect, ignore, take for granted, misshape, and otherwise scar our environments. But the enjoyment humans experience through acts of love to our environments and life systems also loops backward into us and through us. God enjoys creation's enjoyment of itself. The human enjoyment of loving creation is a qualified, interruptible, and halting enjoyment. There are mosquitoes, viruses, dangers, and death that we do not enjoy. Even so, we can take creation's enjoyability as a sign, even a sacramental sign, of God's own hopes for us.

FINDING GOD'S MARK ON INTEGRATED THEOLOGICAL VIRTUES

Divine-human cooperation is close in a moral agent's theological virtues. But what is it, exactly, that hope takes up from faith and moves along to charity? Is it raw grace alone? I believe that this is ecologically unlikely. The theological virtues do not merely convey but also mingle with grace. Where there is interaction, there is mutual influence. The flow that the theological virtues soak up and move along toward moral actions is a dynamic mix of God's and person's motions, together. The theological virtues do not only pass a baton from one to the next. What is passed along seeps into the moral agent's faith, hope, and love. The theological virtues are an interplay, a fertilizing coming together, that feeds, informs, and inspires a person's moral life.

What we learn from the theological virtues, especially hope, is that the theological virtues are all about moral growth. They motivate it, aim it, shape it in the form of love, and fuel it even as they are fueled. Were moral growth unnecessary or impossible, the theological virtues would be nonsensical. So, with these aspects of a moral character model in place, we are ready to imagine the moral virtues, beginning with the cardinal virtues.

NOTES

1. Aquinas, *ST*, II–II, q. 17, a. 7.
2. Aquinas, *ST*, II–II, q. 17, a. 8.
3. Aquinas, *ST*, II–II, q. 51, a. 2; II–II q. 33, a. 1; and I–II q. 65, a. 1.
4. Aquinas, *ST*, I–II, q. 64.
5. Aquinas, *ST*, II–II, q. 4, a. 6.
6. Aquinas notes that the relationships between faith and moral virtues differ between moral agents. Aquinas, *ST*, II–II, q. 4, a. 7.
7. Groppe, *Eating and Drinking*; and *Laudato si'*, para. 5, which notes a 2001 address from Pope John Paul II, para. 4: Pope John Paul II, "General Audience, God Made Man the Steward of Creation," January 17, 2001.

8. Pope Francis, *Laudato si'*; and Pope John Paul II, "General Audience, God Made Man the Steward of Creation."

9. Kirschenmann, "On Becoming Lovers of the Soil," 285.

10. Wirzba, *Food and Faith*; and Groppe, *Eating and Drinking*.

11. Berry, *The Gift of Good Land*; Berry, *What Are People For?*; and Berry, *Another Turn of the Crank*.

12. *Laudato si'*, no. 98.

13. Carl Sagan et al., "Preserving and Cherishing the Earth: An Appeal for Joint Commitment in Science and Religion," January 1990, https://fore.yale.edu/sites/default/files/files/Preserving%20and%20Cherishing%20the%20Earth.pdf.

14. See Journey of the Earth, https://www.journeyoftheuniverse.org/.

15. Swimme and Berry, *The Universe Story from the Primordial Flaring Forth to the Ecozoic Era*.

16. Edwards, *Ecology at the Heart of Faith*, 7.

17. Aquinas, *ST*, II–II, q. 4, a. 2.

18. For our purposes, I use the term "grace" to refer to grace as God's gift, not to name grace's effects within a person. See Aquinas, *ST*, I–II, q. 109–14.

19. Pope Francis, "Lumen Fidei," para. 6.

20. "Catechism of the Catholic Church" (Libreria Editrice Vaticana, Citta del Vaticano, 1993), para. 1815.

21. Aquinas, *ST*, II–II, q. 1; and Brown, "The Theological Virtue of Faith," 226.

22. Aquinas, *ST*, II–II, q. 1, a. 3.

23. Van Wensveen, *Dirty Virtues*, 11 and 49. See also Gosling and Case, "Social Dreaming and Ecocentric Ethics"; and Thompson, "Radical Hope."

24. See this book's preface for more on this.

25. See IPCC, "Climate Change 2022," https://report.ipcc.ch/ar6/wg2/IPCC_AR6_WGII_FullReport.pdf, chap. 8.

26. Lear, *Radical Hope*. Lear's use of Chief Plenty Coups as a "representative anecdote" deserves critique as an example of cultural appropriation that has not grasped this Crow leader's strategies well. See Gosling and Case, "Social Dreaming and Ecocentric Ethics," 710.

27. Lear, *Radical Hope*, 56–57.

28. Bouma-Prediger, *Earthkeeping and Character*, 121–22.

29. Bouma-Prediger, citing Goodall's *Reason for Hope*, notes her practice of naming chimps about whom she wrote. Bouma-Prediger, *Earthkeeping and Character*, 121.

30. Bouma-Prediger, *Earthkeeping and Character*, 122.

31. In "Spes Salvi," see the title following the introductory paragraph. Pope Benedict XVI, "Spes Salvi."

32. Thompson, "Radical Hope," 51.

33. I Corinthians 4:9–13.

34. Bouma-Prediger, *For the Beauty of the Earth*, 144.

35. Bouma-Prediger's work is in a context of Reformed theology and as such represents an important dialogue partner for Catholic ecological virtue ethics.

36. Recent and helpful works demonstrating this include Alexander, *The New Jim Crow*; Jennings, *The Christian Imagination*; Jones, *White Too Long*; Grimes, *Christ Divided*; Washington, *Medical Apartheid*; and Zimring, *Clean and White*.

37. This is argued by several Catholic writers, including Daniel Horan, "The Bishops' Letter Fails to Recognize That Racism Is a White Problem," *National Catholic Reporter*,

February 20, 2019; Horan, *A White Catholic's Guide to Racism and Privilege*; and Massingale, *Racial Justice and the Catholic Church*.

38. Lloyd, "For What Are Whites to Hope?," 171.

39. Lloyd, 172.

40. Lloyd, 173.

41. Aquinas, *ST*, II–II, q. 17, a. 2.

42. Chapter 6 on fortitude also notes the role of imagination.

43. The significance of "where" will be described in chapter 5.

44. Lloyd, "For What Are Whites to Hope?," 142.

45. Lloyd, 176. Lloyd describes the retraining of desires (e.g., for certain kinds of neighborhoods, clothing, or foods) that cultivate hope as poverty.

46. Lloyd, 179.

47. Some Christian traditions tend to conflate optimistic affect with hope as a theological virtue. This exacerbates the suffering of depression because it intimates that lack of faith is the cause of illness. Good resources on this include Lynch, *Images of Hope*; and, more recently, Coblentz, *Dust in the Blood*.

48. For another discussion of this, see Lynch, *Images of Hope*, 31–32; and Coblentz, "Dust in the Blood," 58–59, 67, and chap. 3.

49. "Catechism of the Catholic Church," para. 2091. This text names despair as mutually exclusive with hope and absolutizes it as a rejection of God's promises, which is not true of despair as a mood or a passing experience.

50. Van Wensveen, *Dirty Virtues*, 141.

51. Van Wensveen, 49.

52. See, for example, Berry, *Another Turn of the Crank*; and McDonagh, "The Death of Life."

53. Keenan, *Virtues for Ordinary Christians*, 50.

54. Pope Benedict XVI, *Caritas in Veritate*, para. 7.

55. This "outward" direction implies that faith is at the core of the theological virtues community and that charity contains the moral virtues and links them. Aquinas, *ST*, I–II, q. 65, a. 3. An ecological model of moral character could imagine the entrance and flow direction in several different ways (with grace flowing downward, upward, etc.).

56. Pope Benedict XVI, *Caritas in Veritate*, para. 2.

57. See, for example, Davison, *Participation in God*.

58. For an ecotheological discussion of this participation, see Edwards, *Ecology at the Heart of Faith*, particularly chap. 3; and Edwards, *Partaking of God*.

5

Embedded Within and Without

PRUDENCE AND JUSTICE

Traditional Catholic virtue theory names four cardinal virtues. This chapter describes two of the four, prudence and justice, and chapter 6 describes temperance and fortitude. Like all virtues in an ecological model of moral character, cardinal virtues interact with other participants of a moral character. In such a model, frequent and intense interactivity, forming a community of many different participants, is a definitive trait of a flourishing moral character. Cardinal virtues function to organize sets of these interactions. This means that cardinal virtues offer a way for us to consider the relationships and interactions between participants within a moral character across different scales of focus.

First, let's consider cardinality itself. I argue that because cardinal virtues are the way that a moral character develops and balances itself, they are always excellences of attunement.[1] Cardinal virtues are attentive to the worlds without and within a person. Good cardinal virtues are those that enable good responses to the moral agent's context and to the internal worlds inhabited by the moral agent's theological virtues, will, intellect, passions, and senses.

Pioneer ecological virtue ethicist Louke van Wensveen contributed to ecological virtue theory a vision of cardinal virtues as sets of virtues. Traditional Catholic virtue theory tends to describe cardinal virtues as directing other virtues, but it is difficult to imagine what kinds of ecosystem participants would play roles of directing or governing other participants. Behaviors of prey species may change in response to what predators do, but the reverse is also true. Van Wensveen described cardinal virtues as shaping the communities of virtues that participate within them. In that way, cardinal virtues organize themselves. We can begin to see how this works by considering prudence.

Prudence is defined in traditional Catholic virtue theory as an intellectual virtue that functions as a moral virtue.[2] Prudence brings to moral deliberation its abilities of foresight, circumspection, and caution.[3] The virtue is sometimes named "practical wisdom,"[4] or a well-practiced ability to recognize where and what the good and the right is in a specific situation and to identify how a moral agent's participation in a situation can be good and can create good. Beyond virtue theory, common understanding of prudence often restricts prudence's attention to what is practical even despite moral considerations, particularly when moral considerations seem too challenging. But in virtue theory, prudence attends to situations' circumstances, to the good itself, and to how and where exactly a moral agent herself can best channel goodness into a context, in time.[5] Prudence enables effective moral vision and discernment. Prudence is an ability at the level of the big picture, cosmologically speaking, and draws on a canny understanding of how life can turn out. As such, prudence represents that within which all the moral virtues are nested.

Chapter 3 described nestedness as a cardinal virtue's ability to establish and conform to the "mean" of participating virtues. A cardinal virtue names a community of the shifting nexuses within itself. I will draw on this idea to say that prudence, as Catholic virtue theory's traditional name for the virtue that "orders" all others, acts as the outermost or broadest moral virtue. It is the set of sets comprising the other cardinal virtues and the communities of virtues within and between each of them. One niche of prudence, organizing and balancing the moral virtues, is actually occupied by all the moral virtues and vices.

The nestedness of an ecological model of moral character reminds us that prudence and all the cardinal virtues disappear from view when we consider a moral character on the smaller scale in order to look at individual virtues. Still, the effects of all the virtues' behaviors are at work everywhere in a moral character and on every scale. Furthermore, as the more encompassing elements of a nested system, cardinal virtues contribute to the characteristics of all they contain. Prudence is a characteristic of a moral agent's entire virtues community. It is an excellence of attunement to exterior and interior worlds, including neighboring participants such as the theological virtues, the will, and the intellect. In a sense, prudence is a moral character's ability to tune into resonance with the theological virtues the actual behaviors of its own capacities, including reason, knowledge, observations, senses, emotions, moral virtues, and vices, and to express that resonance as effectively as possible into creation. For example, prudence's capacity of foresight enables the moral agent to "see" both present and future.[6] Yet this capacity is possible only in cooperation with intellect, memory and shrewdness. Circumspection allows prudence to identify and assent to the means of a response to a situation, given the specific circumstances and likely near futures,[7] and prudence brings caution with its firm rootedness in the good itself to help the moral agent step carefully to avoid evil.[8]

THE "DIRTY" CARDINAL VIRTUES

Before we imagine prudence's habitat in the ecological model of moral character, let's first incorporate Louke van Wensveen's insights about cardinal virtues as cardinal. Incorporating her work will show us the role of accepting embodiment in our moral development. Her model also highlights the significance of cardinality's nestedness within a moral agent, the resonance between care for self and care for others, and the thick interreliance between the passions and our moral growth. This ecological model also reveals interaction between hope and fortitude and has implications for how we understand time's flow. Van Wensveen's description of four "dirty" cardinal virtues reveals the characteristics that the cardinal virtues share in common, their links to embodiment, and their interactions with other participants of a moral character.[9] She identifies four sets of ecological cardinal virtues: position, attunement, care, and endurance.

Virtues of Position

For van Wensveen, virtues of position matter because a human person is always in a place. This is a condition of mortal embodiment. The virtues of position help a moral agent accept this and live in accordance with it. Accepting the value of the virtues of position also helps us grow. We can improve morally by accepting our physical embodiment more deeply into our self-understanding. For a Roman Catholic ecological virtue theory, this means expanding on that aspect of our theological anthropology.

Many people inhabit cultures that assume that we (human persons) decide where to be and restructure our places to fit ourselves. We build social and physical structures where we are, and we adjust or alter existing structures when we arrive in new places. The other side of the relationship between person and place is often underestimated: Our places also shape us. For some cultures, the authority of place over self can be difficult to accept. Those of us with more social power, often people who have relocated frequently by choice in pursuit of higher education or specific careers, tend to view locations as objects of our choice. Those of us with economic power acquire homes in places, near and far, and view this as a purchase choice, thereby making another place home. But people who deliberately draw on their locations for identity formation (through cultural practices and social structuring) and those whose relocations have been involuntary or coerced (refugees, first peoples in North America, enslaved and trafficked humans, the incarcerated, and migrants) have a different awareness about the meaning of place. Attending to that awareness can help those of us whose awareness of place is dulled by our power. We need to develop more fully the virtues of position and to understand what we are.

We are earthlings. We are bipeds, shaped and sized as we are and breathing how and what we breathe because of the conditions within which our species evolved. Many of the things that we believe make each of us unique (such as our preferences, dreams, and worldviews) take the specific form that they do because of our physical shape, metabolic cycles and patterns, and emotional-chemical experiences (to name a few). These traits result from our coevolution. We think of space and distance the way we do because our eyes and ears are generally between three and seven feet from the ground or floor. We experience lengths of time in the chunks of hours and years that we do because of our life span, maturity span, the duration of the time we can tolerate being conscious and awake, and our astronomical cycles. We imagine our velocities as fast or slow because of our physical size.[10] Our specific temperature tolerance range comes from the ways our dermal layers respond to light and heat. Nothing about the way we are as a species or as individuals can be explained apart from the conditions of our planet and its other forms of life.

This demonstrates that location is essential to identity and is neither minor nor accidental. Where we are strongly determines who and what we are.[11] We coevolve in places alongside every other form of life and every abiotic element and condition that shares our proximity. As Holmes Rolston III reminds us, "We are finding out who we are by finding out where we are and how we are emplaced there."[12] As an example he speaks of elephants, noting that the location of a savanna or a forest is as necessary to the life of an elephant as her heart and liver. "The outside," he notes, "is as *vital* as the inside."[13] Elephants' hearts and livers are the way they are because of those savannas and forests. Like elephants, we are embedded within our places.

Virtues of position help us to notice what is around us and to be attuned to what is happening there in order to understand how to be there well. This goal is central to virtue theory. After all, for embodied beings, being somewhere well is the same as being well. We are always somewhere in particular, and all livable "wheres" have specific characteristics with which we can attentively cooperate for mutual benefit. Holmes Rolston III calls this virtue "natural attunement" and deems it the source of true "excellence of character."[14]

So, where are we? Moral theologian Steven Bouma-Prediger offers a "battery of questions" about environments to help us in this moral growth. These questions exemplify the kinds of things we should know about the places where we are. As he notes, for most people these questions are difficult to answer. "Ecologically speaking," he asks,

> do you know where you are? . . . What is the soil like around your home? Silty loam? Loamy sand? Sandy clay? . . . What are five agricultural plants in your region? . . . What trees live where you do? . . . What about birds, resident and migratory? . . . What flowers bloom where you live? . . . Which animals are extinct in your neck of the woods? Wolverine, grizzly bear, passenger pigeon, prairie dog? How many days until the moon is full? . . . From where you are reading this, which way is north? From which direction do the prevailing winds blow? From where does your water come? To where does your garbage go?[15]

These are fundamental questions of ecological literacy and self-knowledge. Pope Francis's ecological encyclical emphasized that knowledge, and I add specifically knowledge of these kinds of things, helps our moral growth.[16] This shows us how the intellect's virtues are essential for virtues of position. Van Wensveen's second group of cardinal virtues demonstrates the collaboration between moral and intellectual virtues. These are the virtues of attunement.

Virtues of Attunement

Van Wensveen's virtues of attunement help us in "adjusting ('tuning') our positive, outgoing drives and emotions to match our chosen place and degree of constructive, ecosocial involvement."[17] The virtues of attunement add up to an excellence in habitually noticing and adjusting. They enhance our awareness of our places, as do the virtues of position, but also enable our willingness and skill in responding well to that awareness. Because responses can be acts, emotions, knowledge gained, and moments of stillness, attunement engages the will, the intellect, the senses, and the passions. Van Wensveen also describes engaging the will to adjust our external worlds into resonance with our inner dynamics. Thus, the dynamics of attunement pervade a good moral character. As such, this set of virtues functions in a moral character similarly to prudence's role in traditional Catholic virtue theory.[18]

Steven Bouma-Prediger points to prudence's noticing capacity in his discussion of the vice of ecological foolishness. He says that "because we are enslaved to this vice, ecological services such as natural purification of water are invisible to us,"[19] and thus we name air and water pollution as marginally significant "externalities." Here, a foolishness—or lack of wisdom—impedes our ability to recognize the essential systems of life.

The parallel between attunement and prudence also appears in the work of ecological virtue ethicist Bill Shaw, who has described a close collaboration between attunement and practical wisdom.[20] Shaw argues that the virtue of sensitivity (that is, paying attention habitually, continually, and responsively, which is what I mean by attunement) can be equated with practical wisdom.[21] Shaw defines some terms differently than Catholic virtue theory does, but his meaning of sensitivity aligns well with Catholic virtue traditions' definition of prudence. For Shaw, the moral virtues all connect through this virtue of sensitivity. Sensitivity therefore works with every virtue. It is something they share in common, and because they cooperate with it, sensitivity is also a characteristic of virtues' collaboration itself. Shaw's sensitivity, Catholic virtue theory's prudence, and van Wensveen's attunement virtues, each in their own moral character models, characterize excellences of a moral agent, the whole of the moral agent, and even the interactions between a moral character's participants. We can see here again the nestedness of ecologically envisioned moral character. A trait that is true of a moral agent is true within and between her virtues as well as within and between herself and others, and therefore, in some way, it appears also within and between her communities. Because she herself participates in her communities, her virtues do too. This is what it means to say that cardinal virtues are nested within a moral agent. They have a fractal dynamic, creating patterns that recur across a moral agent's internal and external degrees of scale.

Virtues of Care

Van Wensveen's third cardinal group is the virtues of care. These virtues grow in response to the development of the other cardinal virtues. If we understand ourselves specifically as emplaced and if we come to be, as Rolston III asks, well emplaced, we also become better able to recognize our intrinsic relationality with those with whom we share proximity (and therefore everything). Our awareness of this relationality and our responsiveness to that awareness cultivate good caring.[22]

How does this happen? For humans, at least some degree of caring for and about oneself is inevitable, as the immediacy of pain and suffering demonstrate.[23] Virtues of well emplacedness and an ecological model of moral character hold for us an image of the porous boundaries between our life and others' lives. When we habitually recognize this, the object of our ingrained care for self can expand. For example, the conditions of air, water, ground, and social dynamics determine whether one's own health is possible. When these conditions preclude health, no amount of effort can heal us because we are ecologically embedded beings. When we habitually see that our health is contingent on the ground, air, water, and social dynamics of places, our care for our health becomes care for these elements. Our self-care becomes care for the health of others. As one's practiced and ecologically attuned awareness grows, the scope of one's caring about and caring for widens.

With a boost from attunement, virtues of caring can spread to encompass more forms of life. With this evolution, the caring virtues also reciprocally bolster the virtues of well emplacedness and of attunement and orient the passions more toward holistic flourishing. An ecological model of moral character helps us to visualize the role of the affect in our participation in creation's life systems. In a Catholic virtue theory we name this dimension of the cardinal virtues by speaking of the passions. We describe their complex interactions with moral action and growth. A Catholic ecological model of moral character depicts an interdependence between the passions and the moral growth we are able to sustain. Perseverance in moral growth is essential. This is the focus of van Wensveen's fourth cardinal category: virtues of endurance.

Virtues of Endurance

Virtues of endurance help a moral agent to persevere in ecological awareness and in nurturing all the virtues. This ecological cardinal group parallels fortitude in traditional Catholic virtue theory. Van Wensveen is mindful here of the despair that can accompany ecological awareness of people in our age.[24] Caring for ecosystems leads to a deeper understanding of the ways in which we (humanity) have sickened the lives around us and undermined biodiversity globally. This awareness can overwhelm. We are tempted toward escapism, nihilism, or other forms of withdrawal or disengagement. But actual withdrawal from ecosystems is impossible. We can interact mindfully, obliviously, or some way in between, but interaction is our only option. We cannot even minimize our ecosystem participation. Without endurance, we abandon ecological awareness and avoid the struggle for attunement with our environments. With endurance, we can care enough to be pained by our ecological legacy and our perilous future while still persevering in our effort to cultivate our ecological awareness.

Virtues of endurance enable us to take the long view, and we need this to struggle through doubts and failures toward a penitent, sustainable, and hopeful society. We require endurance today to counteract the vices we have acquired from practices that draw our attention continually to immediate gratification, quick "returns on investments," and quarterly reportable profits. We need a better vision of our relationship with time. Similar to Catholic virtue theory's fortitude, virtues of endurance incorporate into a model of moral character better ways of navigating the flow of time. In this chapter we will see that fortitude, the Catholic virtue analog to van Wensveen's virtues of endurance, works in concert with courage and with the theological virtue of hope.

Louke van Wensveen's way of describing the cardinal virtues gives an ecological and inspiring vision of a good moral character. This model highlights the patterns of a moral character's interactions across many different scales and gives ways to imagine interactions between moral virtues and the intellect, emotions, the will, and each other. Van Wensveen depicts the interactions between our virtues, passions, and intellect and our contexts. All of this reflects vitally organic links between actions and one's internal growth.

Van Wensveen's description also offers an answer to a question raised in chapter 4 about the theological virtues. The question was whether we should imagine the link between prudence and charity as the only locus of communion between the theological and the moral virtues (and vices). Van Wensveen's description of four cardinal virtue communities names one characteristic of each of the four cardinal sets: attunement. Attunement is a virtue that we need to develop within creation. But it is not a virtue that functions in only one area of a moral character. Attunement characterizes the virtues themselves when they are evolving toward balance. The ecological model of moral character should therefore depict many threads linking the theological virtues with moral virtues. Attunement to the good, orientation to love itself, is everywhere. With help from van Wensveen's vision, this chapter next describes prudence and justice in accordance with an ecological model of moral character.

PRUDENCE'S FUNCTIONS

Traditional Catholic virtue theory honors prudence as an apex virtue because of its character-shaping role. One niche it occupies is to note and fill all of a moral character's empty niches. In this way, prudence seeks and maintains balance between all the moral virtues. Attuned to the dynamics of the whole moral character, prudence acts to help a moral agent exercise virtues as needed, balancing out excesses and scarcities of traits.

Prudence also acts as practical wisdom. In this role, prudence helps a moral agent read an environment and decide how to do what she intends to do. Prudence does this by cooperating in a give-and-take dynamic with the intellect, the senses, the passions, and the will. In addition, as noted earlier, Catholic virtue theory traditionally identifies prudence as the bridge between the theological virtues and the moral virtues. Charity motivates and informs prudence in its back-and-forth with the will in order to shape good actions that reflect faith and are also effective and wise.[25]

This is a lot of roles for one virtue to fill. We should examine that critically for a moment. Two possible problems result. First, it can encourage an egocentric virtue ethics, and second, it might indicate that prudence has been defined too expansively.

Problems with Prudence's Many Roles

Moral growth is the main focus of this book's model of moral character. With such a focus, one might too easily identify a moral agent's action deliberations as morally significant merely because they serve as that person's way of growing morally. If moral growth were not our main interest, then this reason for valuing good actions could seem misplaced. Perhaps it smacks of egocentrism to recommend that a moral agent consider first how an action might benefit her own development. Ought we always decide what to do by considering which kinds of exercise our moral character needs at that time? This priority could make all of creation into a tool for one's own self exploration, development, or even edification.

The second and related problem is that these two functions of prudence (balancing one's own moral character and directing one's action) seem quite different from each other. One wonders how these can both be the responsibility of a single virtue. Prudence's internal dynamics receive more enumeration and are distinguished from one another with more care than takes place for other cardinal virtues' moving parts. We discuss foresight, circumspection, and caution or synderesis, judgment, and command, although we do not define these as virtues in themselves.[26] The traditional model of moral character looks "within" prudence while still viewing prudence as a unified whole. This book's ecological model of moral character envisions prudence as a trait to be found everywhere in a moral character, more like a flow or a pattern of motion than a single entity that manifests in several places at different stages of a moral deliberation. Prudence is a dynamic, like a certain kind of spin, a seeping and transforming, or a picking-up and carrying-with of every flow or element it touches. Its behavior alters all the regions of its environment fractally.

This includes the worlds through which a moral agent navigates. Here is the answer to both problems with prudence's many diverse roles: The trajectory of one's moral development is never an exclusively internal matter. A moral agent's moral character, nested within creation, changes many things as she develops.

Virtue theory does prioritize moral growth. Improvement is the purpose of moral analysis. Remember also that moral agency is a capacity of an individual person. A moral agent's agency can and should shape that moral agent's own moral improvement, and no other moral agent can do that work for any other moral character. The only moral character we can change is our own. (This is not to say that the efficacy of our own work is sufficient, as we will soon see.)

In a virtue theory belonging to moral theology, it is important also that human perfection is impossible and that the mission of moral growth is possible only with God's help. We can then frame moral development as a taking in, a soaking up of goodness. Moral growth is a response exercise of gratitude for creation and of regard for its creator. The humble moral journey is among our definitive duties to "till and to keep" what grows in creation.[27]

Traditional Catholic virtue theory attributes to prudence two tasks. Prudence tends to a person's internal worlds and steers her external actions. As the beginning of this section noted, these two functions are very different. Can a single virtue really satisfy both roles? An ecological model of moral character helps here. An awareness of nestedness does not separate a moral agent's internal world from her external world as firmly as traditional virtue theory might depict them. If virtues are internal and practices and actions are external, nestedness reminds us that these realms constantly influence one another. An agent's internal world, including her moral character, is nested within her environments, and as chapter 3 showed, the borders between the inside and the outside are vague and porous. Our character growth is a significant dynamic of our ecological participation. So, a single virtue's dual responsibility to guide decisions and moral development makes sense. The only thing we can do in creation is shape our participation in it. The human will acts to move only the individual moral agent. We can notice what there is and choose our best responses. But the "tilling and keeping" we are to carry out takes place both outwardly and inwardly. Our every action occurs always without and within. These are nested realms of the same effort.

DEFINING PRUDENCE

Prudence is able to effect all of this because of its rootedness in the theological virtues. Aquinas notes that prudence can effect good deeds and moral growth without charity, to an extent. Prudence has some reasons of its own to drive good actions. But if prudence is not linked to charity and the theological virtues, a moral agent's abilities to bring goodness into the world will be limited. Aquinas distinguishes between the possible effects of prudence in terms of the end.[28] Without charity, prudence has no way to act from an orientation toward the "ultimate end," as it lacks both fuel and direction. Prudence's links to character are matters of content and form. Prudence draws something (love) from the theological virtues, and that love is itself a dynamic, a fecund reaching and pulling flow of affirmation and love. Picturing prudence taking in, being fed, and informed by this love allows one to imagine the dynamic of prudence's own behaviors and motions being changed by what it has received. The infusion of love seeded by the gift of the theological virtues grows and spreads into creation through the moral agent because of prudence's rootedness in charity. Without charity, prudence still seeks, enhances, and directs the moral virtues toward a goodness but not toward ultimate goodness.

As a habit, prudence is a moral agent's practiced love response. Prudence is how a moral agent notices, receives, and gives love habitually. In a Catholic virtues ecology model, prudence resembles ecological connectivity itself. Like an ecosystem's cycles of energy, water, or nitrogen exchange, what we call prudence is therefore a way of referring to the whole moral character. It is a moral agent's way of integrating all aspects of herself as living being, human, ecological participant, moral being, and expression of God's love itself.

Prudence, then, encompasses the community of all the sets of moral virtues. As a nexus of the interactions between a person's moral traits, theological virtues, cognitive and passionate capacities, will, and the world outside of the moral agent, prudence attends to what exists, without and within and beyond itself, and with love and judgment responds well to what it notices. This is, again, attunement: a habit of attentive and reasoned responsivity. Attunement characterizes how prudence behaves.

In chapter 4's description of the community of theological virtues, I noted that a moral agent's relationship with God changes the dynamics of her moral character. Now, we can see how this is in an ecological model of moral character. Prudence can be seen as a moral agent's way of embodying an interresponsive translation of God's self-expression into creation. It is a moral agent's way of representing her *imago Dei* self as best as she can. The work of prudence is to draw forth within moral character its attunement to the theological virtues and to shape a moral agent's life fueled by the love conveyed there. Aquinas noted that prudence helps a person's virtues to become more "developed, subtle and flexible,"[29] and the "parts" of the moral character get better at "reinforcing" each other. Therefore, prudence grows itself, adding to the moral agent's community of virtues, increasing their diversity and interrelationality, and enriching the whole person's complexity. Prudence refers to our moral webs, the interrelationality between moral and theological virtues, intellect, passions, senses, and gifts from God.

JUSTICE

In an ecologically imagined moral character, the cardinal virtue of justice is one set of virtues within prudence. Justice describes an aspect of prudence's behaviors. To describe justice, this chapter first summarizes Catholicism's traditional definition of justice, then defines justice for an ecological model of moral character by drawing on Melanie Harris's ecowomanist virtue work. For Harris, justice is a name for "fairness in relation to the self, others, and all life in creation."[30] It is another virtue of attunement, attunement specifically to life's deserving and to systems and structures that cooperate to meet that deserving. For embodied creatures, justice requires an intersectional view and an opposition to dominance.

Traditional Catholic virtue concepts of justice focus on deserving or, in other words, what is due.[31] The meaning of deserving must rest on the basis of what one is, not on one's actions, contributions to others, or successes and failures. For humans, a theological anthropology supplies the foundations of deserving. Humans live, are intrinsically interrelational, and are embodied and finite, and we have grace and bear God's image, and we have reason, original sin, and dignity.

For better or worse, justice is often defined with an eye to conflicting or nonaligned claims of access to tangible and intangible goods. Two fundamental traits among these theological anthropological elements are often used to rank levels or degrees of deserving. The most fundamental of these traits is that we live. We are alive. We share this trait with all living beings, so this is not unique to humans but does establish a morally significant difference between the deserving attributed to living beings in comparison with nonliving entities. A second fundamental trait is humans' capacities for reason and communication. These capacities are evident among humans and nonhuman animals, and we are learning of forms of communication among plant life as well.[32] Ethics debates parse whether and in what ways the capacities of a being affect the relative priority of that being's needs. In all cases, life itself, the gift, deserves on a fundamental level. Life deserves to continue. In creation's life systems, living beings need to occupy certain niches and also need for remaining niches to be occupied by others. Justice recognizes that living beings deserve physical and behavioral spaces. We (physical living beings) deserve physical places to occupy and functions to perform in communities with others who deserve the same so we can all live and flourish.

In traditional Catholic virtue theory, the stakes of forming the virtue of justice are high. Aquinas notes that the virtue of justice is that point at which someone's true virtue really shines,[33] and the *Compendium* and Catholic social teaching similarly note that justice is "the decisive criteria of morality in the intersubjective and social sphere."[34] An ecologically informed theological anthropology recognizes that no human activity takes place outside of that sphere. Justice is a definitive Catholic virtue.

Like all life, humans need specific ecological conditions. Like forms of life with reason and communication, humans also need specific social conditions. With all of creation's species and entities holding moral claims to access what they need, justice requires a willingness to accept complexity. Steven Bouma-Prediger's discussion of justice as "fairness for all" highlights a piece of this complexity.[35] The virtue of justice can grow in a moral agent where attunement and a willingness to struggle are well practiced. Mortality, our overarching reality, complicates justice formation because everyone needs the deaths of others in order to survive.[36]

Our ecosystems demonstrate that mortality is a condition of life, and our theological commitments define humanity in these terms. We value life, but life requires death. There is a tension between feeding life so that it continues and acknowledging that all living beings die. Somehow, we are to see that this is all good. Justice means acting in favor of others' living and living well, but it cannot require that we prevent all death. It does require that we recognize the universal human need to be able to exercise our niche-filling functions. We breathe, eat, excrete, deliberate, and communicate, always in relationship with our ecological neighbors. Important among these for Catholic virtue theory is that we recognize the human drive to pursue genuine relationship with the sacred, with self, and with others and to discern how each of us could inhabit the intersection between all these genuinely as a nexus of our own. Domination works against justice, because life is given to all and to each in our particularity.

In an ecological model, justice's interactions with other participants of the moral character are important. As a habit of observation and response, justice requires intellect. Societies that suppress knowledge of history inhibit justice's growth. Justice also interacts with a moral agent's emotions and passions. Justice is exercised through working to change one's contexts when one's society is unjust and, where there is justice, recognizing and celebrating that.

For a Catholic ecological virtue theory, justice is formed in accordance with insights from ecotheology and from ecologically informed visions of justice. The theological virtues with ecological awareness grant us the insight that Earth and its living beings are gifts, each for its own sake. We and they are efforts God makes to experience this wild created world. Theologian Melanie Harris's virtue theory is indispensable here. Her intersectional approach supports the kind of awareness we all need to counteract domination systematically and systemically.[37] Embodied justice requires intersectional awareness. Creation's complexity exceeds our understanding, and an intersectional awareness helps us to glimpse dynamics we have been unable to understand.

Harris names justice as the virtue that fuels the actions and activism that establish "equality, freedom, and human and environmental rights."[38] She notes that womanist justice opposes injustice. Injustice exists when "a balance of fairness is upset by any social ill, systemic cultural production of evil, or individual act of violence rooted in any form of the logic of domination."[39] These evils, ills, and roots can exist in anyone. Systems of domination plant destructive seeds in persons who can benefit from them and in persons who are harmed by domination's deprivations and violence. The nestedness of an ecological moral character model likewise recognizes this, as chapter 3 demonstrated. When domination is valued, the virtue of justice is impeded in moral agents' characters.

Justice is the community of its interacting subsidiary virtues, in relationship with the neighboring cardinal virtues and the other participants of a moral character. Aquinas noted among these religion,[40] truth, and gratitude.[41] Prudence, the intellect, and compassion help justice to interpret and share action on scales of individual, interpersonal, familial, and community relationalities (among others). Other virtues that comprise justice might include empathy, humility, and simplicity. Steven Bouma-Prediger, working in a rights-based paradigm, names respectfulness as being central to justice.[42]

For Harris, justice requires opposition to "racism, classism, sexism, homophobia, and environmental degradation."[43] But justice is not only a form of opposition. Justice also "celebrates the shared rights of all to have access to basic needs or goods, including water, shelter, education, and health care." She notes in particular the right to "access land" and the importance for human flourishing of "a sense of belonging and place."[44] This form of an "embrace of earth and earth care" must exist alongside "the promotion of land and earth rights." Deprivation of place recurs consistently with other forms of injustice. This is no coincidence. An intersectional analysis enables us to recognize injustice more accurately and insightfully. The intersectional awareness of justice gives an ability to see injustices' roots. This intersection reveals the interactions between systems of domination in our mentalities, events, histories, and institutions.

Justice tends toward holism but does not neglect the specificity of embodiment and life's particularities. In practicing justice, we (individual moral agents) must remember that the conditions of our social and physical environments are simultaneously both cause and effect of the things we do and of our moral character. Ecological nestedness reminds us that our contexts' conditions and ourselves are not completely separable. An ecologically aware definition of justice such as Harris's demonstrates that social and ecological issues are likewise inseparable. Ecologically inflicted injustices compound, amplify, and perpetuate existing injustices. Racist sitings of toxic landfills are enabled by the history of segregated cities. The water crisis in Flint, Michigan, resulted in part from white flight.[45] Health care outcome disparities follow ecological injustices, which follow other social injustices. The intersections of these realms of injustices endure when we refuse or fail to examine them together. As Willis Jenkins has noted, the exposure of bodies to toxins "challenges how ethics conceptualizes injustice" altogether.[46] Our embodiment refuses to recognize the partitions that we force to distinguish between "different areas" of injustice.

The environmental justice movement offers many examples of attunement to justice. This movement gained broader national attention in the 1970s when residents of Afton, North Carolina, implemented sustained resistance to an industrial toxic waste dump.[47] The environmental justice movement counters ecological racism. Ecological racism is the practice of "racial discrimination in environmental policy-making and the enforcement of regulations and laws, the deliberate targeting of communities of color for toxic waste facilities, the official sanctioning of the life-threatening presence and pollutants in our communities, and the history of excluding people of color from leadership in the environmental movement."[48] Ecological racism, evident in statistical correlations, in health outcomes, and throughout our environmental policies, proposals, impacts, structures, and conditions,[49] inflicts generational harms through a tainted supply of life's basic needs: air, water, ground, and place itself. The continuing assault of expensive and unsafe public water in Flint, Michigan, is a widely recognized recent example.

A moral agent with the virtue of justice is able to recognize ecological racism as a manifestation of multiple and interacting injustices. Joshua Bennett, a scholar of Black American literature, demonstrates what this virtue can help us to see. He finds in this literature the insight that dehumanizing efforts enact violence against not only humans but also nonhuman animals. Bennett describes the US history of leveraging anthropocentrism and racism together. In Black literature, Bennett hears rejection of a "triumphalistic rhetoric that would eschew the nonhuman altogether" and finds a plea that we "see animals as 'co-laborers, friends, partners in the field.'"[50] Justice's vision and the intersectional awareness it brings enable a fuller rejection of white dominance and domination. Bennett discerns an "animal promise,"[51] or a way "to leap into a vision of human person-hood rooted not in the logics of private property or dominion but in wildness, flight, brotherhood and sisterhood beyond blood."[52] He also finds in the literature the resistance and joy of an appreciation for a world full of life and of wildness. The literature and the mind of a reader with justice offer and cultivate a fully alive resistance to domination.

This awareness is possible when justice is integrated into us, embedded within the circuitry of our eyeballs, ear canals, and layers of skin. The virtue of justice prepares us to notice. Justice's cooperations with the theological virtues animate justice, keeping it raw and alive and allowing it to move toward what we cannot humanly expect but that God could lead us to experience. An ecologically vivid justice virtue is, among other things, excellent eschatological preparation.

Justice requires interreligious dialogue. The Christian theological anthropology is a necessary foundation for Catholic definitions and visions of justice, but it should not try to stand alone. Theological anthropologies are articulated by humans. Sin operates in our anthropologies and in our views of justice. This is a danger particularly for believers whose faith enjoys significant social and political power. Humility and an honest and willing participation in communities outside the Church can ameliorate this danger. Inviting the discomfort of others' perspectives, experiences, and priorities is necessary because the exclusion of these voices obscures justice. For Christians, this means attending to the voices that speak from non-Christian cosmologies. For white Christians living in the United States, it means adding to our customary sources of moral understanding by attending to the stories and the experience of First Peoples and of migrant workers whose relationships to place are both shaped and threatened by our own practices (e.g., our market demands, diets, and energy source and use). For Catholics, justice formation requires taking in visions of justice that animate Black communities and truly hearing the American stories of abduction, slavery, rape, segregation, and mass incarceration. Justice formation means attending particularly to all who have been involuntarily relocated and dislocated.

Failures to hear what others are saying to us founds the injustices we practice, and this includes failures to hear what our environments have to say. Listening for justice both requires and facilitates ecological awareness.

The cardinal virtues of prudence and justice can thrive in ecological communion with temperance and fortitude. Chapter 6 describes these two in accordance with the ecological model of moral character.

NOTES

1. Rourke, "Prudence Gone Wild."
2. Aquinas, *ST*, II–II, q. 47, a. 4–5.
3. Aquinas, *ST*, II–II, q. 48.
4. Sometimes a dynamic of prudence is defined as "practical reason" instead. See Kerr, *After Aquinas*, 122–23; Kinghorn, "Presence of Mind"; Pinckaers, *The Pinckaers Reader*; Pope, *The Ethics of Aquinas*, 39; Rhonheimer, *Natural Law and Practical Reason*, 93; Stiltner, *Toward Thriving Communities*; and Zalot and Guevin, *Catholic Ethics in Today's World*, 21.
5. Some of this chapter's arguments were first presented in Rourke, "Prudence Gone Wild."
6. Aquinas, *ST*, II–II, q. 47, a. 8.
7. Aquinas, *ST*, II–II, q. 49, a. 7.
8. Aquinas, *ST*, II–II, q. 49, a. 8.
9. Van Wensveen, *Dirty Virtues*. Van Wensveen names these virtues "dirty" as part of her effort to draw our aesthetic away from matter-spirit dualisms and the presumption of Earth itself as inferior or morally tinged. In her work, "dirty" signifies moral virtuousness. This strategy undermines patriarchally motivated judgments about sexuality.
10. See Yong and Hsieh, "Speed–Size Illusion Correlates with Retinal-Level Motion Statistics"; and Emilie Reas, "Small Animals Live in a Slow-Motion World," *Scientific American*, July 1, 2014.
11. John P. Rafferty and John N. Thompson, "Coevolution," in *Encyclopedia Britannica* (Encyclopedia Britannica, January 9, 2020).
12. Rolston, "Environmental Virtue Ethics," 64.
13. Rolston, 164.
14. Rolston, 42. See also Rourke, "Prudence Gone Wild."
15. Bouma-Prediger, *For the Beauty of the Earth*, 2–3.
16. *Laudato si'*, para. 130, 138, and 141. See also Edwards, *Ecology at the Heart of Faith*, chap. 2.
17. Van Wensveen, "Cardinal Environmental Virtues," 177.
18. This argument is spelled out in Rourke, "Prudence Gone Wild."
19. Bouma-Prediger, *Earthkeeping and Character*, 70.
20. Shaw defines prudence as the "wisdom that enlightened, long-term well-being . . . is more likely to advance the good." Shaw's definition of "sensitivity" fits this book's definition of attunement, but his definition of prudence is not very similar to that of Catholic virtue ethics. Shaw, "A Virtue Ethics Approach to Aldo Leopold's Land Ethic," 100–101.
21. Warren Kinghorn echoes this observation, highlighting prudence's way of integrating a moral agent's ways in terms of knowing, acting, thinking, feeling, memory, foresight, and community participation. Kinghorn, "Presence of Mind."
22. Van Wensveen, "Cardinal Environmental Virtues," 176. See also Rourke, "Prudence Gone Wild," 263.
23. See Scarry, *The Body in Pain*.

24. Another discussion of the necessity of despair for hope was presented in chapter 4.

25. Note Aquinas, *ST*, II–II, q. 48, a. 1, which names counsel, synesis, gnome/judgment. See Rourke, "Prudence Gone Wild," 258.

26. The focus on these parts results from disparate numbers of tasks for which this virtue is held responsible. Aquinas's discussion in *ST*, II–II, q. 48–49, is an overview of three possible ways to dissect prudence as he attempts to synthesize his sources' views.

27. Genesis 2:15.

28. Aquinas, *ST*, I–II, q. 65, a. 2.

29. Porter, "The Unity of the Virtues and the Ambiguity of Goodness," 154. See, for example, Aquinas, *ST*, II–II, q. 48, a. 1.

30. Harris's model was introduced in chapter 1. Harris, *Gifts of Virtue*, 120–21.

31. Aquinas, *ST*, II–II, q. 58, a. 1; "Catechism of the Catholic Church," 1807; Pinckaers, *The Pinckaers Reader*, 295; and Porter, "The Virtue of Justice (IIae, Qq. 58-122)," 272.

32. See, for example, Wohlleben, *The Hidden Life of Trees*; and the discussion of Wohlleben's in Sally McGrane, "German Forest Ranger Finds That Trees Have Social Networks, Too," *New York Times*, January 29, 2016.

33. Aquinas, *ST*, II–II, q. 58, a. 3 (it gives a moral character its "luster").

34. Even the *Compendium of Catholic Social Doctrine*, a document focusing centrally on Catholic social teaching, prioritizes its understanding of justice as a virtue, putting virtue front and center in its definition of justice. As a value, justice "accompanies the exercise of the corresponding cardinal moral virtue, which itself is a 'constant and firm will to give their due to God and neighbor.'" Pontifical Council for Justice and Peace, *Compendium of the Social Doctrine of the Church*, para. 201.

35. He notes that justice includes "impartiality when participating in the decision-making process." Bouma-Prediger, *Earthkeeping and Character*, 80.

36. Wirzba, *Food and Faith*.

37. Harris, *Ecowomanism, Religion and Ecology*, 1. See also Harris, "Sacred Blood, Transformation, and Ecowomanism."

38. Harris, *Gifts of Virtue*, 67.

39. Harris, 121.

40. Aquinas, *ST*, II–II, q. 81.

41. Aquinas, *ST*, II–II, q. 80.

42. Bouma-Prediger, "Earthkeeping and Character," 92.

43. Harris, *Gifts of Virtue*, 53.

44. Harris, 120–21.

45. Michigan Civil Rights Commission, "The Flint Water Crisis: Systemic Racism through the Lens of Flint; Report of the Michigan Civil Rights Commission," February 17, 2017.

46. Jenkins, *The Future of Ethics*, 67.

47. Rourke, "Environmental Justice." See also Bullard, *Dumping in Dixie*; and Burwell and Cole, "Environmental Justice Comes Full Circle."

48. Zimring, *Clean and White*, 1–2, quoting Karl Grossman, "From Toxic Racism to Environmental Justice," *E–The Environmental Magazine*, May–June 1992, 31.

49. See Commission for Racial Justice United Church of Christ, "Toxic Wastes and Race." A second report followed twenty years later, finding that the problems persist. This commission studied census data alongside locations' hazardous waste facilities. See United Church of Christ Justice and Witness Ministries, "Toxic Wastes and Race" and "Toxic Wastes and Race at Twenty (1987–2007)." In 1995 the Presbyterian Church USA's 2017

General Assembly prepared a similar report that also found strong "correlation between race, economics, and the location of manufacturing complexes and hazardous storage and waste disposal sites." Presbyterian Church of America, "Hazardous Waste, Race and the Environment" (Presbyterian Church USA, April 28, 2010), 4.

50. Bennett, *Being Property Once Myself*, 3.
51. Bennett, 3.
52. Bennett, 4.

6

Enjoyment in a World of Wounds

FORTITUDE AND TEMPERANCE

This chapter continues chapter 5's description of the cardinal moral virtues as they would be understood in an ecological model of moral character. Chapter 5 described prudence and justice. This chapter's description of temperance demonstrates its links to gratitude and healthy societies. The discussion of fortitude walks us through the relationships between greed and courage to reveal fortitude's connections to hope and imagination. Finally, the chapter will summarize the book's proposed ecological model of moral character by revisiting the traits of a good moral character proposed in the preface.

Because virtues are intrinsically interrelational, no single virtue's cultivation holds the key to a moral agent's opportunities for joy and well-being. Chapter 5's description of justice portrays the ways that the virtue of justice prepares a moral agent to see connections between systems of injustice and justice. There is a hint of good news in what justice helps us to see: the world is not as fragmented as we have taught ourselves, and we, embodied living beings, are likewise integrated into this world. The virtue of temperance similarly demonstrates how we (humans) transcend fragmentation. Temperance speaks of the links between moral character and senses, passions, mood, and emotion. Temperance is a trait whose contemplation brings relief and an unqualified joy. *Laudato si'* points to the effects of temperance with this reminder: the world is not a problem to solve but rather a mystery to "contemplate with gladness and praise."[1]

TEMPERANCE

Temperance seems an obvious fit for environmental virtue ethics, as temperance stands in opposition to consumerism, exorbitant energy use, resource hoarding, and other ecologically damaging practices. Yet for many, temperance implies restraint, moderation, and saying no to excessive enjoyment, even to the point of denying pleasures just because they are pleasurable. Temperance and environmentalism have both received a negative "sour grapes" image unfairly. Neither is about obsessive self-restraint and self-denial.

A Catholic ecological virtue theory defines temperance as a virtue that brings serenity, tranquility, and joy.[2] That this is a moral virtue reflects the fact that enjoyment is good. Enjoyable experiences are good, and enjoyment is both good and right. God's people are enjoined to enjoy.[3] Temperance means being good at enjoyment, or enjoying well in the fullest sense of "well."[4] Temperance is not primarily about deciding the degree or direction of restraint and self-denial. Instead, it is about being "rightly pleased."

In traditional Catholic virtue theory, temperance integrates reason and passions.[5] In an ecological model of moral character, temperance is a community of interactions between the virtues, the passions, affect, intellect, and the will. The interactions between these in temperance is not one in which the will takes input from all and then proceeds out of cold logic. These elements of a moral character interact: they affect one another. An ecologically modeled vision of temperance should find the interactions of these relationships to be very close, too close to easily differentiate reason from emotion or mood from mind.

As a cardinal virtue, temperance is characterized by attunement. Temperance enhances a moral agent's awareness of her own internal pleasure environment. An agent with temperance will have a clear sense of the ways in which all the pleasures relate to each other, to goodness itself, and to the agent's own fullest flourishing.[6] This means having a sense of pleasure that comes from a nuanced understanding of the context within which one enjoys things such as food, drink, sex, fresh air, a cold smooth stone, goosebumps, an energizing rhythm, and sweet fertilized hayfields. Temperance draws enjoyment and ecological awareness together. We (animals, including humans) are meant to enjoy the pleasures of Earth and to enjoy all this in ways and to degrees that are good for us and good for Earth.

Pope Francis describes an example of a widespread inability to enjoy well. He describes abuses of recreational drugs as an example of a global web that exploits the poor, harms the wealthy, encourages deception, and undermines health. The drug abuse of affluent societies is both cause and consequence of our disconnectedness and isolation.[7] Affluent societies' abuse of cocaine particularly hurts lives, behaviors, and the ecological health of impoverished communities such as the places where drugs' raw materials are grown. This example demonstrates several injustices and affective disconnects. Cocaine's status in our laws reflects and powerfully reinforces racist ideologies and structures of incarceration (mandatory minimum sentences, for example).

The lifestyles of this planet's affluent societies require significant obfuscation, distraction, and mind numbing in order to sustain. We require self-deception about agricultural industries in order to be able to enjoy the food we produce (continual assertions that "bacon tastes good" recall Orwellian messaging),[8] and the suffering of starvation must be made invisible for many people in order to accept as normal our own nutritional options and supply systems. As *Laudato si'* notes, we train to become "superficial, aggressive and compulsive consumers" by feeding an "unhealthy anxiety." We embody what Jesus noticed in the restless rich man in Mark 10:21.[9] We incentivize private transportation and present detached homes as a lifestyle ideal, but we must then create methods of purchasable physical exercise to fend off the dangers of excessively sedentary lifestyles. We indoctrinate generations of Americans to overlook, ignore, and deny our nation's history of genocide, land theft, and enslavement, and then we must, against significant resistance, relearn, reeducate, and retrain many of our citizenry in response to the violence and shame that resulted from our ignorance. We report global heights of wealth and leisure but not of happiness, health, or well-being. We do not know what or how to enjoy,[10] and we don't even know that we don't know this. If there is joy to be rediscovered, it will be in this moment's opportunities to cultivate temperance. We do not need the "more" that we think we need. We need only the gift that we already have.

Lisa Fullam's description of a virtue approach to sex can help here. Fullam observes that we (humans) expect too little of sex. She argues that a virtue ethics approach to sex reveals our low and narrow expectations. We define it in narrow terms, limited to only a select few body parts, and find ourselves unable to explain how it relates to sensuality, for example. Fullam argues that when we push ourselves to diminish the meaning, significance, and wisdom that come with our sexual embodiment, we can train ourselves to become insensitive to what sex gives us. We can sink to a flattened existence. When we expect less of sex, we train ourselves to experience sex and sexuality less fully.[11] The result is rigid boundaries, confusion, fear, violence, shame, and emptiness. Temperance can be balanced when we appreciate (meaning we both enjoy and understand well) the many "dimensions" of excellent sex.

Similarly, temperance comes with learning to expect more of creation. Temperance-building practices are practices that train us to see creation grandly. When we think of this world merely or mostly as a resource, we level forests, poison air and water, and endanger life's diversity. We must learn to see our environments as teeming with companions, sensations, and a wide diversity of lives, each of which can teach us about enjoyment. Greater awareness of these lives will help us to live among them with gratitude and well-being, and experiences of gratitude and well-being ease our way to simple and direct engagement of our own created embodiment and embeddedness in creation.

We have role models to help us see in this way. The presence of joy, enjoyment, pleasure, glee, and awe in the writings of environmental virtue ethicists is impossible to miss. Through their eyes, we can see how attentiveness and joy relate. Discovery of the complexity and interactivity of ecosystems within which we live brings joy as we learn that there is and always has been more life around than we ever knew. Joy and enjoyment are embedded into the fabric of creation. It is little wonder that God chose incarnation.

Christian readiness to experience the wonder, awe, playfulness, surpassing calm, and overwhelming scale of creation translates into gratitude before all God's expressions and experiments. An ethical approach should motivate good thought, action, and life in addition to explaining it. Wonder is an important virtue to be gained and experienced from participating more fully in creation. Chapter 7 will describe wonder. Here, we arrive at a supremely faith-filled virtue and a goal of Catholic virtue theory itself: gratitude. The virtue of temperance reaches for the joys that God has already embedded into creation, and the flow of gratitude for this is a cause and consequence of enjoying life and enjoying it well.[12]

FORTITUDE

The final cardinal virtue to discuss is fortitude. Traditional Catholic virtue theory defines fortitude as a kind of endurance, or a tendency to persevere well through adversity or difficulty, particularly through the difficulties involved in moral growth.[13] Fortitude works with virtues such as stamina, persistence, and optimism. We can work our way toward an ecological model of moral character's definition of temperance by thinking first about the vice of greed. This discussion of greed will demonstrate two things: that fortitude contributes to an ecologically attuned moral character and that the way we envision moral character is important.

Like many environmentally minded people, I sometimes blame CEOs or boards of directors of energy companies or the rich and politically powerful for the consequences of our climate's instability. "They are just greedy." This does not represent my best analysis. This conclusion is a way of minimizing the culpability of my own participation in the systems of anthropogenic climate change, allowing me to abandon the search for a meaningful analysis of a harm such as climate instability. As is traditional in scapegoating, this move also dehumanizes those individuals by attributing their actions to a single fundamental moral flaw such as greed. This blaming oversimplifies strangers I'll never meet, absolutizing one particular apparently inexplicable moral deficit, and also misidentifies greed as a mindless or malicious voracity.

Alternatively, we can imagine greed as an extreme failure of generosity, but this is also problematic. (We will return to this point.) This tautological understanding of generosity still gives no good explanation for how greed developed within a person. An insightful description of greed is important, and as ecological models of moral character remind us, we need good descriptions of vices' interactions with other aspects of a moral character in order to understand moral character.

Greed is a failure of courage. Most of us do not live in economic or financial contexts similar to leaders of Exxon and British Petroleum, but we can, with a little discomfort and compassion, imagine the kinds of fears these individuals face. This is important, because courage, more than generosity, is the niche-filling trait that is lacking where greed exists. Courage can help a person to turn away from the opportunities for fast profits that could otherwise appear to be necessary for ensuring the security of his own family. Such opportunities might seem like ways to give one's own children and loved ones rare, fantastic, or even necessary experiences. It could take courage to make decisions that seem to one's peers to endanger the legacy of one's ancestors' financial fortune and legacy. With excessive temerity, one's perceptions of what genuinely counts as "dangerous" becomes extremely off-kilter. This is important, because what frightens us and what we count as dangerous are moral issues. Our epidemic of police killings of Black children have repeatedly demonstrated this point.[14]

Fear about the future is a common experience through which we can imagine why some individuals believe that aggressive mining of coal and gas is necessary.[15] Fear also motivates many to invest retirement savings for the benefit of companies that trade in fossil fuels. Many do this in order to get the sort of return that, we are told, is a commonsense measure of self-protection and planning.[16] Fear of the future sustains practices of greed. A failure of courage eroded the faith of wandering people in a desert when God, according to God's own promise, was providing them with food but only enough for one day at a time.[17] Courage would help one to gather only what was needed for the day. The training that God gives to the people in this story reveals the links between courage and faith and the importance of practices that employ these two virtues together.

Equating greed with heartless voracity is a comforting kind of scapegoating, but naming greed as a failure of courage shows us where we too are vulnerable to greed. This analysis is also more accurate because we (humans who do not own Exxon) are also culpable for our continuing greenhouse gas emissions. A good model of the relationships between greed and our other virtues and vices is important. We need such a model to be able to see ourselves honestly. Like courage, fearfulness interacts with many other participants in a moral character.

Fearfulness (understood as a moral vice, not as the experience of being afraid) affects perception itself. Fearfulness is a kind of anticipation. We expect what we dread. What we habitually fear is influenced by our vices and sins. Anti-Blackness, the vice that we cultivate through participation in our white supremacist systems, offers a significant example for white people such as myself and many others. The anti-Blackness rooted within us is enabled by racist miseducation. The resultant ignorance increases fearfulness. This fearfulness encourages our tendency to activate our vice of anti-Blackness. Racist structures leverage those forms of fearfulness and feed the roots of our racism. Fearfulness also intertwines with the passions, a close relationship evidenced by that fact that it can be defined as a vice or as a mood. Its power over a moral agent can also overwhelm completely the activity of the intellect. As Elaine Scarry's analysis of torture has demonstrated, leveraging a person's fear of disintegration is the means by which torture breaks people instead of killing them.[18] She demonstrates that the aim of torture is to destroy (disintegrate) a living person in order to be able to make use of that person for others' benefit. Dread and pain create a fearfulness that overpowers a moral agent's intellect, fragmenting her internal world into incoherence. The intellect cannot endure it.

Often, greed is defined in opposition to generosity. Consider for a moment what generosity means.[19] Generosity seems to be about giving of one's money, time, attention, energy, opportunities, resources, and so on. Whatever is being given up must be something belonging to the generous person. Generosity as a concept makes sense only when there exists a consensus about the generous person's rightful claim to that which she gives up. When we name an act of giving "generous," we are saying that the generous person had some right to keep what was given but instead chose to give it up. In other words, some claim is sacrificed when generosity is enacted. A moral agent would not be wrong in retaining this claim instead of making the sacrifice, but she is generous in sacrificing. If generosity is supererogatory, is greed simply morally neutral?

Now, consider the other virtues that might encompass or belong within generosity. Imagine first that generosity is a subsidiary virtue within justice.[20] For this to be the case, justice would have to be about going beyond what is morally required of oneself. Justice, if significantly informed by generosity, would be supererogatory, a trait of "going above and beyond" what moral goodness requires. This would mean accepting injustice as a matter of moral neutrality. But this is the opposite of what justice means. Generosity cannot safely be imagined as a participant primarily within justice's purview. Generosity might indirectly bolster or enhance justice for some moral agents—every person's virtues behave a bit differently, and moral growth is a wild process—but imagining generosity as primarily inhabiting justice is problematic.

Imagine instead generosity as a subsidiary of the cardinal virtue of fortitude.[21] Fortitude is a kind of endurance, a tendency to persevere through adversity. In this case, generosity would connect with one's ability to persevere through difficulty and also implies that a moral agent is facing the flow of time in some way. She is thinking ahead and anticipating a different future than her current trajectories would create, and endurance is called for because difficulties do arise when one makes a sacrifice.

Thomas Aquinas's vision recognizes the kinds of difficulties involved in overcoming greed and the ways that moral virtues, such as optimism and stamina, and intellectual virtues, such as foresight, can help to minimize the power of greed. This description of greed's relationships to moral virtues demonstrates the importance of endurance. A person will not feel the pull of greed when she learns to endure the risk of having less than she is accustomed to having. With such endurance, the facade of this kind of risk cracks and falls. A willingness to reject greed is strengthened by the understanding that there will be enough for all, that there is sufficient time, energy, attention, niche space, money, food, and so on. in creation for the lives that fill and need them. Courage empowers such a vision of the future by helping moral agents see that having too much actually does us more harm than good.

This kind of outlook enables a moral agent to participate in creation more fully. When linked closely with fortitude, generosity does not destroy the meaning of justice. The virtue structures we imagine significantly impact our understanding of specific virtues. They show how virtues connect to wider moral issues, such as the meaning of justice itself. After all, it is not only our virtues and vices that are nested within our world. The way we imagine these virtues and vices is also embedded there.

Next, let's describe fortitude in accordance with an ecological model of moral character. Fortitude integrates strength, endurance, perseverance, and patience to sustain a moral agent's efforts when these efforts cannot bring immediate results. When one moral agent decides to live in a more sustainable manner, her decision will not bring substantial immediate ecological benefits. For example, a significant lifestyle change to trade away convenience for a lower carbon footprint will give a moral agent difficulties but no sign of environmental impact. Fortitude enables the motivation we need to adopt sustainable practices and policies. On a larger scale, our societies need this fortitude in order to begin to refit our energy and transportation infrastructures and stop using fossil fuels as sources of energy. Fortitude cooperates closely with hope. As noted in chapter 4, imagination is a virtue that can strengthen that cooperation. On the other hand, fearfulness, a vice that amplifies greed, weakens fortitude.

Humans fear losing control, sacrificing comfort, increasing vulnerability, and being at nature's mercy. Some fear of nature is reasonable for us (furless, clawless, wingless humans), but excessive fearfulness presents dangers. One danger, as we've seen, is a growth of greed. Fearfulness is empowered by hidden and unknowable things. *Laudato si'* shows how the invisibility of the changes we need can be imagined and indirectly perceived. Acknowledging that small acts of ecological responsiveness can seem too tiny to matter, Pope Francis adds that "we must not think that these efforts are not going to change the world. They benefit society, *often unbeknown to us*, for they call forth a goodness which, *albeit unseen*, inevitably tends to spread. Furthermore, such actions can restore our sense of self-esteem; they can enable us to live more fully and to feel that life on earth is worthwhile."[22] This sneaky self-esteem, encouraged by imagination, can be integrated into the webs of fortitude along with courage and hope. If we attend to their cooperation as a form of trustworthy perception, we can strengthen fortitude and the stamina and patience it offers.[23] Our vision can change as fortitude grows.

Theologian Richard Miller offers a view of energy use that demonstrates the cooperation between imagination, fortitude, and vision.[24] When we use the lens of integral ecology in cooperation with fortitude, "coal, oil and natural gas appear as more than hidden resources to be extracted and burned. We can see their fuller dimensions as part of the earth's climate system that has maintained the temperatures in which humans have evolved and civilization has flourished by removing carbon from the atmosphere and sequestering it underground. We can see wild animals as more than predators, nuisances, and potential game. We can attend to their myriad ecological interconnections upon which we depend."[25] Fortitude both enables and exercises this vision.

CARDINAL VIRTUES IN CONTEXT

The cardinal virtues, ecologically defined, are certainly virtues that help people, with all our human particularities, to participate in creation's life, but the larger point in this book is that no list of specific virtues will help us to develop and live in the best ways possible. The structure of virtue theory offers us a chance to shape our integration in creation in ways that are most urgently needed for today. An ecological model of moral character encourages us to develop a complex web of interacting virtue nexuses and to enhance that complexity by adding to our virtues. Envisioning our moral character as an active community with many different participants, as many participants as communities have lives, also gives us new ways to imagine how we might collaborate with the sacred itself in our tilling and keeping of a most important garden: who and what we are.

Decades ago Servais Pinckaers observed that "a virtue-based morality, however precise and imperfect, will always remain incomplete. Its real function is surely to open our minds and hearts to the mystery of the human person and God, so that our actions may participate in the 'unreachable riches of Christ' in his mystery (Eph 3:8)."[26] I echo this reminder and note that Pinckaers's reflection here also names the far side of human agency. There are limits to what we can do to shape our own moral growth. Pinckaers states that "no philosophy, no theology can fill such a role. Only the Holy Spirit possesses the power of the Word who reveals the truth to us interiorly and gives the grace that transforms our hearts and actions." Amen to this also. We will not cultivate ourselves into perfection. But we can choose good models to direct our efforts to become more of what we truly are.

This book began with a description of what a good model of moral character ought to be able to do. Before the final chapter demonstrates this model, with examples, let's look again at the criteria with which we began and notice how this model meets these criteria.

The first trait of a good model of moral character is its ability to support people in our thoughts, efforts, and hopes toward moral growth. This trait orients and encourages us toward that end but does not view that end as a goal to accomplish. Instead, a good model continually inspires us to live a whole life shaped by this pursuit. The model does this in several ways.

Because this model presents virtues and other aspects of the moral character as active and even (metaphorically) alive, it encourages us to attend to our moral evolution. If we imagine surveying a wide, still land of virtues and vices, our moral reflection could fixate on balancing out the peaks and valleys. With an ecological model of moral character, we can imagine better than that. The nestedness trait of this ecological model helps us to recognize cardinal virtues as communities. We gain from this a scale-reflexive view of the details of cardinal virtues' participating virtues and vices. We can pick out and identify exceptions within a cardinal virtue community. We are reminded that these outlier traits demonstrate our lives' moral trajectories so that we can learn from them. The image can open for us our dynamic contexts, such as our social structures, aspirations, and complete personal histories. We can name the thin spots within our moral character as empty niches. This helps us imagine the relationships between different cardinal virtue communities and recognize the areas we tend to overlook. The nestedness of an ecological model imparts a richer and animated view of moral character.

This model's observation that each virtue is universally individuated (different within each moral agent it inhabits) offers us more subtle and complex visions of the virtues. The model resists reducing virtue ethics to a list of virtues to be recommended to each person as a checklist of what makes for a good person. Instead, we each bear the responsibility to notice our own internal worlds and to name where there is thinness, isolation, or closed-off areas that need more diversity or more connection.

The model reminds us that each individual has a different moral balance to moderate within and between her own cardinal communities. What is good and what is needed varies with a moral character's context and history. The model depicts the external and internal influences moving our moral, intellectual, and theological development. Our way of filling (behavioral) spaces shapes who we are.

This model also warns us about the stakes of shaping our moral character. The virtues we have shape what we are likely to notice. In fact, because our interpretation of what we meet is itself carried out by our moral character, our virtues and vices inform what we are likely to encounter, miss, or misinterpret. Interpretation of our worlds does not sit outside of what counts as morality. This model bolsters virtue theory's readiness to help us with this perception and motivates our work to morally improve how well we perceive.

The ecological model's way of describing hope is an important part of how it supports our moral growth. Hope is central to moral development exactly because growth is the goal. Hope counterfeits can be expressed carefully with this model's thick descriptions of relationship and cooperation. Hope is a channel to faith, and we can expand hope's connection when we mingle it with imagination, meditation, and prayer. We can cognitively recognize its power and presence even when deep in despair. As chapter 4 noted, despair is not a death of hope but rather a sign of its power. In these ways, the ecological model supports and encourages moral reflection and development.

The second trait of a good model proposed in the preface was that a good model of moral character reveals both a totality (the whole person) and the many dynamics within that totality. The ecological model of moral character presents a human person as a whole and also represents this whole's internal complexity. The participants of a person's moral character interact, creating patterns of incidents and pathway among neighbors. This reinforces for us that our good traits are those that are well integrated among many other traits. The model's description of connections between moral and theological virtues is an example. The relationships involving the passions is another. Virtues are virtues because they are integrated into a community.

Although a person is whole, the permeability of borders in this model motivates us to imagine beyond the discrete parts of a system. To imagine these interacting participants is to think about how they move together and about what moves all of them. At its center we can recognize the divine-human collaboration, a mutual responsiveness, taking place deep within where faith and God meet.

The nestedness presented by this model shows us that our moral traits are as embedded within our environments as we are. This helps us more clearly see the reciprocity of the causes that create our characters' swirling dynamics. World shapes virtue.

The model also demonstrates that virtue shapes the world. The nestedness of this model allows us to account for a moral agent as both shaper and recipient of the world. The model does this while still respecting an indeterminacy across the scales of moral life. The model respects the loose reflexivity and supports thoughtful moral examination of persons, cardinal virtues, virtues' interactions and relationships, social structures, and whole societies.

The third trait of a good moral character model follows the second. A good model demonstrates and embraces complexity and does not reduce a moral character into a simple discrete system or a human person into a total accumulation of traits, habits, and skills. In addition, a good model considers moral agency without making moral agency the singular defining trait of a person or of humanity. A Catholic ecological model of moral character recognizes God as the first Mover while appreciating genuine human agency. The model reflects each of these while respecting the ambiguities where divine and human agencies meet, because the model values collaboration as a defining feature of all life's systems.

The model embraces additional forms of complexity. For example, the concept of ecological niches indicates that imperfect traits and vices can aid moral growth. This model's capacity to incorporate a moral agent's own trajectory of moral development allows virtue theory to view vices more comprehensively, not simply as problems to solve or extinguish but instead as part of our continuing story. The model encourages us also to consider how vices play roles (positively and negatively) in our moral development. This offers hope and a motivation to keep moving toward increasing goodness. This capacity reflects thoughtful theological anthropology too. The roles of moral vices remind us that sinfulness is not only a theological reason for salvation's necessity, an influence of which to be wary, or an explanation for suffering. Sinfulness is also a (postlapsarian) condition of life. In this, virtue theory can speak to systematic theology. Virtue theory holds a particularly strong potential to merge with ecotheological traditions in Christian theology.

The model's vision of our nestedness within creation describes us (humans) as niche creators and participants. This vision reminds us that we are moral agents and also animals, emitters, consumers, observers, and observed. We are in need of this model's theological anthropological emphasis on humans not as the apex of creation but instead as embedded within and subject to creation's conditions.

The fourth trait of a good model of moral character is that it is viable according to scientific observation and casual observation. A good model can make sense to scholars of ethics, sociology, psychology, the humanities, and any exploration of humankind. A good model is ready to facilitate engagement between moral theology and scholarship of many disciplines.

In the ecological model of moral character, the concept of nestedness helps us think across scale, and the dynamics of interactions across the scales should be informed by psychological and sociological tools. Though scaling a moral theory upward or downward is treacherous (intention and agency do not work the same way at different levels of scale), the scales of moral life are in some way mutually responsive. This model helps virtue theory work on multiple scales. Partnership with these models and metaphors that are already under development can help virtue theory navigate across scales of moral life.

Even on the scale of individual human persons, moral growth is unpredictable. Casual observers of the ups and downs of personal development recognize this, and any model that claims otherwise will not ring true. The ecological model helps virtue theory to reflect what casual observation recognizes: we cannot simply, directly, or quickly propel our moral growth.

One reason for this unpredictability is that we cannot directly exercise many of our virtues and vices. The ecological model takes account of this by showing how weak causal contributions accumulate within us. This model demonstrates that changes can cascade, which creates a more encouraging system of moral thought, making more of virtue theory's strength as an ethic of aspiration.

The fifth trait of a good model is that it demonstrates awareness of sinfulness and as such does not participate in unjust social systems. While a good model resonates with the common understanding of an era's people, it does not conform to ideologies that deny human value, absolutize power imbalance, or represent systemic oppression as inevitable or necessary. Binary gender essentialism is one model to avoid and counteract. Extreme individualism is another. So, in the context of twenty-first-century North America, a good model prioritizes marginalized perspectives, presenting obstacles to racism, xenophobia, patriarchy, and heteronormativity. A good model integrates, urging cooperation, and does not fragment or merge neatly into patriarchal, ecocidal, racist, or colonialist narratives.

This model reflects life itself and does not centrally employ social structures or anthropocentric worldviews. The model's initial insight is that virtues are best imagined not as entities but rather as loci or nexuses where vectors meet. This insight counteracts the fragmentation of individualizing social imaginaries. The model portrays virtues and vices only in relationship. They cannot be imagined in isolation. The virtues themselves are relationship loci. As the nexuses of the vectors of relation patterns, virtues are constantly mutually shaping influences, and all their changes can at any time rebound and amplify or diffuse.

Interrelationality is definitive.[27] The passions' interactions with reason have a messiness in this model that particularly demonstrates this strength. The passions manifest in moral action and development but also in other premoral dynamics. The relationship between the passions and reason is one example.

This model also represents the permeability of the boundaries between individuals, recognizing the constant mutual influencing we share with others both with and beyond our own awareness.

The sixth trait is that a good model helps us to understand morality across multiple scales of observation. This is our most significant need of virtue theory.

The nestedness aspect of this model gives us new language to envision moral character as a dynamic within an ecosystem and within societies. There is a reciprocal influence between the larger contexts of ecosystem and society and the moral character of one who lives there. Moral agents absorb environments' physical, religious, political, legal, and social elements. These then manifest within us in the moral character and in our physical being. The nestedness aspect of moral character gives us a way to consider closely how our participation in societies and ecosystems affects our moral development. We can examine the meaning and significance of participation with more complexity, taking into account indeterminacy and mutual reflexivity. The power of tiny effects is evident when we maintain awareness of the nestedness of virtues and vices as well as passions and intellects and of persons and social groups and bioregions.

The seventh and final trait of a good model is that it reflects grace's wild movement, which allows for unpredictability, demonstrates our roots in God, and offers visions of how these roots draw on our grounding and our ground. In this, the model facilitates ecumenical and interreligious dialogue between ethicists and others across opposing views of human agency and freedom. The porosity of borders between a moral agent and God helps us think differently about practices and participation. This final trait describes a person as participating in God through her actions, life, and being, and demonstrates God's participation in a person. Goodness itself and responses to goodness seep into one another.

The model gives us a vision of seepage through all the layers of our embeddedness, through the layers of the three theological virtues. As the model demonstrates, faith is both received and nurtured. With faith two agencies meet, and the context of a whole moral character is part of a description of faith in this model.

The ambiguity of moral agency in this model is a strength because it invites us to allow for the wildness of the creator/creation relationship. This is integrative pneumatology. The closer we look at what we are like and how we direct ourselves, the more we are also able to see God's doings and not only our own. Likewise, the closer we look at what God does in the world, the more we end up noticing the fruits of a collaboration between creator and species.

Chapter 7 will consider some subsidiary virtues and then will demonstrate what this model can do for virtue theory with a unique reading of the integral ecology presented in Pope Francis's ecological encyclical *Laudato si'*.

NOTES

1. *Laudato si'*, para. 12.
2. Aquinas, *ST*, II–II, q. 141, a. 2. See also Cates, "The Virtue of Temperance."
3. For more on this, see, for example, works by Catherine Keller and Elaine Padilla; Groppe, *Eating and Drinking*; and *Laudato si'*, para. 222–23.
4. Cates, "The Virtue of Temperance," 324.
5. Aquinas, *ST*, II–II, q. 141, a. 2.
6. Cates, "The Virtue of Temperance," 322.
7. Pope Francis's description of a rich man can easily be read as an illustration of this experience of restlessness and unhappiness, even for one who has plenty. *Laudato si'*, para. 226.
8. Robert Hackett, "Why Bacon Is Suddenly Everywhere," *Fortune*, May 19, 2015, https://fortune.com/2015/05/19/bacon/.

9. *Laudato si'*, para. 226.

10. *Laudato si'*, para. 204.

11. Fullam, "Sex in 3-D," 166.

12. Rourke, "God, Grace, and Creation."

13. Aquinas, *ST*, II–II, a. 123, a. 1, and II–II, a. 123, a. 2, respondeo 2.

14. Bryan Massingale, "The Assumptions of White Privilege and What We Can Do about It," *National Catholic Reporter*, June 1, 2020, 4–5. For a discussion of police fearfulness of Black people and juries' sympathy with that fearfulness, see Jamelle Bouie, "'Fear' Was a Viable Defense for Killing Philando Castile," *Slate Magazine*, June 23, 2017.

15. Some of these arguments are executed in Kolb, *The Natural Gas Revolution*. For more context, see also Kolb, *Too Much Is Not Enough*.

16. That is, this may be taught to us if these businesses do give a larger return on investment. This itself is worth questioning but is beyond this book's ability to address.

17. Exodus 16.

18. Scarry, *The Body in Pain*.

19. Aquinas, *ST*, I–II, q. 65, 66, and 117, a. 2, and II–II, q. 117.

20. Aquinas ruled out generosity as a subsidiary virtue of justice in *ST*, II–II, q. 117, a. 5. See also Bonnie Kent's discussion of generosity's relationship to magnificence and magnanimity. Kent, "Habits and Virtues (Ia IIae, qq. 49-70)," 123–24.

21. Aquinas, *ST*, I–II, q. 65, a. 1, and II–II, q. 117, a5.

22. *Laudato si'*, pars. 211–212 (emphasis added).

23. Aquinas notes that fortitude collaborates with the passions. Aquinas, *ST*, II–II, q. 134, a. 4.

24. Chapter 4 described imagination's cooperation with hope.

25. Miller, "Integral Ecology," 14.

26. Pinckaers, *The Pinckaers Reader*, 303.

27. I must thank theologian Charles Curran for encouraging me to link virtue theory models with relationality after I first presented this idea to the Catholic Theological Society of America.

7

Down to Earth with
the Integral Ecology

ROLE MODELS

This final chapter showcases the ecological model of moral character. We will begin with a look at three virtues of particular significance to Catholic ecological virtue theory. Previous chapters' discussions of theological and cardinal virtues helped us think about structures of good moral character in accordance with an ecological model of moral character. Now, we can shift our attention to virtues traditionally called "subsidiary." This will sharpen our vision of good moral character with more particularity. We will begin with definitions and discussions of wonder, integrity, and solidarity. Each of these moral virtues demonstrates the intimate relationships and ecological dynamics between the participants of a good moral character. Wonder demonstrates that virtues and emotions shape and define one another and that the intellect can feed the virtues with what they need. Integrity demonstrates that remembering our nestedness within creation helps us to identify the ways in which our moral agency can cooperate with God. Solidarity demonstrates that moral virtue needs imagination to help a moral agent recognize reality well.

After the discussion of these virtues the chapter returns to Pope Francis's ecological encyclical *Laudato si'* to argue that this encyclical is a document driven by virtue ethics. The encyclical's integral ecology in particular is a call for an ecological model of moral character. Then, the chapter describes three role models: two individuals and one group that can serve as models of good and ecologically modeled moral character in action.

SUBSIDIARY VIRTUES

We can learn more about the ecological dynamics within our moral characters by imagining the "smaller" participants, the less often discussed virtues and the vices. They exist among and between the other moral character participants and exhibit interactions we might not expect to see. These virtues' participation in moral character are described less often in traditional Catholic virtue theory. Yet the activity of each of these three virtues (wonder, integrity, and solidarity) within a moral character adds important layers to a good model of moral character. An ecologically attuned description of wonder can help us imagine moral virtues' reliance on the passions and the intellect. Integrity, a "gateway virtue" to solidarity, goes to the heart of ecological virtue theory.[1] Solidarity, a "quintessential" moral virtue for Catholic and for ecological well-being, offers us the reward of healing from deceptive habits and isolation.[2]

Wonder

Wonder is among the moral virtues often praised by philosophical ecological virtue ethicists. In chapter 6 we saw that temperance and wonder grow with awareness of our environments and that joy and gratitude are nurtured along with this growth. Defining wonder as a participant of an ecological model of moral character reveals an intricate cooperation between virtues and emotions.

Wonder is the tendency to experience awe or an unexpected attraction to something (such as a place, an object, a being, or a phenomenon). An experience of wonder is often an enjoyable version of the feeling of being overwhelmed. Religion scholars such as Otto and James offer well-known analyses of this kind of experience as the definitive element of religious participation.[3]

As a moral virtue, though, wonder is harder to explain. Moral virtues are tendencies to do certain kinds of acts well, but what act does wonder uniquely enable? Wonder is a tendency not to do something but instead to feel something. Wonder is a capacity for certain emotional responses. Other moral virtues are also like this: gratitude, affection, sensuousness, mournfulness, enthusiasm, joyfulness, anger, and awe.[4] These virtues' strong affective component indicates a thick intertwining between moral virtues and the passions.

Virtues with an affective quality make new demands of a model of moral character. Because a good moral character model informs and inspires moral formation, the ecological model of moral character must be able to describe practices or actions that cultivate affective virtues. But a moral agent cannot resolve to feel a certain emotion and then begin feeling it.

As a child, I hated being told to be more grateful. If I wasn't feeling grateful already, how could I simply start feeling more grateful? I even noticed that thanking someone after being admonished to do so brought me resentment at least as often as gratitude. Going through the motions of acting as if I were grateful backfired. It seems that cultivating affective virtues is not as simple or direct as merely doing the things a moral agent does when feeling that way. You can't make a flower grow taller by pulling up on the stem. So, how can someone who rarely feels wonder acquire the virtue of wonder?

An ecological model of moral character can answer this problem well because it acknowledges and values weak and indirect causes. Wonder is indirectly nurtured. A moral agent can strengthen wonder indirectly by nurturing something else, something other than wonder.[5] In a wondrous creation, knowledge about the world feeds wonder.

Ecofeminist theologian Sally McFague observed that wonder results from the study of different species.[6] This book has demonstrated that increasing a moral agent's knowledge helps virtues' development because moral and intellectual virtues rely on one another. Naturalists and ecological writers support McFague's observation. Conservationists, farmers, philosophers, and scientists frequently exhibit wonder in their writings. Even when they aim simply to observe and describe, they frequently slip into a tone that demonstrates admiration, enjoyment, and even ecstasy.[7] Pope Francis, himself a practiced scientific observer, reminds us about this as he links intellectual and affective development in *Laudato si'*.[8]

The virtue of wonder, then, attends to the intellect. The feeling of wonder carries a cognitive component. One person watching the stars on a bitterly cold winter night might hold along with her gaze an understanding of the size and remoteness of these sustained explosions and of the incomprehensible distance of cold emptiness between them and herself. A different person might watch them with the knowledge that these slowly migrating points of light are the same that watched and guided her ancestors and her heroes and that they will continue to guide from above the lives of her children's children. When paired with these varieties of knowledge, the observation of neighboring stars is more powerfully evocative of emotion. Reflection on the stars, whether it brings to mind the life cycles of gaseous explosion or the world of one's descendants, enhances the aesthetic experience of looking upward. At the same time, a feeling of wonder can motivate methodical observation of phenomena, thereby fertilizing knowledge and intellectual exercise. The virtue nexus we call wonder represents a self-sustaining dynamic linking mind and mood, knowing and feeling.

If gaining knowledge about creation brings us to wonder, it follows that creation, for any being able to know, is wondrous, created by an awesome Creator expressing creativity into creation. In a way, wonder itself is "infused into our environment,"[9] present and ready for us to soak it up. Having the moral virtue of wonder means having a ready response that resonates well with the wonderfulness that is here.

Wonder is good for us, and its loss is symptomatic of harmful practices. Ecologists and farmers practice observation and knowledgeable responses to ecosystems, but many people do not. Many of our practices and cultural values work against being still and observing environments. Simply observing a place just to see what is there, to watch, is not rewarded or valued in many societies. The pressure to be productive, to be always doing something, opposes wonder cultivation. Pope Francis comments on this: "Nature is filled with words of love, but how can we listen to them amid constant noise, interminable and nerve-wracking distractions, or the cult of appearances? Many people today sense a profound imbalance which drives them to frenetic activity and makes them feel busy, in a constant hurry which in turn leads them to ride rough-shod over everything around them."[10] Slowness or stillness can prepare us to discover wonder.

Theological ethicist David Cloutier identifies our "practices of speed" as a "spiritual disease," which is reinforced by our glamorization of being busy.[11] (After all, being busy signifies being important.) C. S. Lewis also noticed this effect of speed. He reflected on his childhood awareness of place before cars were omnipresent. "I measured distances by the standard of man, man walking on his own two feet. . . . The truest and most horrible claim made for modern transport is that it 'annihilates space.' It does. It annihilates one of the most glorious gifts we have been given. It is a vile inflation which lowers the value of distance, so that a modern boy travels a hundred miles with less sense of liberation and pilgrimage and adventure than his grandfather got from traveling them."[12] Theologian Cara Anthony calls this "hypermobility" and recommends a practice to counteract the spiritual harms it causes.[13] The practices of fast travel undermine the "virtues of place" that were described in chapter 5, that set of cardinal virtues we need in order to cultivate attunement. Busyness demotivates our ecological awareness and knowledge and makes wonder more difficult to ignite.

For Christian ethics, wonder also nurtures other moral virtues, such as the humility that a person of faith must be able to experience. A wonder-humility partnership is an enjoyable experience in its own right. Moments in which wonder is felt can transform a person. This is a virtue that can connect our imaginations to the very roots of God's relationships with creation, in the shock of remembering the first thought presented to us in the Bible's creation accounts: that this is indeed all very good.

Integrity

Integrity is another important subsidiary virtue requiring a careful definition. The popular understanding of the virtue of integrity is that it is a tendency to act in accordance with one's existing beliefs or principles.[14] This definition implies a consistency over time and across situations. We praise someone's integrity when her ways of acting do not change with different kinds of situations. This is contrasted with hypocrisy, or behaving differently in different situations in order to gain benefits. This fits with a view of integrity similar to that of "structural integrity," in which something is fixed in place to the degree that it would continue to maintain its same shape even if its context were to threaten or weaken it. Integrity in this understanding signals a constancy and an ability to stay intact or even unchanging in all circumstances.

There is value in this. But integrity also means integrating, which can include changing our internal worlds in response to our environments. An ecologically attuned understanding of integrity values responsive change. Situational nonresponsiveness is not a particularly ecological trait. Ecological attunement does not tend to look to some unchanging core of something as a way to understand that thing. Therefore ecological integrity as an ecologically attuned virtue points toward excellent integration. As an ecological virtue, integrity is a virtue of integration between the exterior and the interior. This understanding of integrity appreciates that the boundaries between a moral agent and her environment are porous and permeable.

The worlds without and within a moral agent continually and mutually influence one another. A moral agent, as a freely moving *imago Dei*, is ecologically virtuous in her ability to identify and respond well to both of these dynamics: the dynamics of all creation and those that her own moral character are drinking in through her faith.

Ecological ethicists who have discussed integrity have addressed it mainly as a trait of ecosystems that humans ought to protect. When the term "integrity" appears in ecological ethics, it often refers to ecosystems rather than a human moral trait.[15] This could indicate that there is not much potential for this virtue in the eyes of ecological virtue ethics. On the other hand, liberation theologian Leonardo Boff has demonstrated that an ecologically attuned definition of integrity participates significantly in virtue thinking.

Boff is not known as a virtue ethicist, but he does display a virtue sensibility. For example, consider his praise of a "mental ecology": "Mental ecology strives to achieve a psychic *integration* of human persons so as to make them gentler in their relationships with the natural and social environment and to bring them into a more lasting harmony with the universe in reverence and balance."[16] In other words, our ways of moving on Earth ought to match our mental or "internal" ways of moving.

Boff arrives at this integration from his discussion of gentleness. He argues that we can and should strive for gentleness, outwardly and inwardly, first because both are necessary but also because our distinct efforts to practice gentleness will enhance one another to form a habit, or a "mental ecology." Boff describes an integration of one's self with one's environments, affirming that our environments within and without can resonate or at least harmonize together. The connectedness described and prescribed by integrity understood this way is evident on a larger scale in Boff's work. This ecologically attuned liberation theology demonstrates the integrated nature of social, economic, political, and ecological liberation.

This kind of integration is valued by virtue theory. Virtue theory, after all, assumes that our way of living (our actions, practices, and behaviors) shapes our internal landscapes in persistent ways. At the same time, our internal landscape manifests actions, practices, and behaviors. Our actions reveal our moral traits. In a way, ecological virtue ethics is all about integrity. We reflect our environments within our moral character, and we express our moral character into our environments. We absorb traits, and we emanate traits. These dynamics were described in the discussions of nestedness in chapter 4.

The virtue of integrity means acknowledging our nestedness. The virtue of integrity recognizes our nestedness within our contexts and in the nested layers of traits that are within us. Integrity is a tendency to act in accordance with these layers. Our agency functions at a locus between our characteristics and the characteristics of our contexts. We make choices about when, where, and how these inner and outer conditions will meet and fit. For example, compassion within a moral agent and cruelty of her society can encounter one another in a moral agent. She exercises her agency to decide how that encounter will take place. She can absorb cruelty into herself, or she can allow her compassion to emerge outward from herself to be expressed into the world of her context. Through our exercise of moral agency, we can shape our own specific nestedness. A moral agent with integrity recognizes that her moral character is a participant in her contexts, that her contexts are participating in the shape of her moral growth, and that her agency makes her responsible for deciding how to guide the shaping influences of all of these. She recognizes her own participation as a means of world building for the good. She can enact and actualize her own unique nexus of God's love and her own moral formation, knowledge and intellect, and passions into the world. For Catholic ethics, this awareness and the willingness to be fully in the world in this way prepares a moral agent to develop a further moral virtue: the virtue of solidarity.

Solidarity

Solidarity is about allowing our interconnectedness with others to guide our actions well. Interconnectedness is not avoidable, but in order for solidarity to be a moral virtue, it must be true that we have some choice about this. We can choose to live either in accordance with our interconnectedness or in ways that deny it. The possibility of choosing to live either way is what makes this a moral trait.

But to what degree can we deny our interdependence? Independence from others is possible only to an extremely limited degree. To some extent, living in accordance with reality is not a moral choice so much as a requirement for survival. So, there must be more to solidarity than a recognition of reality. If the awareness that integrity cultivates within a moral agent can expand with a faith-informed sensitivity to wider contexts and if that moral agent accepts and then acts in accordance with that awareness, then the virtue solidarity can grow.

Moral theologian Meghan Clark notes that the principle of solidarity has a "feel" to it. "It translates into the willingness to give oneself for the good of one's neighbor, beyond any individual or particular interest."[17] As a skill, solidarity helps us to ensure "that nothing is lacking in the common cause" and seek "points of possible agreement where attitudes of separation and fragmentation prevail." This is aided by awareness of the ways in which we are indebted to (all) others and a willingness to learn to love these sustaining interrelationalities.[18] Mutual indebtedness is a very ecological concept.

Accepting our indebtedness to others is difficult. Those of us with social and economic power find it easy to overlook our dependence on those who have less than we do. We are well motivated to overlook this because we value independence or at least the illusion of independence. But we are dependent. Thinking about food makes this quite clear. For example, in fields far from their families, migrant workers grow and gather the food that I eat. How many hours of work and how many people's labor go into growing a tomato I eat in March to satisfy my nonseasonal craving?

Further, the lives of these workers are burdened in multiple ways by the privileges and customs of my life and the social norms of my context. The harvesters of my vegetables often receive impossibly low compensation and perform difficult labor in order to escape the violence, poverty, terror, and oppression of lives lived south of the US border. The means by which crops are tended endangers these workers' health. The acquisition and by-products of the fuels that give me energy to heal, travel, read at night, cook, drink, and eat have resulted in a global atmospheric chemistry that destroys other people's homes and amplifies the wildness of their weather. The true costs of my clothing, housing, food, and transport are being borne by others, human and nonhuman. Fiscal economies translate labor, mine and others', and facilitate exchanges, but these exchanges do not result in equanimity. Others' survival struggles are made more difficult as a result. The virtues of integrity and solidarity require and enable us to face honestly the full costs of our lives.

This situation is not healthy for any of us. The social practices that exempt some from struggle while further burdening others who are already more vulnerable require continual deception. Duplicitous social structures and carefully disguised oppression hide what is being done, exacerbating our ignorance and warping our understanding of humanity and of creation. Theologian M. Shawn Copeland gave a name to this problem: "structural historical amnesia."[19] This vice is the opposite of solidarity. Our racism, classism, ableism, heterosexism, and other patriarchal tendencies also represent a willful social ignorance and a contrived and duplicitous isolationism.

Practices of solidarity help us to perceive reality more clearly and honestly. For those of us who live protected by structures of privilege and the scaffolding of deception that such structures require, solidarity means thrusting ourselves out of our current situations of inordinate power, wealth, safety, and leisure into the danger, deprivation, threat, hunger, exposure, and vulnerability within which others are embedded because of the global consequences of our own lifestyles. This step is necessary for our moral growth and is absolutely a requirement for practitioners of a faith that names a person such as Jesus Christ as God incarnate.

As we saw in chapter 4's discussion of hope, the vices that counterfeit solidarity are insidious and important to recognize. Theologian Maureen O'Connell warns that solidarity can be twisted into a cliché or, worse, a reinforcement of exactly what solidarity's spirit aims to destroy: marginalization, suppression, exclusion, coercion, and ignorance.[20] Solidarity is possible only when our community awareness is intact, keen, honest, wide, and open to the discomfort of learning more. Misnaming this virtue is particularly dangerous because it directly engages power. Genuine solidarity employs an accurate and effective interpretation of power: what it is, where and how it moves, whom it tends to benefit. Accidental and deliberate misunderstandings of power enable counterfeit vices of solidarity to undermine relationality and ultimately the common good itself.[21]

A moral agent requires intellectual effort and imagination in order to develop solidarity.[22] Theologian and environmentalist Russell Butkus's definition of solidarity highlights solidarity's connection to an intelligent and accurate recognition of the world. Solidarity is "the consistent habit of character expressed in the recognition of our fundamental interrelatedness ... that takes explicit shape in determined active engagement to create, promote and restore the universal common good of creation."[23] The recognition we gain from solidarity can shift us into an unexpected and unfamiliar self-contextualizing. The cultivation of solidarity can be painful and glorious because it is an awakening from ignorance and self-deception. This chapter's next discussion might tempt us toward such an awakening with echoes of Pope Francis's hints at the benefits that will follow from healing from our fragmentation and experiencing the feeling that solidarity gives.

EXAMPLES OF ECOLOGICAL MORAL CHARACTER

It is appropriate to end a book that proposes a new moral character model with some example or case study to put it through its paces. One might expect a "green virtue" illustration, such as an obviously environmentally oriented case study, to appear here, but exclusively environmental ethics cases are not necessary to demonstrate ecological ethics theories. There are two reasons this is true.

The first reason is that exclusively environmental ethics cases do not exist. A decision or a situation that is about ecology is also always about other things (such as economics, racism, technology, family, or global politics). Any situation that seems to call for ecological virtuousness will also require virtuous participation in parenting, health care, and business. The work of ecological integrity requires us to learn to see the ecological contours of all the situations we move through. In fact, the better case to demonstrate an ecological virtue model is one that on the surface does not appear to be an environmental ethics sort of case at all.

The second reason that overtly environmental ethics cases are unnecessary is that a moral agent's moral character is what it is in all the situations that person encounters.[24] A good model for moral character helps us imagine and improve moral character in every kind of context.

The stories that begin each chapter of Steven Bouma-Prediger's book *Earthkeeping and Character* offer glimpses of full-bodied ecological character and what it has to give. His profiles of role models are also helpful, sketching the stories of a few individuals' demonstrations of ecologically excellent moral character. Wangari Maathai,[25] Crow chief Plenty Coups,[26] Susan Drake Emmerich,[27] and Jane Goodall[28] are some. I can personally attest to his description of the character, personality, and legacy of Reverend Kent Busman, under whose leadership I have worked and learned at Camp Fowler of Speculator, New York.[29]

This chapter will conclude with three brief examples to demonstrate good and ecologically attuned moral character, but first we will consider a case study that illustrates specifically Catholic ecological moral character, with attention to multiple scales of its nestedness. This example is buried in Pope Francis's *Laudato si'*. *Laudato si'* demonstrated that thinking about virtues ecologically does not pull our attention toward a narrowly ecological reading of all situations. The encyclical also does not ask us to balance social justice or personal faith commitment against an ecological concern, as some representatives of Christianity at times suggest. *Laudato si'* is a plea not for turning from one tight focus to another but instead for opening up. A life of Christian faith involves the whole person. Such a life undermines social and ecological injustices and delights in and amplifies justice. A person of ecologically attuned moral character notices and responds to all life's dynamics, including creatures' social structures. A life of virtue is a virtuous participation in life itself.[30]

LAUDATO SI' AND ECOLOGICAL VIRTUE ETHICS

Laudato si' is Pope Francis's 2015 ecological encyclical. At first blush, its moral lessons seem grounded entirely in Catholic social teaching. In the English translation of the encyclical's more than two hundred paragraphs, the word "virtue" appears only five times (half the number of mentions of "duty").[31] Nevertheless, this encyclical is a demonstration of ecological virtue ethics. The dearth of virtue language does not disprove this. As a pastorally motivated letter written for the broadest possible audience, *Laudato si'* avoids the technical language of moral theology's theories.[32] Lay language makes the document approachable. (My anecdotal experience suggests that it succeeded. With its promulgation several parishes in my diocese launched reading groups, summer public talks, and adult education classes to help local Catholics gather to read it together. Many readers in these groups expressed gratitude at the encyclical's hospitality, tone, and vocabulary.)[33]

This encyclical's call for an "integral ecology" is a thoroughly virtue-minded plea. Virtue thinking is its DNA. This is discernible in several places. First, the encyclical describes the carpenter, wanderer, observer, and storyteller Jesus Christ as a moral role model. Second, the encyclical names several specific virtues even though it often refers to these as "attitudes" or "mindsets" instead of virtues.[34] Third, the encyclical describes the nestedness of human moral character within creation as a participant in the systems of life.

A Role Model in *Laudato si'*

The first demonstration of virtue theory is in part 7 of the encyclical's second chapter with a creative virtue-style reflection. Here, *Laudato si'* presents Jesus Christ's gaze as a model of "attentiveness to the beauty of the world."[35] The gospels indicate that Jesus Christ noticed his environments habitually. Ecotheologian Denis Edwards has also observed that environmental details often appear in Jesus's stories and as a focus of his attentions.[36] An overtly virtue-styled analysis might at this point describe how this virtue of attentiveness could have been shaped by the practices of the person Jesus Christ, and indeed *Laudato si'* does speculate on this, imagining that Jesus's vocational practice of carpentry helped him to develop his awareness of environments.[37] We can conclude that work with our hands, or practices of cooperation with materials in order to make something with them, is a behavior that can shape ecological virtues. The encyclical offers Jesus Christ as a role model of ecologically attuned moral character.

The Encyclical's Praise of Virtues

For the second way this encyclical demonstrates virtue theory, *Laudato si'* directly calls readers to cultivate virtues.[38] The encyclical suggests that a person who learns to stop and admire beauty will be able to "reject self-interested pragmatism." The same paragraph adds that the "mindset" of people is important because it influences people's behavior and also notes that the cultivation of a "life of virtue" is "essential" to Christian life.[39] Integrating the Christian vocation into our relations with the rest of creation is part of a Christian's life of faith. The encyclical encourages readers to do this through a method that resembles virtue ethics' way of thinking. For example, we are to make a habit of "assessing the impact of our every action and personal decision on the world around us."[40] This describes the virtue of attunement, and as we saw in chapter 5 of this book, attunement is a core characteristic of an ecological model of moral character. Pope Francis describes this habit as a path for us to experience "ecological conversion," and this conversion is imagined as a "profound interior" redirection of all aspects of a person and a community.[41]

The encyclical also constructs a portrait of a vice. As is consistent with the encyclical's tone, this vice portrayal is threaded through the document but not labeled as a "vice" in so many words. The document describes in several places a utilitarian mindset of consumerism.[42] This mindset, evident in politics, in social practices, and attitudes in daily life, is characterized by a complete trust in markets to shape our world well. In addition, this mindset irresponsibly urges short-term private gains and ignores the harms it adds to the lives of the vulnerable. Thus, this mindset is a misdirected faith bolstered by a resistance against noticing widely.

This sounds a lot like a vice, in fact, and a vice that connects resistances against faith, attunement, and compassion. "Mindset" is often defined as a "fixed attitude, *disposition* or mood."[43] The term has also been defined as "a fixed mental attitude or disposition that predetermines a person's responses to and interpretations of situations; an *inclination* or a *habit*."[44] "Mindset" is a good word choice to refer to "vice." This harmful human trait is an unbalanced conglomeration of vices, including a misdirected or deficient faith and an isolating denial of reality's connectedness (a deficient solidarity).

The encyclical also names many moral virtues. These include honesty,[45] responsibility,[46] sobriety,[47] humility,[48] innocence,[49] self-control, willingness to learn, courage,[50] care,[51] simplicity,[52] justice/justness, generosity, and tenderness.[53] *Laudato si'* sometimes calls these "attitudes."[54] The encyclical gives no technical definition of "attitude," but, again, nontechnical definitions seem reasonable for reading such a pastoral exhortation. An attitude is a sort of trait, disposition, behavior style, or inclination.[55] Attitudes are imperceptible as they influence our way of interpreting reality but are quite visible in the responses we tend to give to what we notice. A moral agent's attitude can be felt by the moral agent herself in a gut reaction, the first assumption, or a default preliminary response that occurs to her prior to deliberation. This is a tendency that may or may not be overridden or hidden by further thought or a second look. Even when not displayed, an attitude is still present as a baseline. Attitude is invisible, mutable, and habitual, manifesting when acted on and accumulating to resemble an enduring trait, very much like a virtue.

The Encyclical's Portrayal of Our Moral Nestedness within Creation

The third way this encyclical demonstrates ecological virtue thinking is in its understanding of human moral character as nested within creation. The nestedness of an ecological virtue theory appears as this encyclical acknowledges the interrelationality between individuals' and societies' moral characters.

This can be difficult to track, as the encyclical zooms in and out across scale quickly, moving between a focus on the human experience of being an individual and the wider scales of human societies. This focus shift reflects a human experience of always being both an individual and a social participant. Let's consider one particularly insightful example. The document warns that our "flood" of consumer goods "can baffle the heart."[56] We can read this discussion as a portrayal of a hypothetical (but familiar) person. The encyclical's description of this baffled person demonstrates a skillful ecological virtue theory analysis.

According to *Laudato si'*, a baffled heart can result from the mere presence of an overwhelming "flood" of things to consume. But this flood cannot simply be a happenstance present condition to be experienced. It is also a product of an economic system that necessitates the continual regeneration of goods to be consumed. Therefore, this flood signifies not only the presence of a threat but also a degrading practice (continually generating and consuming goods) in which we participate. This practice works in concert with related practices.

In one related practice, residents of the United States such as myself often identify economic growth as an important indicator of the health of our society. Our fixation on the financial aspects of economics and on the economic aspects of well-being is a habit that we learn, trust, and reinforce. The all-encompassing absorption of our interest in consumer goods and financial exchange overwhelms other concerns that the heart may hold.[57] An unbalanced moral character results. Virtue theory recognizes that a moral character can trap itself in a cycle of mutually supporting vicious practices, and the encyclical echoes this understanding in several places, such as its famously frequent reminders that "everything is connected." Our individual selves and our social selves, our psychological worlds and our "external worlds," our "doing" and our "being," and our practices and our attitudes are all connected and interconnected.

We are baffled, Pope Francis is saying, not only by our aisles and shelves of things to purchase but also by everything we do and believe in order to keep these aisles and shelves continually full of buyable things and to keep our wallets and attentions ready to choose and acquire from among them. The heart is baffled at the sheer number of things to acquire, at the attention these things require (make them, want them, learn about them, choose them, sell them, buy them, upgrade them), and at the suspicion that these things create not a fountain of plenty but rather a drowning flood.

Liberation theologian Leonardo Boff said, "There is an internal ecology just as surely as there is an external ecology, and they mutually condition each other."[58] In *Laudato si'*, we read from Pope Benedict's 2005 homily, "The external deserts in the world are growing, because the internal deserts have become so vast."[59] These thoughts reflect the nestedness highlighted in an ecological model of moral character. The dynamics of a person's external world are describable social and ecological systems. The same is true of a person's internal world, which is no less complex and wild than an ecosystem or a society. A good model of moral character helps us to describe these internal systems of interactions. Furthermore, ecologically nested as all these systems are, they influence one another. Participation in ecological and social systems changes our character's development, and our moral character, moving as it does within our ecological and social systems, changes those systems, sometimes as reinforcement, sometimes steering these systems' development, and sometimes even subverting them. This is the very soul of virtue thought. It is also what *Laudato si'* means when it speaks of an integral ecology.

The Integral Ecology as a Call for an Ecological Model of Moral Character

Laudato si' offers an idea of an "integral ecology" in order to move us more deeply into what Boff and Benedict XVI had both observed: we are nested into creation, and how we respond to our nestedness has moral significance. The integral ecology introduced in the encyclical's fourth chapter engages the mutual influence between humans' internal and external worlds and asks that we participate in this mutual influence deliberately and well.

Vincent Miller notes that the encyclical's "integral ecology can be read in three related ways."[60] First, it is an assertion about reality: everything is, in essence, interconnection. This recalls a fundamental claim of ecotheology and of this book: relationships are fundamental, whether one is defining the participants of a moral character, an ecosystem, or the universe. The second way to understand Pope Francis's integral ecology is as a way of seeing interconnectedness. It is a habitual perception or lens that recognizes interconnectedness as intrinsic to the fabric and meaning of creation. This lens is accurate. The third way of understanding integral ecology is as a moral principle that guides us (humans) in living out our recognition of the first claim. Miller notes in contrast other lenses such as the technocratic paradigm and certain economic systems' adamant fixation on short-term profit.

Evolution of the Integral Ecology

The evolution of the integral ecology concept began in Pope John Paul II's *Centesimus Annus* in 1991. In part 4 of *Centesimus Annus*, Pope John Paul II describes consumerism's erosion of our quality of life, noting that it fuels a pursuit of "'having' rather than 'being.'"[61] He notes that this relates to "the ecological question," which has at its roots an "anthropological error."[62] That error is our belief that we can "make arbitrary use of the earth, subjecting it without restraint to [our] will, as though it did not have its own requisites and a prior God-given purpose." This reflects the Catholic social teaching principle of the universal destination of goods. This observation also presages the "baffled heart" that cannot find in consumerism the happiness and fulfillment that consumerism promises to deliver.

Pope John Paul II then notes concern about species' habitat preservation and extinction (adding, even in 1991, that we should be more worried about this than we are). Each species is needed because of its role in "the balance of nature." But, he adds, we also expend "too little effort" "to safeguard the moral conditions of an authentic 'human ecology.'"[63] We need to learn to "respect the natural and moral structure with which he [sic] has been endowed." Here, we see a version of this book's claim that human life is embedded, ecologically and morally, within the planet's systems of life.

The nestedness of ecologically understood moral character appears as Pope John Paul II expands on the connections between moral agency and this human ecology. Our decisions "create a human environment," and this also means that our decisions "give rise to specific structures of sin." We are reminded, then, that these structures "impede[d] the full realization of those who are in any way oppressed by them."[64] These kinds of decisions cut people out of the human ecology and the social ecology, isolating them. As we know from ecology, such isolation means death. Pope John Paul II shows how we bring harm and death to others when we do not attend to how our own actions exacerbate injustice, and he demonstrates how this takes place by describing the social and ecological embeddedness of a human person's moral character. The human ecology concept traces a vision of a moral character's effects on its social and ecological surroundings.

Following Pope John Paul II, Pope Benedict XVI takes up the concept of a "human ecology." He introduces it similarly to Pope John Paul II and then integrates it more closely with nonhuman elements of creation: "Nature, especially in our time, is so integrated into the dynamics of society and culture that by now it hardly constitutes an independent variable."[65] Pope Benedict specifies examples of desertification and its multiple causal links to human poverty. He reinforces this point using virtue theory. "Just as human virtues are interrelated, such that the weakening of one places others at risk, so the ecological system is based on respect for a plan that affects both the health of society and its good relationship with nature."[66] Here, the "human ecology" is a sort of human-sized mirror of creation's systems of interrelationality in terms of mutual interdependence and in terms of God's intention for creation's interdependence. This parallel between moral character and ecosystems echoes the model presented in this book.

The "integral ecology" of Pope Francis's *Laudato si'* develops the human ecology idea into a thicker, more organic connectivity. Recall from chapter 2 in the current book that the term "ecology" refers primarily to a category of scientific disciplines, or the study of the systems of life. Popes John Paul II and Benedict XVI addressed the actual interrelationalities among the participants in a system and not the study of these systems themselves, so at first glance "human ecology" might sound like a misnomer. However, as we (humans) study ecosystems, we are also participating in them, so the two concepts are not as far apart as they might seem. Our understandings of ecosystems manifest into those ecosystems, participating in how they behave. As Thomas Berry and others have demonstrated, our very storytelling about the universe moves the story and shapes the universe itself.[67]

In *Laudato si'*, the "ecology" of "integral ecology" refers to both the systems of interrelationality themselves and humanity's attitudes toward these interrelationalities, as Miller pointed out. In other words, *Laudato si'* looks at the ecology of ecology. The encyclical explores the relationships between life's relationship webs and examines how we (humans) spin among these webs as we move, observe, interpret, and reflect. Pope Francis takes a step beyond his predecessors in this regard.

Laudato si' notes that "the human person grows more, matures more and is sanctified more to the extent that he or she enters into relationships, going out from themselves to live in communion with God, with others and with all creatures. In this way, they make their own that trinitarian dynamism which God imprinted in them when they were created."[68] Miller agrees, noting that engaging and diving into relationships and into communion makes us more fully what we are.[69] He finds in Pope Francis's integral ecology concept an expansion of ecological insights about relationally such that "the existence of human *society* is as much a matter of relationships with other species as it is a matter of economic development."[70] This observation is absolutely correct, and it is absolutely what we must incorporate more thoroughly into Christian theological anthropologies.

An "integral ecology" warns us that when we cut people and lives out of relationalities (such as structures of educational systems, food distribution, medical care), we not only bring isolation (and therefore death) for them and sickness or impoverishment for ourselves but also amplify through a feedback loop the wrongs of our own participation in structures of sin. Isolation can be fecund. Through exiles, closets, pogroms, mass incarcerations, captivities, enslavements, forced relocations of people from land, genocides, and extinctions, entire communities are sickened and destroyed, and all creation suffers.

What, then, are we to do? The integral ecology means remembering and understanding connections. Every discipline and profession and mentality is linked. Our problems are likewise deeply intertwined, which means that we must learn "a distinctive way of looking."[71] An integral ecology means habitually contextualizing ourselves and our interactions within our many environments (social, religious, ecological, professional, personal, political, economic, etc.).[72] Virtue theory's overlap with this integral ecology is its ability to help us habitually contextualize our moral character as well as the participants of our moral character within these same environments. This is an integral ecology's moral character. If we understand the links between ourselves and our systems, we will not be tempted to seek the "solutions" offered by a technocratic paradigm. This is important, because any technological or scientific progress without accompanying moral progress threatens humanity.[73] Such lopsided developments amplify power while suppressing wisdom. The integral ecology is both our awareness of interrelationality and our faithful cooperation with all our spheres of interrelationality. Internal ecology is integration work, sustainable with a moral habit of integrity. Among other things, internal ecology inspires us to ask what need Earth has of us.[74] Miller correctly links solidarity, that essential element of Catholic life, with the integral ecology. Integral ecology expands solidarity to mean not only humans' but all creation's interdependence,[75] and solidarity is a habit we can each shape through practices that nurture our awareness.

Laudato si' presents St. Francis as a role model to demonstrate a kind of person who recognizes the "inseparable bond between concern for nature, justice for the poor, commitment to society, and interior peace."[76] The document argues that affection characterized Francis's bonds with creation, from sun to individual neighboring creatures. This affect warmed Francis's life and united him intimately with the cycles of life. His asceticism followed from this communion including even with wildlife, as his legends describe. We are not asked to scold wolves, but we must learn to see them as peers, as created creatures of God's own. US environmentalism pioneer Aldo Leopold learned this, finding in his encounter with a wolf the catalyst for his ecological conversion to "thinking like a mountain."[77]

Affection, born from attentiveness, can begin this habit. In other words, a passion can sprout from attunement and cultivate a joyful asceticism. This is a conversion supported by an ecological model of moral character.

To understand what this might look like for our day, let's recall first one of our most pressing problems: global warming.

Global Warming and the Integral Ecology

As this book's preface noted, our world's climate has warmed by about one degree Celsius since the Industrial Revolution.[78] This warming results from human activity. Our energy source choices emit greenhouse gases into the atmosphere.[79] The resulting atmospheric makeup leads to other changes, including globally higher average temperatures. Our use of fossil fuels changes the global climate.

Our climate's increasing temperature has led to species extinctions, changes in our oceans, and more frequent extreme weather events, more frequent forest fires, more invasive species, and more frequent droughts.[80] Each of these patterns is a distinct problem, and these problems also interact with each other. Each of these changes causes additional changes. The interactions of climate warming's consequences further accelerate the pace of global warming.[81] This is an example of reciprocal causation, discussed in chapter 2.

Global warming is an example of a complex problem. In their book *An Introduction to Christian Environmentalism*, theologians Kathryn Blanchard and Kevin O'Brien describe a typology that explains what this means. Simple problems can be solved by following a series of steps. Complicated problems involve more steps to follow and require a fuller grasp of the situation at hand, but they can still be solved by following a series of instructions. Complex problems change even as we address them. No list of instructions can be detailed enough to serve as a solution. "Solving" a complex problem is never perfectly done and may even be impossible.[82] Ecological problems are complex. They involve changing dynamics, causes that are weak, indirect, or reciprocal and systems that are porous, interacting, and impossible to predict with precision. Because ecosystems are nested, any solutions applied on the scale of a problem will have some kind of effect on other scales. Thinking about one scale only will not help.[83]

The integral ecology described in *Laudato si'* is a habit of seeking "comprehensive solutions" to complex problems. That is, when problems have multiple and interacting dimensions, as ecological problems always do, we should employ comprehensive solutions,[84] not solutions that neatly or simply answer all dimensions of a problem at once. We need solutions that take into account problems' full complexity.

In the face of climate instability, our aim should not be solutions that end all problems with one sweep. Instead, we should seek responses that are attuned to a problem's simultaneously social and environmental nature and to its moral and religious contexts.[85] Responses must also be sustainable, which is possible only if they make use of a well-informed vision of humans as ecological participants and moral agents. Comprehensive solutions encourage good moral development among all participants and stake bearers. One sign of a good comprehensive solution is that it is good for the persons who participate in it. A good comprehensive solution involves practices that help people to be good people. A good moral character dances between attention to specific aspects of a problem at hand and its tendrils extending into other areas and to attention to the dynamics and interactions that brought about the problem. This requires integrated education, which in turn means (among other things) that researchers and teachers must study and learn in academic freedom.[86] Comprehensive solutions respect ecological problems' complexity and are nurtured by education that encourages people to recognize the links between areas of knowledge. An integral ecology reveals and encourages this way of thinking.

An integral ecology also means that some of our practices must be left behind. In academia, we should reduce practices that perpetuate excessive specialization. Pope Francis calls us to shape academia with an eye to the world's urgent need for "a humanism capable of bringing together the different fields of knowledge, including economics, in the service of a more integral and integrating vision."[87]

Three examples, one of a group and two of individuals, follow to demonstrate versions of an integral ecology's moral character.

EXAMPLES OF MORAL CHARACTER, ECOLOGICALLY UNDERSTOOD

One example is Canisius University's collaboration of faculty staff and students through an informally recognized sustainability initiative. Inspired by Loyola University Chicago's sustainability institute, this group aims to guide the university's culture by eroding barriers between the academic, student life, and physical plant realms of the university. In the spirit of an integral ecology, the work transgresses many traditional academic norms and hierarchies. Faculty have learned to work under the direction and supervision of the university's facilities director. Professors have turned to student government for direction and guidance. Students have learned how to communicate with facilities and food services employees. Personal relationships have formed among faculty, staff, students, and administrators over power tools between mounds of dirt and around shredded tarps flapping in the wind. These relationships at times have snuck around or squirmed to fit between official university procedures and rules. The group has navigated an awkward space among the university's structures. These efforts to integrate "physical, curricular, social, economic and spiritual" realms have maintained a community garden, a strip of land where food grows, insects are protected, city schoolchildren are introduced to lawn mowers and worms, and faculty get lessons about native plants from the dean's administrative assistant.[88] This garden holds open a gap in the borders between the university and the neighborhoods within which it lives. Together we integrate gardening know-how with social justice organizing and commitment to a community.

In parish life, an integral ecology could mean fostering collaborations between committees or social groups that do not normally intersect. It could also mean inculcating into one's religious community a deep recognition of the collaborations between God and creation. One such example is Kent Busman, ordained pastor of the Reformed Church of America in the regional synod of Albany. Reverend Busman directs the denomination's summer camp in Speculator, New York, alongside one of a series of Adirondack lakes.[89] He manages the camp, supervises the staff and volunteers, and participates in the madcap adventures of each week's camping experience. Busman dresses as old-timey fur-trapper "French Louie" to teach campers about wilderness fire drills, leads nightly singalongs, trains and shepherds his staff, pays the bills for the facility, and conducts outreach to the churches that support and send generations of their children to the camp. Under his leadership, campers acclimate to a culture of awareness about the sources of the food they eat, the leech field that processes their waste, the prevention of swimmer's itch, the social structures that lead to homelessness, and images of atonement, Christian Reformed style. As Bouma-Prediger notes, Busman "embodies a hunger for justice and exhibits a pursuit of love. In all this he exudes an infectious joy, such that all who come to Fowler—campers, volunteers, staff—catch the spirit of this holy place."[90] Busman assumes and inhabits a link between environment and faith. He demonstrates a faith complexly integrated with the moral virtues of ecological attentiveness: patience, prudence, exuberance, and honesty. His full-bodied demonstration of the collaboration of faith and ecological well-being has spread through many Reformed Church of America churches and communities of central New York and the Adirondacks. Busman is a model of a moral character that integrates theological and moral virtues with intellect and passions.

Sometimes a moral character of integrated ecological awareness appears when a moral agent steps outside of professional bounds to respond to a crisis that she is uniquely prepared to understand and professionally well placed to resolve. In medical practice, an integrated and ecological moral character is modeled by Dr. Mona Hanna-Attisha. This pediatrician of Michigan State University and Hurley Children's Hospital, hearing of problems with the water in her city of Flint, speedily organized a study of the levels of lead in blood for the children of the city to bring attention to a public health crisis. In the face of character assaults and public attacks on her research competence, she used her professional skills and resources to carry out this study, which was crucial to undermining authorities' efforts to hide the dangers in the public water supply in Flint, Michigan.[91] Rather than "staying in her own lane," Hanna-Attisha forcefully made known what she saw happening. She saved the lives and the futures of many of Flint's youngest and most vulnerable residents.[92] Her response to the problem demonstrated her well-attuned recognition of the ways that racism, pediatric medicine, and environmental negligence conspire. She also understood complex truths: that people and structures can be complicit and brutal and also sorry for their own wrongdoing. Hanna-Attisha was able to learn from experts with methods and goals that side-stepped or even potentially threatened her own and to maintain a focus on the reasons why she did what she did (the well-being of the children of Flint) while still accepting the complexity of the problem.

CONCLUSION

As a uniquely virtue-infused exhortation, *Laudato si'* asks us to see ourselves differently. We are wholes, we are parts, and we are relationship creators. This change of vision is a form of healing. An integral ecology "includes taking time to recover a serene harmony with creation, reflecting on our lifestyle with creation, reflecting on our lifestyle and our ideals, and contemplating the creator who lives among us and surrounds us."[93] This is "an attitude of the heart."[94] It requires a fully ecological Catholic virtue ethics. Attunement's role in prudence became evident in this book's chapter 5. The integral ecology that Pope Francis imagines ultimately calls for habits of attunement. It is "the sort of sustained attention we need to develop" in order to survive and grow.[95] Integral ecology is a foundational step for a lifetime of growth and development. We can enjoy this process when we understand ourselves as embodying with agency the places where God and creation encounter one another and participating in these intersections. From these places, the view of creation and of morality is marvelous. That is the gift of an ecological model of moral character.

NOTES

1. Rourke, "A Catholic Virtues Ecology."
2. Pope John Paul II, "Sollicitudo Rei Socialis," para. 38.

3. See Otto, *The Idea of the Holy*; and James, *The Varieties of Religious Experience*. For a useful summary of both, see Herling, *A Beginner's Guide to the Study of Religion*, 62–67.

4. Some of these are cataloged as frequently named ecological virtues in Van Wensveen, *Dirty Virtues*, 164.

5. Elements of this argument can be found in Rourke, "A Catholic Virtues Ecology," 196–97.

6. McFague, *The Body of God*, 121.

7. Rourke, "A Catholic Virtues Ecology," 196–97. See, for example, Rachel Carson's writings about the sea. Carson, *The Sea around Us*; and Carson, *The Edge of the Sea*.

8. See, for example, *Laudato si'*, para. 138 and 141.

9. Rourke, "A Catholic Virtues Ecology," 197.

10. *Laudato si'*, para. 225.

11. Cloutier, *Walking God's Earth*, 17.

12. Lewis, *Surprised by Joy*, 167.

13. Anthony, "Walking as Resistance to Hypermobility."

14. Much of the following section describing "integrity" is developed from Rourke, "Good Chaos, Bad Chaos, and the Meaning of Integrity in Both"; and Rourke, "A Catholic Virtues Ecology."

15. See Westra, *An Environmental Proposal for Ethics*; and Westra, *Living in Integrity*. Westra's definition of integrity focused on a steady persistence through circumstances. This fits Westra's priority, which has been to restrain human influence on environments in order to conserve critical wild spaces.

16. Boff, *Cry of the Earth, Cry of the Poor*, 6–7 (emphasis added).

17. Clark, "Anatomy of a Social Virtue," 194.

18. Clark, 195. For more on indebtedness as a morally and ecologically significant concept, see Ka, "Environment," 221.

19. Copeland, "Memory, #BlackLivesMatter, and Theologians," 1.

20. O'Connell, "The Dance of Open Minds and Hearts."

21. The idea of reverse racism is one example of this kind of error. See Horan, *A White Catholic's Guide to Racism and Privilege*; and Massingale, *Racial Justice and the Catholic Church*.

22. O'Connell, "The Dance of Open Minds and Hearts," 80.

23. Butkus, "Solidarity," 185.

24. I disagree in this respect with Jason Kawall and Ronald Sandler. See Kawall, "Inner Diversity," 29; and Sandler, *Character and Environment*, 10–11.

25. Bouma-Prediger, *Earthkeeping and Character*, 97–98.

26. Bouma-Prediger, 110.

27. Bouma-Prediger, 70–72.

28. Bouma-Prediger, 121–22.

29. Camp Fowler is a children's summer camp of the Reformed Church of America, a significant Christian denomination in central New York state. The camp emphasizes ecological awareness and skills and faith development.

30. *Laudato si'*, para. 202.

31. *Laudato si'*, para. 69, 88, 211, 217, and 224. Paragraph 69 does not actually refer to moral virtue.

32. By "pastorally motivated document" I mean that this encyclical's topics, language, and tone indicate an intended audience beyond clergy, theologians, and ethicists. It is meant for all to read and to understand.

33. These groups met in the diocese of Rochester at St. John the Evangelist (July 2015), St. Monica's (September 2015), the Church of the Transfiguration (May 2016), the SouthEast Rochester parish (July and August 2016), and the mother house of the Sisters of St. Joseph (October 2016).
34. The term "attitude" appears fourteen times, and "mindset" appears eight times. Each of these are used to refer to habits of thought, or tendencies to think, act, and believe in a certain way.
35. *Laudato si'*, para. 97.
36. Edwards, *Ecology at the Heart of Faith*, 51.
37. *Laudato si'*, para. 98.
38. *Laudato si'*, para. 215.
39. *Laudato si'*, para. 217.
40. *Laudato si'*, para. 208.
41. *Laudato si'*, para. 217–18 and 219.
42. See *Laudato si'*, 123, 181, 196, 210, 215, and 219.
43. "Mindset," dictionary.com (emphasis added).
44. "Mindset," *The American Heritage Stedman's Medical Dictionary* (Houghton Mifflin 2002) (emphasis added).
45. *Laudato si'*, para. 138, 169, and 229.
46. *Laudato si'*, para. 169, 25, 67, and 105.
47. *Laudato si'*, para. 11, 126, and 223–24. Paragraph 126 also notes protectiveness and respectfulness.
48. *Laudato si'*, para. 223 and 242.
49. *Laudato si'*, para. 66.
50. *Laudato si'*, para. 169.
51. *Laudato si'*, para. 11.
52. *Laudato si'*, para. 222.
53. *Laudato si'*, para. 242.
54. *Laudato si'*, para. 220, 226, and 227.
55. According to online dictionaries, "attitude" refers to a "manner, disposition, feeling, position," a "position or posture of the body," and the "inclination of the three principal axes of an aircraft." Attitude is also "the way a person views something or tends to behave towards it, often in an evaluative way." "Attitude," dictionary.com, http://dictionary.reference.com/browse/attitude.
56. *Laudato si'*, para. 222.
57. See, for example, Martha C. Nussbaum, "What Makes Life Good?," *The Nation*, April 13, 2011; and Nussbaum, *Creating Capabilities*.
58. Boff, *Cry of the Earth, Cry of the Poor*, 6 (emphasis added).
59. *Laudato si'*, para. 217, quoting Pope Benedict XVI, "Homily for the Solemn Inauguration of the Petrine Ministry," 710.
60. Miller, "Integral Ecology," 11.
61. Pope John Paul II, "Centesimus Annus," para. 36.
62. Pope John Paul II, 37.
63. Pope John Paul II, 38.
64. Pope John Paul II, para. 38.
65. Pope Benedict XVI, "Message for the Celebration of the World Day of Peace 2007," para. 8; and Pope Benedict XVI, *Caritas in Veritate*, para. 51. A thoughtful analysis of

gender would benefit the document in discerning more carefully between divine agency (what God created) and human agency (what social structures humans have assembled). We await the magisterium's willingness to take up this question seriously.

66. Benedict XVI, *Caritas in Veritate*, para. 51.

67. As Denis Edwards noted, "Scientific cosmology and evolutionary biology offer fundamental resources for an ecological theology of the human. . . . They situate the human in relation to the history of the universe and the history of life on Earth." Such a theology can, he continues, "build on the resources of the Christian tradition concerning the identity of the human being before God." Edwards, *Ecology at the Heart of Faith*, 7. See also Swimme and Berry, *The Universe Story from the Primordial Flaring Forth to the Ecozoic Era*.

68. *Laudato si'*, para. 240.

69. Miller, "Integral Ecology," 11 and 19.

70. Miller, 18 (emphasis added), citing *Laudato si'*, para. 137.

71. *Laudato si'*, para. 111.

72. I am grateful to Dr. Dan DiLeo, director of the Peace and Justice Project at Creighton University, who in a 2016 private conversation helped me to think through this concept. See DiLeo, *All Creation Is Connected*.

73. *Laudato si'*, para. 4.

74. *Laudato si'*, para. 160.

75. Miller, "Integral Ecology," 15.

76. *Laudato si'*, para. 10.

77. See Leopold, *A Sand County Almanac, and Sketches Here and There*, 120. For more on this famous story and its context, see Lorbiecki, *Aldo Leopold*; and Meine, *Aldo Leopold*.

78. IPCC, "Climate Change 2021," 6.

79. International Energy Agency (IEA), *Net Zero by 2050: A Roadmap for the Global Energy Sector* (May 2021), "Summary for Policy Makers," 13.

80. IPCC, "Synthesis Report of the IPCC Sixth Assessment Report (AR6)," 34–35.

81. For example, the deoxygenation of ocean waters kills the life of coral reefs, which in turn eliminates ecosystems that could otherwise reabsorb greenhouse gas emissions. IPCC, "Synthesis Report," 34 and 36.

82. Blanchard and O'Brien, *An Introduction to Christian Environmentalism*, 7. They draw on Frances Westley, Michael Quinn and Brenda Zimmerman, *Getting to Maybe: How the World Is Changed* (Toronto: Vintage Canada, 2007), 6–11.

83. For more on scale, see O'Brien, *An Ethics of Biodiversity*.

84. *Laudato si'*, para. 60 and 139.

85. *Laudato si'*, para. 139.

86. *Laudato si'*, para. 140.

87. *Laudato si'*, para. 141.

88. "Sustainability Initiative," Canisius University, https://www.canisius.edu/academics/our-schools/college-arts-sciences/sustainability-initiative. Disclosure: I am a founding member of this group.

89. Bouma-Prediger, *Earthkeeping and Character*, 127–29. My own experiences of Kent Busman and of working at Camp Fowler have informed my description of this role model, offered first by Bouma-Prediger.

90. Bouma-Prediger, *Earthkeeping and Character*, 129.

91. Hanna-Attisha, *What the Eyes Don't See*.

92. Kim Kozlowski, "Hanna-Attisha Tells MSU Grads to Stand Up, Speak Out," *Detroit News*, May 6, 2016, https://www.detroitnews.com/story/news/local/michigan/2016/05/06/michigan-state-commencement-hanna-attisha/84026134/; Russ White, "Mona Hanna-Attisha: 'Flipping the Story' in Flint," Mlive, February 24, 2016, https://www.mlive.com/environment/2016/02/mona_hanna-attisha_flipping_th.html; David Wahlberg, "Flint Doctor Used Epic Systems Records to Expose Lead Crisis," *Wisconsin State Journal*, January 30, 2016, https://madison.com/news/local/health-med-fit/flint-doctor-used-epic-systems-records-to-expose-lead-crisis/article_ef462592-f27b-5ed0-a2ff-33232902ab74.html; "High School Friend Sounded First Alert to Flint's Dr. Mona Hanna-Attisha," Michigan Radio, February 16, 2016, https://www.michiganradio.org/health/2016-02-16/high-school-friend-sounded-first-alert-to-flints-dr-mona-hanna-attisha; and Mona Hanna-Attisha, *What the Eyes Don't See*.

93. *Laudato si'*, para. 225.

94. *Laudato si'*, para. 226.

95. Miller, "Integral Ecology," 19.

Bibliography

Alexander, Michelle. *The New Jim Crow: Mass Incarceration in the Age of Colorblindness*. New York: New Press, 2010.

Anthony, Cara. "Walking as Resistance to Hypermobility: The Camino de Santiago Pilgrimage." *Spiritus: A Journal of Christian Spirituality* 18, no. 1 (2018): 1–13.

Aquinas, Thomas. *Summa Theologica*. Christian Classics Ethereal Library. https://www.ccel.org/a/aquinas/summa/home.html.

Auerbach, Michael J. "Stability, Probability, and the Topology of Food Webs." In *Ecological Communities: Conceptual Issues and the Evidence*, ed. Donald R. Strong et al., 413–36. Princeton, NJ: Princeton University Press, 1984.

Austin, Nicholas. "Normative Virtue Theory in Theological Ethics." *Religions* 8, no. 211 (2017): 1–9. https://doi.org/doi:10.3390/rel8100211.

Barron, Robert. *The Priority of Christ: Toward a Postliberal Catholicism*. Grand Rapids, MI: Brazos Press, 2007.

Bell, Catherine M. *Ritual Theory, Ritual Practice*. New York: Oxford University Press, 1992.

Bennett, Joshua. *Being Property Once Myself: Blackness and the End of Man*. Cambridge, MA: Harvard University Press, 2020.

Berges, Sandrine. *A Feminist Perspective on Virtue Ethics*. New York: Palgrave Macmillan, 2015. https://cando.canisius.edu/record=b2310598.

Berry, Thomas. *The Dream of the Earth*. San Francisco: Sierra Club Books, 2006.

———. "The New Story: Comments on the Origin, Identification and Transmission of Values." *CrossCurrents* 37, nos. 2–3 (Summer/Fall 1987): 187–99.

Berry, Wendell. *Another Turn of the Crank*. Washington, DC: Counterpoint, 1995.

———. *The Gift of Good Land: Further Essays Cultural and Agricultural*. San Francisco: North Point, 1981.

———. *What Are People For?* San Francisco: North Point, 1990.

Blanchard, Kathryn, and Kevin O'Brien. *An Introduction to Christian Environmentalism: Ecology, Virtue, and Ethics*. Waco, TX: Baylor University Press, 2014).

Bloomfield, Jay A., Scott O. Quinn, Ronald J. Scrudato, Dean Long, Arthur Richards, and Frank Ryan. "Atmospheric and Watershed Inputs of Mercury to Cranberry Lake, St. Lawrence County, New York." In *Polluted Rain*, ed. Taft Y. Toribara, Morton W. Miller, and Paul E. Morrow, 175–210. Environmental Science Research. Boston: Springer US, 1980. https://doi.org/10.1007/978-1-4613-3060-8_9.

Boff, Leonardo. *Cry of the Earth, Cry of the Poor*. Ecology and Justice. Maryknoll, NY: Orbis Books, 1997.

———. *Ecology & Liberation: A New Paradigm*. Maryknoll, NY: Orbis Books, 1995.

Bouma-Prediger, Steven. *Earthkeeping and Character: Exploring a Christian Ecological Virtue Ethic*. Grand Rapids, MI: Baker Academic, 2019.

———. *For the Beauty of the Earth: A Christian Vision for Creation Care*. 2nd ed. Grand Rapids, MI: Baker Academic, 2010.

Brown, Stephen F. "The Theological Virtue of Faith: An Invitation to an Ecclesial Life of Truth (IIa IIae, qq. 1–16)." In *The Ethics of Aquinas*, ed. Stephen J. Pope, 221–31. Moral Traditions Series. Washington, DC: Georgetown University Press, 2002.

Bullard, Robert D. *Dumping in Dixie: Race, Class, and Environmental Quality*. Boulder, CO: Westview, 2008.

Burger, Joanna, Mark Pokras, Rebecca Chafel, and Michael Gochfeld. "Heavy Metal Concentrations in Feathers of Common Loons (Gavia Immer) in the Northeastern United States and Age Differences in Mercury Levels." *Environmental Monitoring and Assessment* 30, no. 1 (March 1, 1994): 1–7. https://doi.org/10.1007/BF00546196.

Burwell, Dollie, and Luke W. Cole, "Environmental Justice Comes Full Circle: Warren County Before and After." *Golden Gate University Environmental Law Journal* 1, no. 9 (2007): 9–40.

Butkus, Russell. "Solidarity: Does the Modern Catholic Rights Tradition Have Anything to Offer Environmental Virtue Ethics?" *Environmental Ethics* 37 (Summer 2015): 169–86.

Byrd, Allison. "Common Loon (Gavia Immer) Biogeography and Reproductive Success in an Era of Climate Change." Master's thesis, University of Maine, 2013. https://umaine.edu/olsenlab/wp-content/uploads/sites/384/2020/01/Byrd2013.pdf.

Cafaro, Philip. "Patriotism as Environmental Virtue." In *Virtue Ethics and the Environment*, ed. Philip Cafaro and Ronald Sandler, 185–206. Dordrecht, Netherlands: Springer, 2010.

———. "Thoreau, Leopold, and Carson: Toward an Environmental Virtue Ethics." In *Environmental Virtue Ethics*, ed. Ronald D Sandler and Philip Cafaro, 31–46. Lanham, MD: Rowman & Littlefield, 2005.

Cafaro, Philip, and Ronald Sandler. *Virtue Ethics and the Environment*. 1st ed. Dordrecht, Netherlands: Springer, 2010.

Callicott, J. Baird. *Thinking like a Planet: The Land Ethic and the Earth Ethic*. New York: Oxford University Press, 2013.

Calow, Peter P. *Blackwell's Concise Encyclopedia of Ecology*. Hoboken, NJ: Wiley, 1999. http://ebookcentral.proquest.com/lib/canisius/detail.action?docID=428016.

Card, Claudia. *Virtues and Moral Luck*. Madison: University of Wisconsin–Madison Law School, 1985.

Carson, Rachel. *The Edge of the Sea*. Boston: Houghton Mifflin, 1955.

———. *The Sea around Us*. New York: Simon and Schuster, 1958.

———. *Silent Spring*. Boston: Houghton Mifflin, 1962.

Cassel, Eric J. "The Nature of Suffering and the Goals of Medicine." *New England Journal of Medicine* 306, no. 11 (March 18, 1982): 639–45.

"Catechism of the Catholic Church." Libreria Editrice Vaticana, Citta del Vaticano, 1993. https://www.vatican.va/archive/ENG0015/_INDEX.HTM.

Cates, Diana Fritz. "The Virtue of Temperance (IIa IIae, qq. 141–170)." In *The Ethics of Aquinas*, ed. Stephen J. Pope, 321–39. Moral Traditions Series. Washington, DC: Georgetown University Press, 2002.

Cebes, ed. *Cebes' Tablet: Facsimiles of the Greek Text, and of Selected Latin, French, English, Spanish, Italian, German, Dutch, and Polish Translations.* Renaissance Text Series. New York: Renaissance Society of America, 1979.

Centers for Disease Control and Prevention. "Coronavirus Disease 2019 (COVID-19)—Environmental Cleaning and Disinfection Recommendations." Centers for Disease Control and Prevention, February 11, 2020. https://www.cdc.gov/coronavirus/2019-ncov/prevent-getting-sick/cleaning-disinfection.html.

Cessario, Romanus. *The Moral Virtues and Theological Ethics.* Notre Dame, IN: University of Notre Dame Press, 2009.

Cherrett, J. M., and A. D. Bradshaw, eds. *Ecological Concepts: The Contribution of Ecology to an Understanding of the Natural World.* Brookline Village, MA: Blackwell Scientific Publications, 1989.

Clark, Meghan J. "Anatomy of a Social Virtue: Solidarity and Corresponding Vices." *Political Theology* 15, no. 1 (2014): 26–39. https://doi.org/10.1179/1462317X13Z.00000000060.

Cloutier, David. *Walking God's Earth: The Environment and Catholic Faith.* Collegeville, MN: Liturgical Press, 2014.

Coblentz, Jessica, *Dust in the Blood: A Theology of Life with Depression.* Collegeville, MN: Liturgical Press, 2022.

Coldsnow, Kayla D., Brian M. Mattes, William D. Hintz, and Rick A. Relyea. "Rapid Evolution of Tolerance to Road Salt in Zooplankton." *Environmental Pollution* 222 (March 1, 2017): 367–73. https://doi.org/10.1016/j.envpol.2016.12.024.

Commission for Racial Justice United Church of Christ. "Toxic Wastes and Race: A National Report on the Racial and Socio-Economic Characteristics of Communities with Hazardous Waste Sites." United Church of Christ, 1987. http://www.ucc.org/.

Cooper, Gregory. "Generalizations in Ecology: A Philosophical Taxonomy." *Biology and Philosophy* 13, no. 4 (October 1998): 555–86. https://doi.org/10.1023/A:1006508101996.

Copeland, M. Shawn. "Memory, #BlackLivesMatter, and Theologians." *Political Theology* 17, no. 1 (March 17, 2016): 1–3.

Cornell Lab of Ornithology. "Common Loon Life History." All about Birds, accessed July 16, 2019. https://www.allaboutbirds.org/guide/Common_Loon/lifehistory.

Costanza, Robert, and Michael Mageau. "What Is a Healthy Ecosystem?" *Aquatic Ecology* 33, no. 1 (March 1, 1999): 105–15.

Daly, Daniel. "Critical Realism, Virtue Ethics, and Moral Agency." In *Moral Agency within Social Structures and Culture: A Primer on Critical Realism for Christian Ethics,* ed. Daniel K. Finn, 89–100. Washington, DC: Georgetown University Press, 2020. http://press.georgetown.edu/book/georgetown/moral-agency-within-social-structures-and-culture.

———. "Structures of Virtue and Vice." *New Blackfriars* 92, no. 1039 (2011): 341–57.

Davison, Andrew. *Participation in God: A Study in Christian Doctrine and Metaphysics.* Cambridge: Cambridge University Press, 2019.

Deane-Drummond, Celia. "Living Narratives: Defiant Earth or Integral Ecology in the Age of Humans?" *Heythrop Journal* 59, no. 6 (2018): 914–28. https://doi.org/10.1111/heyj.13013.

Deane-Drummond, Celia, and Rebecca Artinian-Kaiser. *Theology and Ecology across the Disciplines: On Care for Our Common Home.* London: Bloomsbury Publishing, 2018.

Dickins, T. E., and R. A. Barton. "Reciprocal Causation and the Proximate-Ultimate Distinction." *Biology & Philosophy* 28, no. 5 (September 2013): 747–56.

DiLeo, Daniel. *All Creation Is Connected: Voices in Response to Pope Francis Encyclical on Ecology.* Winona, MN: Anselm Academic, 2018.

Dillon, Dana. "The Vital Cell: Subsidiarity and a Family-Centered Approach to Accompanying Persons with Mental Illness." Presentation at the Annual Meeting of the College Theology Society, May 30, 2020.

Edwards, Denis. *Ecology at the Heart of Faith*. Ossining, NY: Orbis Books, 2014.

———. *How God Acts: Creation, Redemption, and Special Divine Action*. Theology and the Sciences. Minneapolis, MN: Fortress, 2010.

———. *Partaking of God: Trinity, Evolution, and Ecology*. Collegeville, MN: Liturgical Press, 2014.

Erhard, Nancie. *Moral Habitat: Ethos and Agency for the Sake of Earth*. Albany, NY: SUNY Press, 2012. http://ebookcentral.proquest.com/lib/canisius/reader.action?docID=3407425.

Finn, Daniel K. *Moral Agency within Social Structures and Culture: A Primer on Critical Realism for Christian Ethics*. Washington, DC: Georgetown University Press, 2020. http://press.georgetown.edu/book/georgetown/moral-agency-within-social-structures-and-culture.

Fitzgerald, John T., and L. Michael White, eds. *The Tabula of Cebes*. Texts and Translations, Graeco-Roman Religion Series, 24.7. Chico, CA: Scholars Press, 1983.

Fontaine, Colin. "Abundant Equals Nested." *Nature* 500, no. 7463 (August 2013): 411–12. https://doi.org/10.1038/500411a.

Frasz, Geoffrey. "Benevolence as an Environmental Virtue." In *Environmental Virtue Ethics*, ed. Ronald D. Sandler and Philip Cafaro, 121–34. Lanham, MD: Rowman & Littlefield, 2005.

———. "Environmental Virtue Ethics: A New Direction for Environmental Ethics." *Environmental Ethics: An Interdisciplinary Journal Dedicated to the Philosophical Aspects of Environmental Problems* 15, no. 3 (September 1, 1993): 259–74.

———. "What Is Environmental Virtue Ethics That We Should Be Mindful of It?" *Philosophy in the Contemporary World* 8, no. 2 (September 1, 2001): 5–14.

Fullam, Lisa. "Sex in 3-D: A Telos for a Virtue Ethics of Sexuality." *Journal of the Society of Christian Ethics* 27, no. 2 (Fall/Winter 2007): 151–70.

Gallagher, David M. "The Will and Its Acts (Ia IIae, qq. 6–17)." In *The Ethics of Aquinas*, ed. Stephen J. Pope, 69–89. Moral Traditions Series. Washington, DC: Georgetown University Press, 2002.

Gardner, A., and A. Grafen. "Capturing the Superorganism: A Formal Theory of Group Adaptation." *Journal of Evolutionary Biology* 22, no. 4 (2009): 659–71. https://doi.org/10.1111/j.1420-9101.2008.01681.x.

Gosling, Jonathan, and Peter Case. "Social Dreaming and Ecocentric Ethics: Sources of Non-Rational Insight in the Face of Climate Change Catastrophe." *Organization* 20, no. 5 (September 1, 2013): 705–21. https://doi.org/10.1177/1350508413489814.

Grimes, Katie Walker: *Christ Divided: Antiblackness as Corporate Vice*. Minneapolis, MN: Fortress, 2017.

Groppe, Elizabeth. *Eating and Drinking*. Minneapolis, MN: Fortress, 2010.

Grossman, Karl. "Of Toxic Racism and Environmental Justice." *E: The Environmental Magazine*, June 1992.

Guelke, Jeanne Kay. "Looking for Jesus in Christian Environmental Ethics." *Environmental Ethics* 26, no. 2 (May 1, 2004): 115–34. https://doi.org/10.5840/enviroethics200426225.

Hanna-Attisha, Mona. *What the Eyes Don't See: A Story of Crisis, Resistance, and Hope in an American City*. New York: Random House, 2018.

Harris, Melanie. "Ecowomanism: An Introduction." In *Ecowomanism, Religion and Ecology*, ed. Melanie Marris, 3–12. Boston: Brill, 2017. https://brill.com/view/title/35249.

———, ed. *Ecowomanism, Religion and Ecology*. Boston: Brill, 2017. https://brill.com/view/title/35249.

———. *Gifts of Virtue, Alice Walker, and Womanist Ethics*. New York: Palgrave Macmillan, 2010.

———. "Sacred Blood, Transformation, and Ecowomanism." *Reflections: Crucified Creation: A Green Faith Rising*, Spring 2019. https://reflections.yale.edu/article/crucified-creation-green-faith-rising/sacred-blood-transformation-and-ecowomanism.

Hart, John. *Sacramental Commons: Christian Ecological Ethics*. Nature's Meaning. Lanham, MD: Rowman & Littlefield, 2006.

Hawksley, Theodora. "How Critical Realism Can Help Catholic Social Teaching." In *Moral Agency within Social Structures and Culture: A Primer on Critical Realism for Christian Ethics*, ed. Daniel K. Finn, 9–18. Washington, DC: Georgetown University Press, 2020.

Herling, Bradley L. *A Beginner's Guide to the Study of Religion*. 2nd ed. London: Bloomsbury Academic, 2016.

Hill, Thomas, Jr. "Comments on Frasz and Cafaro on Environmental Virtue Ethics." *Philosophy in the Contemporary World* 8, no. 2 (September 1, 2001): 59–62.

———. "Ideals of Human Excellence and Preserving Natural Environments." In *Environmental Virtue Ethics*, ed. Ronald D. Sandler and Philip Cafaro, 47–60. Oxford, UK: Rowman & Littlefield, 2005.

Hill, Thomas E. "Finding Value in Nature." *Environmental Values* 15, no. 3 (2006): 331–41.

Hintz, William D., and Rick A. Relyea. "A Review of the Species, Community, and Ecosystem Impacts of Road Salt Salinisation in Fresh Waters." *Freshwater Biology* 64, no. 6 (2019): 1081–97. https://doi.org/10.1111/fwb.13286.

Hölldobler, Bert and Edward O. Wilson. *The Superorganism: The Beauty, Elegance, and Strangeness of Insect Societies*. W. W. Norton & Company, 2009.

Holmes, Rolston, III. "Ecology: A Primer for Christian Ethics." *Journal of Catholic Social Thought* 4, no. 2 (2007): 293–312.

Hoose, Bernard. *Proportionalism: The American Debate and Its European Roots*. Washington, DC: Georgetown University Press, 1987.

Horan, Daniel P. *A White Catholic's Guide to Racism and Privilege*. Notre Dame, IN: Ave Maria Press, 2021.

Hulme, Mike. "Climate Change and Virtue: An Apologetic." *Humanities* 3, no. 3 (2014): 299–312. http://dx.doi.org.ezproxy.canisius.edu/10.3390/h3030299.

Intergovernmental Panel on Climate Change (IPCC). "AR5 Climate Change 2013: The Physical Science Basis—IPCC." IPCC, 2013. https://www.ipcc.ch/report/ar5/wg1/.

———. "Climate Change: The IPCC 1990 and 1992 Assessments." IPCC, June 1992. https://www.ipcc.ch/report/climate-change-the-ipcc-1990-and-1992-assessments/.

———. "Climate Change 2021: The Physical Science Basis; Summary for Policymakers." IPCC, 2021. https://www.ipcc.ch/report/ar6/wg1/downloads/report/IPCC_AR6_WGI_SPM_final.pdf.

———. "Climate Change 2022: Impacts, Adaptation and Vulnerability. Contribution of Working Group II to the Sixth Assessment Report of the Intergovernmental Panel on Climate Change." IPCC, 2022. https://report.ipcc.ch/ar6/wg2/IPCC_AR6_WGII_FullReport.pdf.

———. "Global Warming of 1.5°C (SR15)." IPCC, 2018. https://www.ipcc.ch/site/assets/uploads/sites/2/2022/06/SPM_version_report_LR.pdf.

———. "Synthesis Report of the IPCC Sixth Assessment Report (AR6)." IPCC, 2023.

International Energy Agency. "Net Zero by 2050: A Roadmap for the Global Energy Sector." IEA, May 2021. https://iea.blob.core.windows.net/assets/deebef5d-0c34-4539-9d0c-10b13d840027/NetZeroby2050-ARoadmapfortheGlobalEnergySector_CORR.pdf.

James, William. *The Varieties of Religious Experience*. Cambridge, MA: Harvard University Press, 1985.

Jamieson, Dale. *Reason in a Dark Time: Why the Struggle against Climate Change Failed and What It Means for Our Future*. New York: Oxford University Press, 2014.

Jenkins, Willis. *Ecologies of Grace: Environmental Ethics and Christian Theology*. Oxford: Oxford University Press, 2008.

———. *The Future of Ethics: Sustainability, Social Justice, and Religious Creativity*. Washington, DC: Georgetown University Press, 2013.

Jennings, Willie James. *The Christian Imagination: Theology and the Origins of Race*. New Haven, CT: Yale University Press, 2010.

Jensen, Steven J. "Virtuous Deliberation and the Passions." *The Thomist: A Speculative Quarterly Review* 77, no. 2 (April 2013): 193–227.

Jessup, Christine M., et al. "Big Questions, Small Worlds: Microbial Model Systems in Ecology." *Trends in Ecology & Evolution* 19, no. 4 (April 1, 2004): 189–97.

Johnson, Elizabeth A. *Ask the Beasts: Darwin and the God of Love*. London: Bloomsbury, 2014.

Johnson, Jerald B., and Kristian S. Omland. "Model Selection in Ecology and Evolution." *Trends in Ecology & Evolution* 19, no. 2 (February 1, 2004): 101–8.

Johnstone, Brian V. "The Meaning of Proportionate Reason in Contemporary Moral Theology." *Thomist* 49 (1985): 223–47.

Jones, Robert P. *White Too Long: The Legacy of White Supremacy in American Christianity*. New York: Simon and Schuster, 2020.

Judson, Olivia P. "The Rise of the Individual-Based Model in Ecology." *Trends in Ecology & Evolution* 9, no. 1 (January 1, 1994): 9–14.

Ka, Hannah. "Environment." In *Asian American Christian Ethics: Voices, Methods, Issues*, ed. Grace Y. Kao and Ilsup Ahn, 203–21. Waco, TX: Baylor University Press, 2016. https://muse.jhu.edu/chapter/1836112.

Kaczor, Christopher. "Double-Effect Reasoning from Jean Pierre Gury to Peter Knauer." *Theological Studies* 59, no. 2 (May 1998): 297–316.

———. *Proportionalism and the Natural Law Tradition*. Washington, DC: Catholic University of America Press, 2002.

Kahm, Nicholas. *Aquinas on Emotion's Participation in Reason*. Washington, DC: Catholic University of America Press, 2019.

Karasov, William H. "Digestive Physiology: A View from Molecules to Ecosystem." *American Journal of Physiology-Regulatory, Integrative and Comparative Physiology* 301, no. 2 (June 8, 2011): R276–84. https://doi.org/10.1152/ajpregu.00600.2010.

Karban, Richard. *How to Do Ecology: A Concise Handbook*. Princeton, NJ: Princeton University Press, 2006.

Kawall, Jason. "Inner Diversity: An Alternative Ecological Virtue Ethics." *Philosophy in the Contemporary World* 8, no. 2 (September 1, 2001): 27–35.

Keenan, James F. "How Catholic Are the Virtues?" *America* 176 (June 7, 1997): 16–22.

———. "Learning the Virtue of Justice." *Church* 9 (1993): 38–40.

———. "Virtue Ethics: Making a Case as It Comes of Age." *Thought* 67 (June 1992): 115–27.

———. "Virtue Ethics and Sexual Ethics." *Louvain Studies* 30, no. 3 (Fall 2005): 180–97.

———. *Virtues for Ordinary Christians*. Lanham, MD: Rowman & Littlefield, 1996.

Kent, Bonnie. "Habits and Virtues (Ia IIae, qq. 49–70)." In *The Ethics of Aquinas*, ed. Stephen J. Pope, 116–30. Moral Traditions Series. Washington, DC: Georgetown University Press, 2002.

Kerr, Fergus. *After Aquinas: Versions of Thomism*. Oxford, UK: Blackwell, 2002.

Kinghorn, Warren. "Presence of Mind: Thomistic Prudence and Contemporary Mindfulness Practices." *Journal of the Society of Christian Ethics* 35, no. 1 (May 13, 2015): 83–102. https://doi.org/10.1353/sce.2015.0009.

Kirschenmann, Frederick: "On Becoming Lovers of the Soil." In *Cultivating an Ecological Conscience: Essays from a Farmer Philosopher*, ed. Constance L. Falk, 284–89. Lexington: University Press of Kentucky, 2010).

Knauer, Peter. "The Hermeneutic Function of the Principle of Double Effect." *Natural Law Forum* 12 (1967): 132–62.

Kolb, Robert W. *The Natural Gas Revolution: At the Pivot of the World's Energy Future*. Upper Saddle River, NJ: Pearson Education, 2013.

———. *Too Much Is Not Enough: Incentives in Executive Compensation*. Financial Management Association Survey and Synthesis Series. New York: Oxford University Press, 2012.

Kormondy, Edward J. *Concepts of Ecology*. 2nd ed. Concepts of Modern Biology Series. Englewood Cliffs, NJ: Prentice-Hall, 1976.

Krebs, Charles J. *Why Ecology Matters*. Chicago: University of Chicago Press, 2016.

Kuhn, Anne, Jane Copeland, John Cooley, Harry Vogel, Kate Taylor, Diane Nacci, and Peter August. "Modeling Habitat Associations for the Common Loon (Gavia Immer) at Multiple Scales in Northeastern North America." *Avian Conservation and Ecology* 6, no. 1 (2011): 4. https://doi.org/10.5751/ACE-00451-060104.

Kutsch, Werner L., et al. "Environmental Indication: A Field Test of an Ecosystem Approach to Quantify Biological Self-Organization." *Ecosystems* 4, no. 1 (January 1, 2001): 49–66.

Laland, Kevin N., John Odling-Smee, William Hoppitt, and Tobias Uller. "More on How and Why: Cause and Effect in Biology Revisited." *Biology & Philosophy* 28, no. 5 (September 2013): 719–45.

Langan, John. "Augustine on the Unity and the Interconnection of the Virtues." *Harvard Theological Review* 72, nos. 1–2 (January 1, 1979): 81–95.

Larson, Douglas W., Uta Matthes, and Peter E. Kelly. *Cliff Ecology: Pattern and Process in Cliff Ecosystems*. Cambridge Studies in Ecology. Cambridge: Cambridge University Press, 2000.

Lear, Jonathan. *Radical Hope: Ethics in the Face of Cultural Devastation*. Cambridge, MA: Harvard University Press, 2009.

Leopold, Aldo. *A Sand County Almanac, and Sketches Here and There*. New York: Oxford University Press, 1987.

Lewis, C. S. *Surprised by Joy: The Shape of My Early Life*. New York: Harcourt, Brace & World, 1955.

Lloyd, Vincent. "For What Are Whites to Hope?" *Political Theology* 17, no. 2 (March 2016): 168–81.

Lorbiecki, Marybeth. *Aldo Leopold: A Fierce Green Fire*. Helena, MT: Falcon, 1996.

Lynch, William F. *Images of Hope: Imagination as Healer of the Hopeless*. Baltimore: Helicon, 1965.

MacIntyre, Alasdair C. *After Virtue: A Study in Moral Theory*. 2nd ed. Notre Dame, IN: University of Notre Dame Press, 1984.

———. *Dependent Rational Animals: Why Human Beings Need the Virtues*. Chicago: Open Court, 1999.

Martinsen, Ellen S., Inga F. Sidor, Sean Flint, John Cooley, and Mark A. Pokras. "Documentation of Malaria Parasite (Plasmodium Spp.) Infection and Associated Mortality in a Common Loon (Gavia Immer)." *Journal of Wildlife Diseases* 53, no. 4 (June 30, 2017): 859–63. https://doi.org/10.7589/2016-08-195.

Massingale, Bryan N. *Racial Justice and the Catholic Church*. Maryknoll, NY: Orbis Books, 2014.

McCann, Kevin S. *Food Webs*. Monographs in Population Biology 50. Princeton, NJ: Princeton University Press, 2012.

McDonagh, Sean. "The Death of Life: A Challenge to Christians." *Ecotheology* 7, no. 2 (January 2003): 202–12.

McFague, Sallie. *The Body of God: An Ecological Theology*. Minneapolis, MN: Augsburg Fortress, 1993.

———. "The Loving Eye vs the Arrogant Eye." *Ecumenical Review* 49, no. 2 (April 1997): 185–93.

McRae, Brad H., et al. "Using Circuit Theory to Model Connectivity in Ecology, Evolution, and Conservation." *Ecology* 89, no. 10 (2008): 2712–24.

Meilaender, Gilbert. "Josef Pieper: Explorations in the Thought of a Philosopher of Virtue." *Journal of Religious Ethics* 11, no. 1 (March 1, 1983): 114–34.

———. *The Theory and Practice of Virtue*. Notre Dame, IN: University of Notre Dame Press, 1984.

Meine, Curt. *Aldo Leopold: His Life and Work*. Madison: University of Wisconsin Press, 1988.

Meshram, Dilip, D. Catherine, Neha Badhe, Snehal Khedkar, Ritesh Vijay, and Tapas Nandy. "Zooplankton Diversity as Indicators of Pollution in Warm Monomictic Dal–Nigeen Lake." *Sustainable Water Resources Management* 4, no. 4 (December 1, 2018): 897–904. https://doi.org/10.1007/s40899-017-0183-7.

Miller, Vincent. "Integral Ecology: Francis' Moral and Spiritual Vision of Interconnectedness." In *The Theological and Ecological Vision of Laudato Si': Everything Is Connected*, ed. Vincent Miller, 11–28. London: Bloomsbury, 2018.

Morito, Bruce. *Thinking Ecologically: Environmental Thought, Values, and Policy*. Halifax, Nova Scotia: Fernwood, 2002.

Narvaez, Darcia. "The Co-Construction of Virtue: Epigenetics, Development and Culture." In *Cultivating Virtue: Perspectives from Philosophy, Theology, and Psychology*, ed. Nancy E. Snow, 251–78. New York: Oxford University Press, 2015.

Nash, James A. "Ecological Integrity and Christian Political Responsibility." *Theology and Public Policy* 1 (Fall 1989): 32–48.

Nussbaum, Martha C. *Creating Capabilities*. Cambridge, MA: Harvard University Press, 2011.

O'Brien, Kevin J. *An Ethics of Biodiversity: Christianity, Ecology, and the Variety of Life*. Washington, DC: Georgetown University Press, 2010.

O'Connell, Maureen H. "The Dance of Open Minds and Hearts: Aesthetic Solidarity as Antidote to an Anemic Solidarity." *Political Theology* 15, no. 1 (2014): 74–87. https://doi.org/10.1179/1462317X13Z.00000000063.

Odum, Eugene. *Fundamentals of Ecology*. Philadelphia: W. B. Saunders, 1953. http://hdl.handle.net/2027/mdp.39015001918880.

Odum, Howard T. *Ecological and General Systems: An Introduction to Systems Ecology.* Revised ed. Niwot: University Press of Colorado, 1994.

———. *Environment, Power, and Society for the Twenty-First Century: The Hierarchy of Energy.* New York: Columbia University Press, 2007.

———. *Systems Ecology: An Introduction.* New York: Wiley, 1983.

Otto, Rudolf. *The Idea of the Holy.* Oxford: Oxford University Press, 1958.

Pavé, Alain. *Modeling of Living Systems: From Cell to Ecosystem.* 1st ed. Somerset, NJ: Wiley, 2012.

Pieper, Josef. *Fortitude, and Temperance.* New York: Pantheon Books, 1954.

———. *The Four Cardinal Virtues: Prudence, Justice, Fortitude, Temperance.* 1st ed. New York: Harcourt, Brace & World, 1965.

———. *Prudence.* New York: Pantheon Books, 1959.

Pinckaers, Servais. *The Pinckaers Reader: Renewing Thomistic Moral Theology.* Edited by John Berkman and Craig Steven Titus. Washington, DC: Catholic University of America Press, 2005.

Pontifical Council for Justice and Peace. *Compendium of the Social Doctrine of the Church.* Washington, DC: USCCB Publishing, 2005. http://www.vatican.va/roman_curia/pontifical_councils/justpeace/documents/rc_pc_justpeace_doc_20060526_compendio-dott-soc_en.html.

Pope, Stephen J., ed. *The Ethics of Aquinas.* Moral Traditions Series. Washington, DC: Georgetown University Press, 2002.

Pope Benedict XVI. *Caritas in Veritate.* June 29, 2009. http://www.vatican.va/holy_father/benedict_xvi/encyclicals/documents/hf_ben-xvi_enc_20090629_caritas-in-veritate_en.html.

———. "Homily for the Solemn Inauguration of the Petrine Ministry." Libreria Editrice Vaticana, April 24, 2005. http://w2.vatican.va/content/benedict-xvi/en/homilies/2005/documents/hf_ben-xvi_hom_20050424_inizio-pontificato.html.

———. "Message for the Celebration of the World Day of Peace 2007." The Vatican, January 1, 2007. http://www.vatican.va/holy_father/benedict_xvi/messages/peace/documents/hf_ben-xvi_mes_20061208_xl-world-day-peace_en.html.

———. "Spes Salvi." Libreria Editrice Vaticana, November 30, 2007. http://www.vatican.va/content/benedict-xvi/en/encyclicals/documents/hf_ben-xvi_enc_20071130_spe-salvi.html.

Pope Francis. *Laudato si'.* The Vatican, 2015. http://w2.vatican.va/content/francesco/en/encyclicals/documents/papa-francesco_20150524_enciclica-laudato-si.html.

———. "Lumen Fidei." June 29, 2013. http://w2.vatican.va/content/francesco/en/encyclicals/documents/papa-francesco_20130629_enciclica-lumen-fidei.html.

Pope John Paul II. "Centesimus Annus." Libreria Editrice Vaticana, May 1, 1991. http://w2.vatican.va/content/john-paul-ii/en/encyclicals/documents/hf_jp-ii_enc_01051991_centesimus-annus.html.

———. "General Audience, God Made Man the Steward of Creation." January 17, 2001. http://w2.vatican.va/content/john-paul-ii/en/audiences/2001/documents/hf_jp-ii_aud_20010117.html.

———. "Sollicitudo Rei Socialis." Libreria Editrice Vaticana, December 30, 1987. http://www.vatican.va/content/john-paul-ii/en/encyclicals/documents/hf_jp-ii_enc_30121987_sollicitudo-rei-socialis.html.

Porter, Jean. *Justice as a Virtue: A Thomistic Perspective.* Grand Rapids, MI: Eerdmans, 2016.

———. *Recovery of Virtue.* Louisville, KY: Presbyterian Publishing, 1990.

———. "The Unity of the Virtues and the Ambiguity of Goodness: A Reappraisal of Aquinas's Theory of the Virtues." *Journal of Religious Ethics* 21, no. 1 (Spring 1993): 137–63.

———. "The Virtue of Justice (IIae, qq. 58-122)." In *The Ethics of Aquinas*, ed. Stephen J. Pope, 272–86. Moral Traditions Series. Washington, DC: Georgetown University Press, 2002.

Powell, S. "How Ecology Shapes Caste Evolution: Linking Resource Use, Morphology, Performance and Fitness in a Superorganism." *Journal of Evolutionary Biology* 22, no. 5 (2009): 1004–13.

Presbyterian Church of America. "Hazardous Waste, Race and the Environment." Presbyterian Church (USA), April 28, 2010. https://www.pcusa.org/resource/hazardous-waste-race-and-environment/.

Radde-Gallwitz, Andrew. "Gregory of Nyssa on the Reciprocity of the Virtues." *Journal of Theological Studies* 58, no. 2 (October 2007): 537–52.

Rafferty, John P., and John N. Thompson. "Coevolution." In *Encyclopedia Britannica*. Encyclopedia Britannica, Inc., January 9, 2020. https://www.britannica.com/science/coevolution.

Ramade, François. "Qualitative and Quantitative Criteria Defining a 'Healthy' Ecosystem." In *Evaluating and Monitoring the Health of Large-Scale Ecosystems*, ed. David J. Rapport, Connie L. Gaudet, and Peter Calow, 43–61. Berlin: Springer, 1995.

Rapport, David J. "Ecosystem Health: An Emerging Integrative Science." In *Evaluating and Monitoring the Health of Large-Scale Ecosystems*, ed. Connie L. Gaudet and Peter Calow, 5–31. NATO ASI Series 28. Berlin: Springer-Verlag, 1995. https://doi.org/10.1007/978-3-642-79464-3_1.

———. "What Constitutes Ecosystem Health?" *Perspectives in Biology and Medicine* 33, no. 1 (Autumn 1989): 120–32. https://doi.org/10.1353/pbm.1990.0004.

Rapport, David J., Connie L. Gaudet, and Peter Calow. *Evaluating and Monitoring the Health of Large-Scale Ecosystems*. Berlin: Springer Science & Business Media, 2013.

Razavi, Roxanna N., Susan F. Cushman, John D. Halfman, Trevor Massey, Robert Beutner, and Lisa B. Cleckner. "Mercury Bioaccumulation in Stream Food Webs of the Finger Lakes in Central New York State, USA." *Ecotoxicology and Environmental Safety* 172 (May 15, 2019): 265–72. https://doi.org/10.1016/j.ecoenv.2019.01.060.

Reas, Emilie. "Small Animals Live in a Slow-Motion World." *Scientific American*, July 1, 2014. https://doi.org/10.1038/scientificamericanmind0714-11a.

Rhonheimer, Martin. *Natural Law and Practical Reason: A Thomist View of Moral Autonomy*. New York: Fordham University Press, 2000.

Roberts, Alan, and Ken Tregonning. "The Robustness of Natural Systems." *Nature* 288, no. 5788 (November 1980): 265–66.

Rolston, Holmes, III. "Ecology: A Primer for Christian Ethics." *Journal of Catholic Social Thought* 4, no. 2 (2007): 293–312.

———. *Environmental Ethics: Duties to and Values in the Natural World*. Ethics and Action. Philadelphia: Temple University Press, 1988.

———. "Environmental Virtue Ethics: Half the Truth but Dangerous as a Whole." In *Environmental Virtue Ethics*, ed. Ronald D. Sandler and Philip Cafaro, 61–76. Lanham, MD: Rowman & Littlefield, 2005.

Rourke, Nancy M. "A Catholic Virtues Ecology." In *Just Sustainability: Ecology, Technology, and Resource Extraction*, ed. Christiana Z. Peppard and Andrea Vicini, 194–204. Maryknoll, NY: Orbis Books, 2015.

———. "The Consequences of Fossil Fuel Addiction in Schoharie County." *Journal of Moral Theology* 6, Special issue no. 1 (2017): 125–43.

———. "Environmental Justice: May Justice and Peace Flow like a River." In *A Just Peace Ethic: A Primer to Building Sustainable Peace and Breaking Cycles of Violence*, ed. Eli Sasaran McCarthy, 93–108. Washington, DC: Georgetown University Press, 2020.

———. "The Environment Within: Virtue Ethics." In *Green Discipleship: Catholic Theological Ethics and the Environment*, ed. Tobias L. Winright, 163–82. Winona, MN: Anselm Academic, 2011.

———. "God, Grace, and Creation: Shaping a Catholic Environmental Virtue Ethic." In *God, Grace, and Creation*, ed. Philip J. Rossi, 222–34. Maryknoll, NY: Orbis Books, 2010.

———. "Good Chaos, Bad Chaos, and the Meaning of Integrity in Both." In *An Unexpected Wilderness: Christianity and the Natural World*, vol. 61, ed. Colleen Carpenter, 79–89. College Theology Society Annual Volumes. Maryknoll, NY: Orbis Books, 2016.

———. "Pope Francis' Encyclical and Catholic Magisterial Statements on Ecological Ethics." In *Nature and the Environment in Contemporary Religious Contexts*, ed. Muhammad Shafiq and Thomas Donlin-Smith, 101–22. Newcastle upon Tyne, UK: Cambridge Scholars Publishing, 2018.

———. "Prudence Gone Wild." *Environmental Ethics: An Interdisciplinary Journal Dedicated to the Philosophical Aspects of Environmental Problems* 33 (Fall 2011): 249–66.

———. "Where Is the Wrong? A Comparison of Two Accounts of the Principle of Double Effect." *Irish Theological Quarterly* 76, no. 2 (May 2011): 150–63.

Russell, Daniel C. "Aristotle on Cultivating Virtue." In *Cultivating Virtue: Perspectives from Philosophy, Theology, and Psychology*, ed. Nancy E. Snow, 17–48. New York: Oxford University Press, 2015.

Sagan, Carl, Hans Bethe, S. Chandrasekhar, Paul J. Crutzen, and Dyson J. Freeman. "Preserving and Cherishing the Earth: An Appeal for Joint Commitment in Science and Religion," January 1990. http://fore.yale.edu/publications/statements/preserve/.

Sandler, Ronald L. *Character and Environment: A Virtue-Oriented Approach to Environmental Ethics*. New York: Columbia University Press, 2007.

———. "The External Goods Approach to Environmental Virtue Ethics." *Environmental Ethics* 25, no. 3 (Fall 2003): 279–93.

———. "A Virtue Ethics Perspective on Genetically Modified Crops." In *Environmental Virtue Ethics*, ed. Ronald Sandler and Philip Cafaro, 215–32. Oxford, UK: Rowman & Littlefield, 2005.

Sandler, Ronald and Philip Cafaro, eds. *Environmental Virtue Ethics*. Lanham, MD: Rowman & Littlefield, 2005.

Scarry, Elaine. *The Body in Pain: The Making and Unmaking of the World*. New York: Oxford University Press, 1985.

Scheid, Daniel. *The Cosmic Common Good: Religious Grounds for Ecological Ethics*. New York: Oxford University Press, 2016.

Schneberger, Edward. *The Black Crappie: Its Life History, Ecology and Management*. Madison, WI: Department of Natural Resources, 1972.

Schoch, Nina, Michale J. Glennon, David C. Evers, Melissa Duron, Allyson K. Jackson, Charles T. Driscoll, John W. Ozard, and Amy K. Sauer. "The Impact of Mercury Exposure on the Common Loon (Gavia Immer) Population in the Adirondack Park, New York, USA." *Waterbirds* 37, no. sp1 (April 2014): 133–46. https://doi.org/10.1675/063.037.sp116.

Schockenhoff, Ebhard. "The Theological Virtue of Charity (IIa IIae, 11. 23–46)." In *The Ethics of Aquinas*, ed. Stephen J. Pope, 221–31. Moral Traditions Series. Washington, DC: Georgetown University Press, 2002.

Scrudato, R. J., D. Long, and Robert Weinbloom. "Mercury Contribution to an Adirondack Lake." *Environmental Geology and Water Sciences* 9, no. 3 (October 1, 1987): 131–37. https://doi.org/10.1007/BF02449945.

Shadle, Matthew. "Culture." In *Moral Agency within Social Structures and Culture: A Primer on Critical Realism for Christian Ethics*, ed. Daniel K. Finn, 73–88. Georgetown University Press, 2020. http://press.georgetown.edu/book/georgetown/moral-agency-within -social-structures-and-culture.

Shaw, Bill. "A Virtue Ethics Approach to Aldo Leopold's Land Ethic." In *Environmental Virtue Ethics*, ed. Ronald D. Sandler and Philip Cafaro, 93–106. Lanham, MD: Rowman & Littlefield, 2005.

Sinclair, James S., and Shelley E. Arnott. "Local Context and Connectivity Determine the Response of Zooplankton Communities to Salt Contamination." *Freshwater Biology* 63, no. 10 (2018): 1273–86. https://doi.org/10.1111/fwb.13132.

Slingerland, Edward. "The Situationist Critique and Early Confucian Virtue Ethics." In *Cultivating Virtue: Perspectives from Philosophy, Theology, and Psychology*, ed. Nancy E Snow, 135–71. New York: Oxford University Press, 2015.

Slobodkin, Lawrence B. *A Citizen's Guide to Ecology*. New York: Oxford University Press, 2003.

Smith, Robert Leo. *Ecology and Field Biology*. 5th ed. New York: HarperCollins, 1996.

Smyth, J. Jones. "The Tablet of the Theban Cebes." *Southern Literary Messenger* 15, no. 10 (October 1849): 539–46.

Snow, Nancy E. *Cultivating Virtue: Perspectives from Philosophy, Theology, and Psychology*. New York: Oxford University Press, 2015.

Spicer, John. *Biodiversity: A Beginner's Guide*. London: Oneworld Publications, 2012.

Srinivasan, Umesh, Krishnapriya Tamma, and Uma Ramakrishnan. "Past Climate and Species Ecology Drive Nested Species Richness Patterns along an East-West Axis in the Himalaya." *Global Ecology and Biogeography* 23, no. 1 (2014): 52–60. https://doi.org/10 .1111/geb.12082.

Stager, Curt. "Update on the Ecological Condition of Adirondack Lakes." *Wild Earth* 6, no. 1 (Spring 1996): 29–33. https://www.environmentandsociety.org/sites/default/files/key _docs/wild_earth_6_1_small_1.pdf.

Stephen, Prothero. *Religion Matters: An Introduction to the World's Religions*. New York: Norton, 2020.

Stiltner, Brian. *Toward Thriving Communities: Virtue Ethics as Social Ethics*. Winona, MN: Anselm Academic, 2016.

Swimme, Brian, and Thomas Berry. *The Universe Story from the Primordial Flaring Forth to the Ecozoic Era: A Celebration of the Unfolding of the Cosmos*. 1st ed. San Francisco: HarperSanFrancisco, 1992.

Tessman, Lisa. *Burdened Virtues: Virtue Ethics for Liberatory Struggles*. Oxford: Oxford University Press, 2005.

———. "Critical Virtue Ethics: Understanding Oppression as Morally Damaging." In *Feminists Doing Ethics*, ed. Peggy DesAutels and Joanne Waugh, 79–100. Rowman & Littlefield, 2001.

Thompson, Allen. "Radical Hope for Living Well in a Warmer World." *Journal of Agricultural and Environmental Ethics* 23, no. 1–2 (2010): 43–59. http://dx.doi.org.ezproxy.canisius .edu/10.1007/s10806-009-9185-2.

Tribe, Michael A., Michael Eraut, and Roger K. Snook. *Ecological Principles*. Cambridge: Cambridge University Press, 1975.

Trimiew, Daryl. "Presidential Address." Presented at the annual meeting of the Society of Christian Ethics, Chicago, IL, January 8–11, 2009.

Tuttle, Carrie M., and Martin D. Heintzelman. "A Loon on Every Lake: A Hedonic Analysis of Lake Water Quality in the Adirondacks." *Resource and Energy Economics* 39 (February 1, 2015): 1–15. https://doi.org/10.1016/j.reseneeco.2014.11.001.

United Church of Christ Justice and Witness Ministries. "Toxic Wastes and Race at Twenty (1987–2007)." United Church of Christ, 2007. http://www.ucc.org/environmental-ministries_toxic-waste-20.

United States Environmental Protection Agency, and Office of Chemical Safety and Pollution Prevention. "Basic Information about Mercury." Overviews and Factsheets. Environmental Protection Agency, August 20, 2015. https://www.epa.gov/mercury/basic-information-about-mercury.

Valleau, Jamie, and Robin Summers. "Rock Salt Keeps Roads Safe in Winter—at a Serious Environmental Cost." *Quartz*, accessed July 16, 2019. https://qz.com/1538968/the-environmental-cost-of-using-rock-salt-on-roads-in-winter/.

Van Wensveen, Louke. "Attunement: An Ecological Spin on the Virtue of Temperance." *Philosophy in the Contemporary World* 8, no. 2 (Fall/Winter 2001): 67–78.

———. "Cardinal Environmental Virtues: A Neurobiological Perspective." In *Environmental Virtue Ethics*, ed. Ronald D. Sandler and Philip Cafaro, 173–96. Lanham, MD: Rowman & Littlefield, 2005.

———. *Dirty Virtues: The Emergence of Ecological Virtue Ethics*. Amherst, NY: Humanity Books, 1999.

———. "Ecosystem Sustainability as a Criterion for Genuine Virtue." *Environmental Ethics: An Interdisciplinary Journal Dedicated to the Philosophical Aspects of Environmental Problems* 23, no. 3 (September 1, 2001): 227–41.

———. "The Emergence of Ecological Virtue Language." In *Environmental Virtue Ethics*, ed. Ronald D. Sandler and Philip Cafaro, 15–30. Lanham, MD: Rowman & Littlefield, 2005.

Ward, Kate. "Toward a Christian Virtue Account of Moral Luck." *Journal of the Society of Christian Ethics* 38, no. 1 (2018): 131–45. https://doi.org/10.1353/sce.2018.0008.

Washington, Harriet A. *Medical Apartheid: The Dark History of Medical Experimentation on Black Americans from Colonial Times to the Present*. New York: Doubleday, 2006.

Westley, Frances. Michael Quinn, and Brenda Zimmerman. *Getting to Maybe: How the World Is Changed*. Toronto: Vintage Canada, 2007.

Westra, Laura. *An Environmental Proposal for Ethics: The Principle of Integrity*. Studies in Social and Political Philosophy. Lanham, MD: Rowman & Littlefield, 1994.

———. *Living in Integrity: A Global Ethic to Restore a Fragmented Earth*. Studies in Social, Political, and Legal Philosophy. Lanham, MD: Rowman & Littlefield, 1998.

White, Kevin. "The Passions of the Soul." In *The Ethics of Aquinas*, ed. Stephen J. Pope, 103–15. Moral Traditions Series. Washington, DC: Georgetown University Press, 2002.

Wimberley, Edward T. *Nested Ecology: The Place of Humans in the Ecological Hierarchy*. Baltimore: Johns Hopkins University Press, 2009.

Winner, Lauren F. *The Dangers of Christian Practice: On Wayward Gifts, Characteristic Damage, and Sin*. New Haven, CT: Yale University Press, 2018.

Wirzba, Norman. *Food and Faith: A Theology of Eating*. New York: Cambridge University Press, 2011.

Wohlleben, Peter. *The Hidden Life of Trees: What They Feel, How They Communicate—Discoveries from a Secret World*. Vancouver: Greystone Books, 2016.

Worster, Donald. *Nature's Economy: A History of Ecological Ideas*. Cambridge: Cambridge University Press, 1994.

Worthen, Wade B. "Community Composition and Nested-Subset Analyses: Basic Descriptors for Community Ecology." *Oikos* 76, no. 3 (1996): 417–26. https://doi.org/10.2307/3546335.

Yong, Zixin, and Po-Jang Hsieh. "Speed-Size Illusion Correlates with Retinal-Level Motion Statistics." *Journal of Vision* 17, no. 9 (August 1, 2017): 1–11. https://doi.org/10.1167/17.9.1.

Zalot, Jozef D. and Benedict Guevin. *Catholic Ethics in Today's World*. Winona, MN: Saint Mary's Press, 2008.

Zhao, Li-Xia, et al. "The Shaping Role of Self-Organization: Linking Vegetation Patterning, Plant Traits and Ecosystem Functioning." *Proceedings of the Royal Society B: Biological Sciences* 286, no. 1900 (April 10, 2019): 20182859.

Zimring, Carl A. *Clean and White: A History of Environmental Racism in the United States*. New York: New York University Press, 2015.

Index

About the Author

Nancy M. Rourke has a PhD in theology from St. Patrick's Pontifical University (Maynooth, Ireland). She is an associate professor of religious studies and theology at Canisius University and an adjunct professor at St. John Fisher University. Rourke teaches courses in Catholic ethics and religious studies and writes in areas of environmental ethics, health care ethics at the end of life, and metaethics. She is a coeditor of *Theological Literacy in the Twenty-First Century* (Eerdmans) and the author of several articles on Christian ecological ethics and Catholic bioethics. Rourke resides in Rochester, New York, where she and her spouse live with rescued cats, musical instruments, and a great love for our planet.